AF608344

Juergen

Words by Johann König

It's more of a friendship between Juergen and me. It started when he photographed me for some Russian magazine that was never published. The publisher was imprisoned for tax evasion or something. Pretty crazy story. That was some 10 years ago. Juergen had come into my gallery on Dessauer Straße and took a picture of me and at some point he said: why don't you take your top off? So, there I was, topless. The way Juergen photographs is very physical. It's a highly concentrated matter, a bit like sex. Because he so weirdly penetrates you. It really is like sex. He doesn't say much, and he sweats a lot, at least that's how I remember it. It begins, and then there's not a lot of talk. Actually all he ever says is "This is good" or the like. And then it's over. It doesn't take long, but it's also not shooting from the hip. Even though it often looks like it. It's rather a mixture of a kind of 'from-the-hip' and a completely exhausting shoot. There are other photographers who get on your nerves with their ideas.

But anyone who lets themselves be photographed is somehow exhibiting themselves. That's what Juergen plays with. Somehow he captured my vanity but then again counteracted it, because I am looking into the camera full of confidence with my belly hanging out over my belt. It's everything but an attractive photo of me. The funny thing is that he was photographing Lars Eidinger on the same day. And we all went out together that night. Juergen and I were kicked out of Felix, this mediocre disco, because we were partying so hard. Then we did a König Souvenir party for documenta, and Lars was the DJ. There were t-shirts with Juergen's photos of that day in Berlin with Lars or myself on them. Lars was wearing the one with himself, of course!

Juergen had this series in the *ZEITmagazin*, where he would tell a personal story about each photo. He exhibited them in Vienna. That's why I went there. Afterwards I was supposed to meet up with him in some disco. And on the way there, walking through the Stephansplatz, I met my wife. It was a funny situation: I had walked bang into her and asked her and her friend if they would like to come with us. I didn't know them from Adam, but it was Art Week in Vienna and Lena had made a big impression on me. That's the story of how I got to know my wife through Juergen. We always say that if we ever celebrate our wedding, then he will be the one to take the pictures.

Juergen manages to make everyone equal. It doesn't matter if they are stars or not. And that the stars are just people. When I showed Juergen in my gallery in Berlin his photograph of Kate Moss lying in a wheelbarrow sold very well. But I don't think that it's the best picture because it looks somewhat contrived. It's very aesthetic, and actually his things are always good if they are not so aesthetic. When Juergen shows that people are strong but also fragile. Nobody really looks good with him, at least not good in terms of actual fashion photography. That's what makes him so special: that he was the first to break with all these aesthetic ideas and the 'how-to-look' picture.

His series *Paradis* with Charlotte Rampling and Raquel Zimmermann at the Louvre is a masterpiece. It has something of a Freudian childhood dream about being in the museum alone at night with these two superwomen, both naked.

I find that what's interesting about Juergen is that he is so no-frills. And that's the beauty of it. I am thinking of the 1996 photo of Kristen McMenamy with "Versace" written on her chest with lipstick. The photo totally contradicted the prevailing image of beauty. But she looks so comfortable with herself in this picture. It was a total break with the etiquette of fashion photography. I look at it from the perspective of being a guardian of art: Juergen brought art into fashion photography. His photos are often quite brown. And that became such a success! It's been copied everywhere. And that's what brings it back around to being German. Wood paneling and beer, the cosy fairytale parlor, the forest, Bavarian Munich, sausage, deer antler trophies and stuff like that: that's what comes to mind. That's maybe Juergen's charm, the authentic and sweet-ugly. I also think of the times when I was a kid and I thought it was great to go to other kids' homes, where there was ugly wallpaper, tablecloths, seating arrangements and wall-to-wall carpeting. At our house, we had a Franz West sofa, art on the walls and herringbone parquet. The other kind gives off a kind of warmth.

Actually, Juergen is the ideal cosmopolitan because he sees himself as an EU emigrant, an international who's done with that pompous German bullshit. I have him to thank for the EUnify Hoodie. I mean this blue hoodie with the circle of stars representing Europe, where a star is missing [signifying Brexit] and which we released for König Souvenir. Juergen had photographed Virgil Abloh for the cover of *System* magazine. And because he is wearing that hoodie it became a worldwide mega-hit.

If you look at Juergen's early Nirvana photos, they're also really good, but he became only really direct and open with Kristen McMenamy. In the process, he has also come to an openness of the portrayed, who dare to show themselves just as they are. What makes Juergen's portraits so sexy is that real sex is so much more unpleasant. You sweat, you make every effort, and there is sand in the bed, it smells, you have complexes.... sex is much more animalistic than it is portrayed in photography. Juergen goes a step further: he takes a picture like you've arrived at home. The dress is no longer fitting just right or the belly is indeed hanging over your belt.

That's why he's so successful in the fashion industry, he scratches at the shell to show us what it's all about: wanting to be wanted. One is how you want it, and the other pushes that point: how you know what it is. With Juergen, nudity means honesty, showing how one is. Really good sex is also about honesty; bad sex is about the image of how you think it should be. If you accept yourself and your stigmas, then you can overcome them. And that's why Juergen's work is so exciting.

Maybe there is a parallel between Juergen and me. I came to be a gallerist out of necessity. I really wanted to work with artists, and the only thing that allowed me to do that directly was the gallery. Juergen also came indirectly to photography, through re-training, because when he was working in a workshop for string instruments, as his father had done, he developed an allergy against the wood dust. I did the gallery for the same reason. My father wasn't a gallerist, but a curator. In the end, we are obviously seeking out the recognition of our fathers. And then Juergen developed this allergy, which was probably not completely un-psychosomatic, and so he came to photography. He says that when he looked through the camera for the first time, he realized that that was his thing.

Also, the photos he took at the childrens' hospice are about being human. These photos of disabled children are so strong because the human in Juergen's work is so important. You would think that that's so normal. But when people know that they are being photographed, they immediately change their attitude. Juergen takes a hell of a lot of pictures, and he picks out the moments where a human is a human. He builds trust and even prefers the moments that are said to be unfavorable. And you go along with it, because that's the way he is. Today it's becoming more and more rare that one shows how one really is. I think that the true relevance of his work has yet to be seen. His photo of Yves Saint Laurent gets better with every passing year that Saint Laurent is no longer alive. He only had one minute and took 20 seconds to take this picture.

It is important that you follow your intuition. Sometimes you are wrong, and it's not always the right advisor, but basically it's simply about honesty. My dad always advised me not to take any big risks. And it's also not wrong to stay on the safe side. But I explicitly decided against staying on the safe side and succeeded nonetheless. One would have to ask Juergen how he came to his thing at all, how he came to trust it. Juergen was definitely important to me, and I'm glad we know each other.

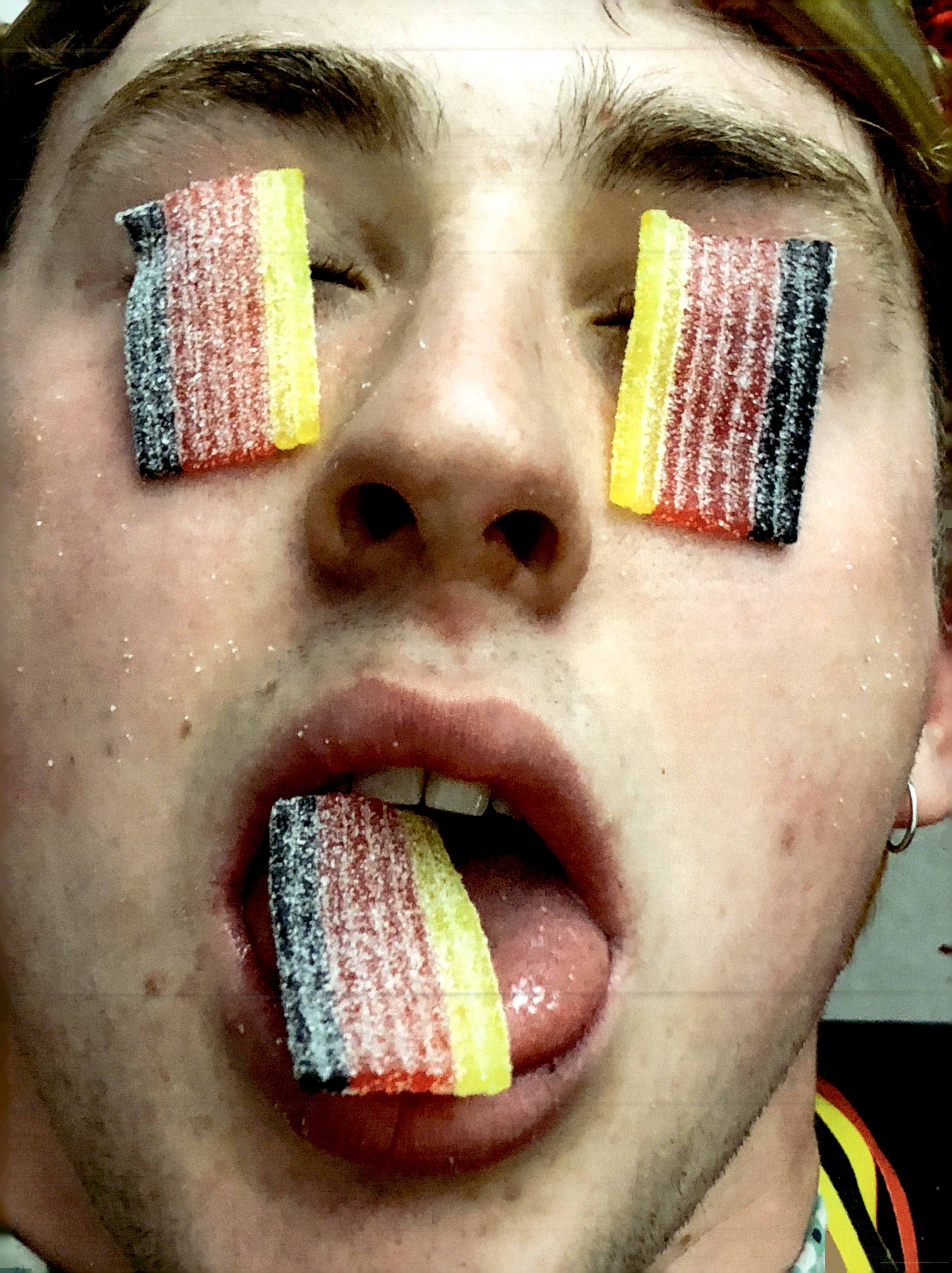

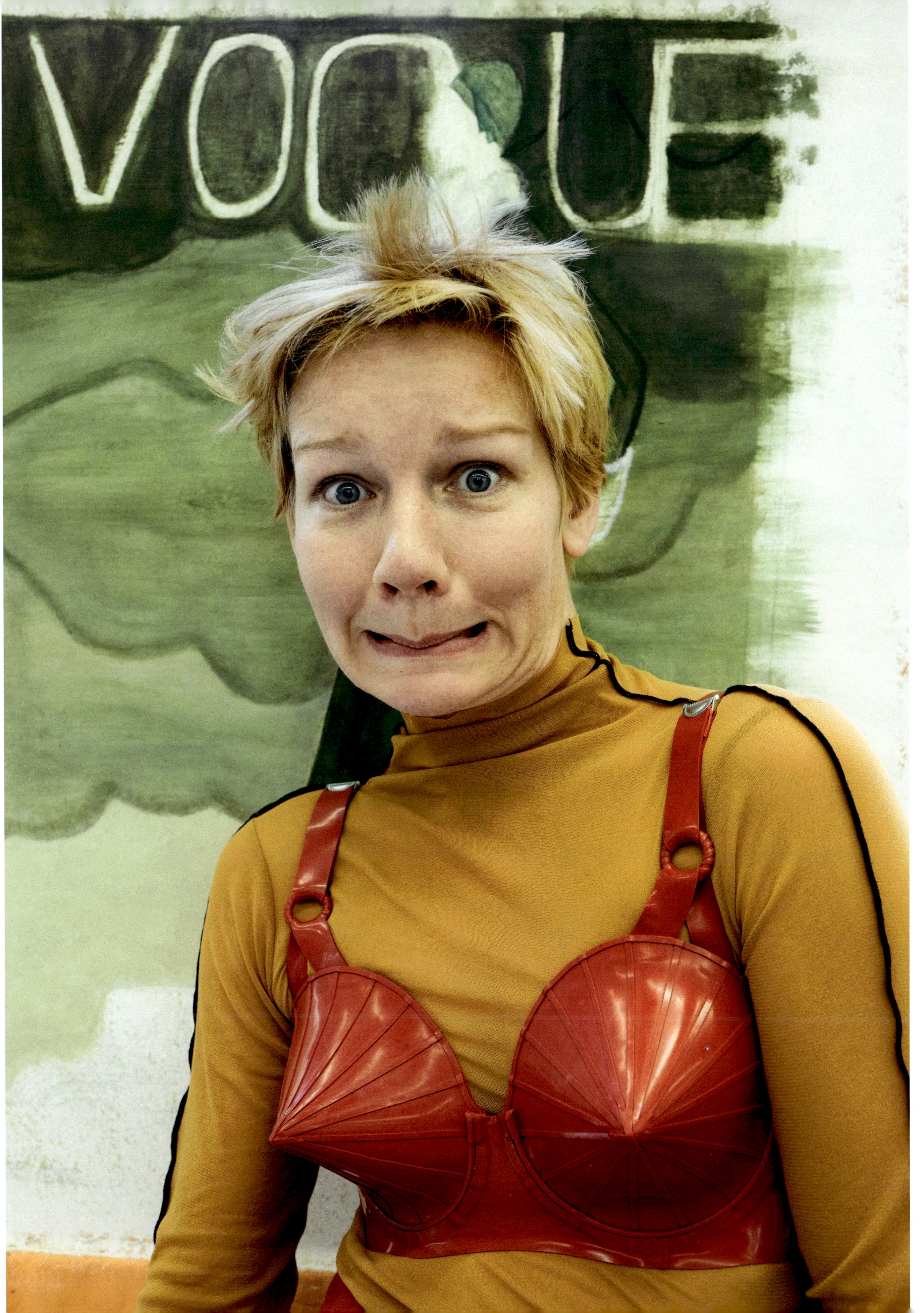

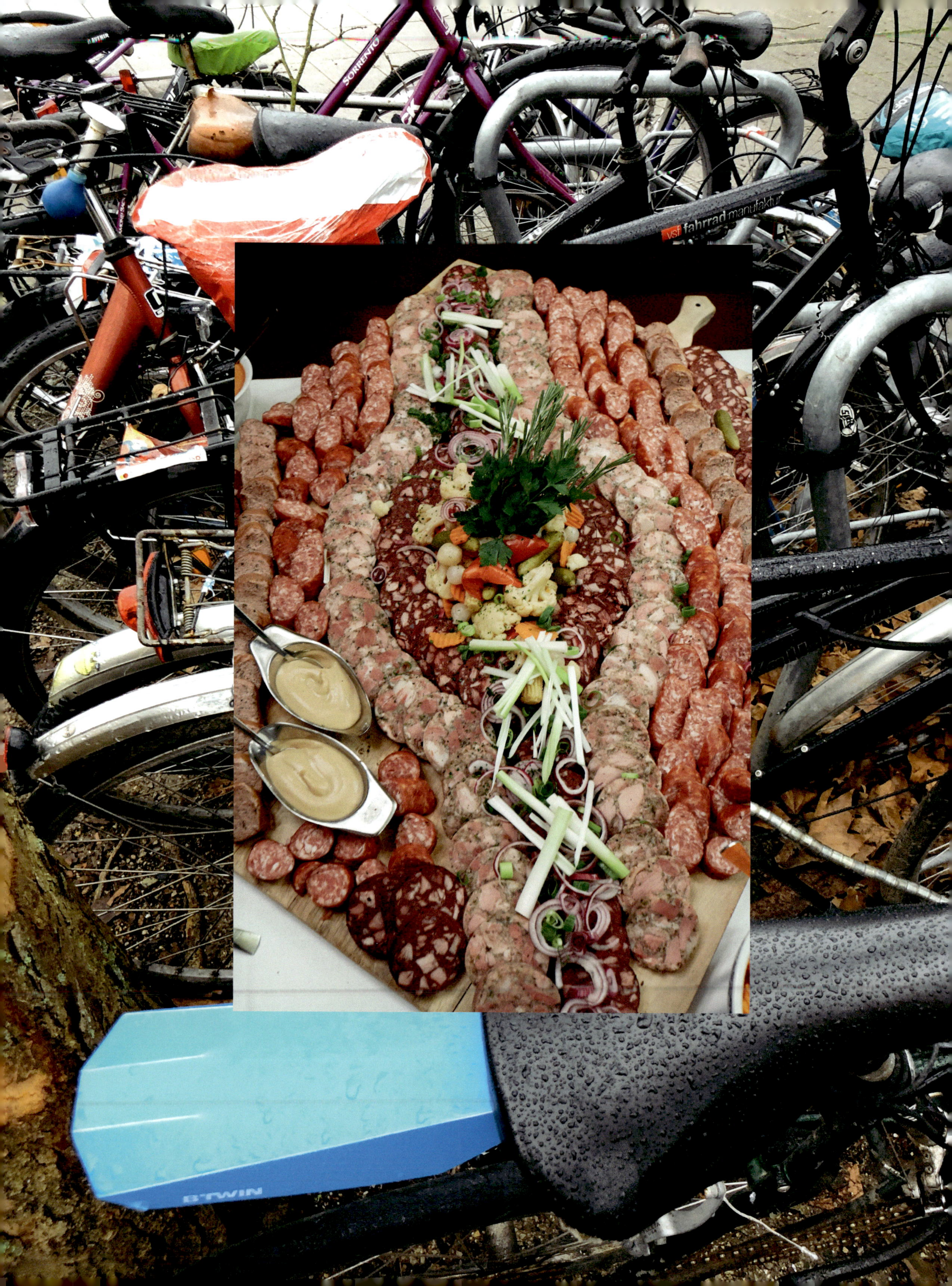
SORRENTO
vsf fahrrad manufaktur
B'TWIN

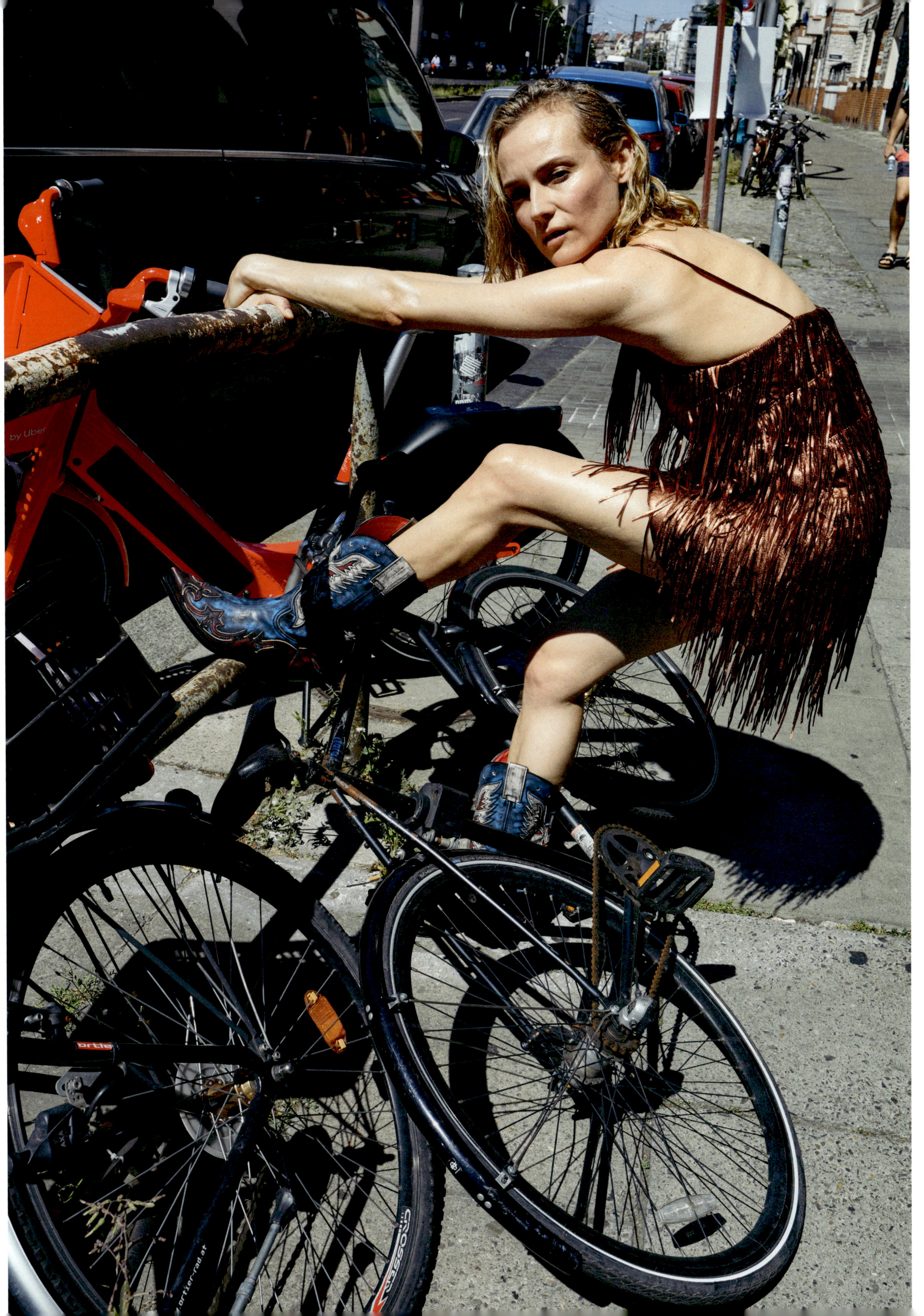
by Uber

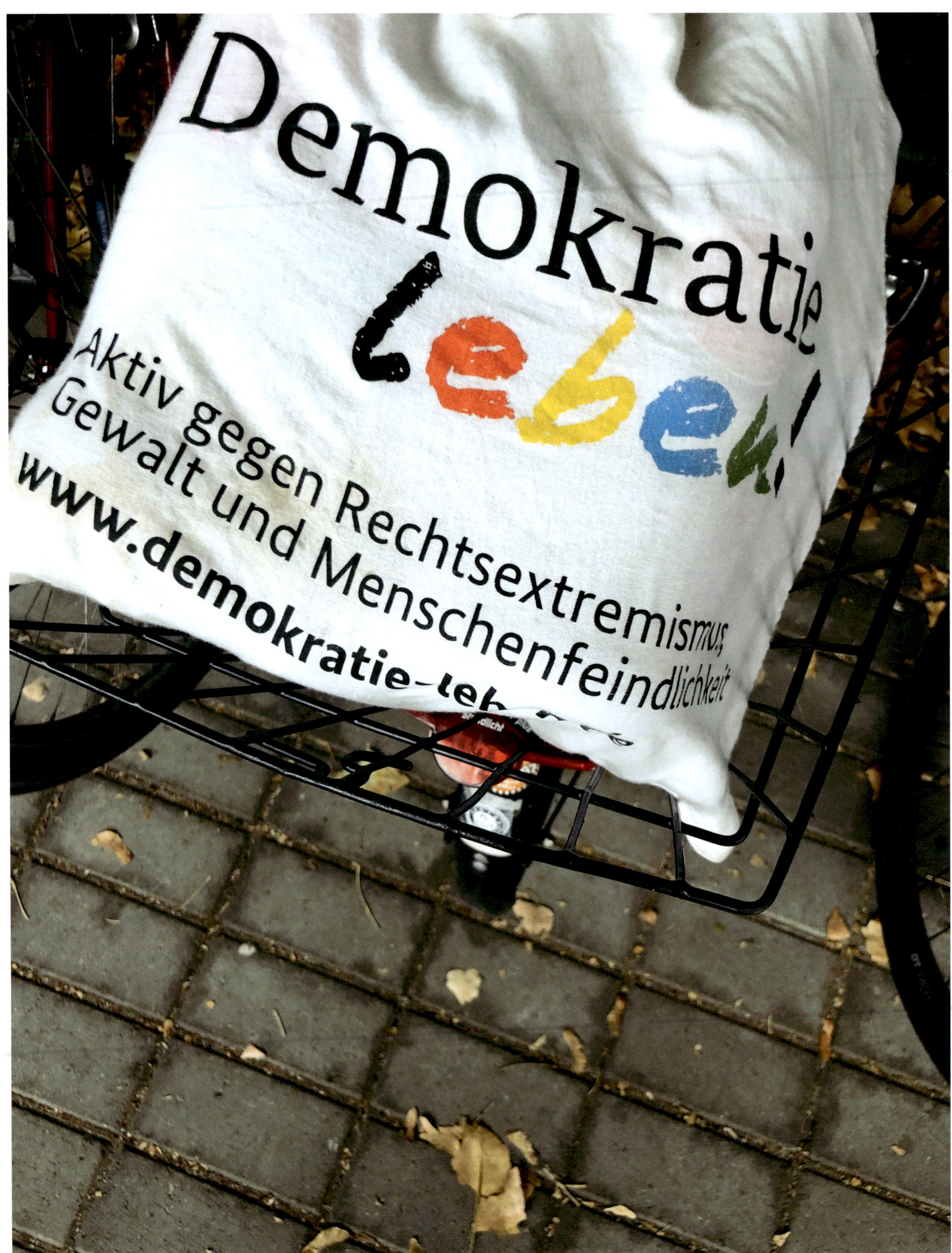
Demokratie
leben!
Aktiv gegen Rechtsextremismus,
Gewalt und Menschenfeindlichkeit
www.demokratie-

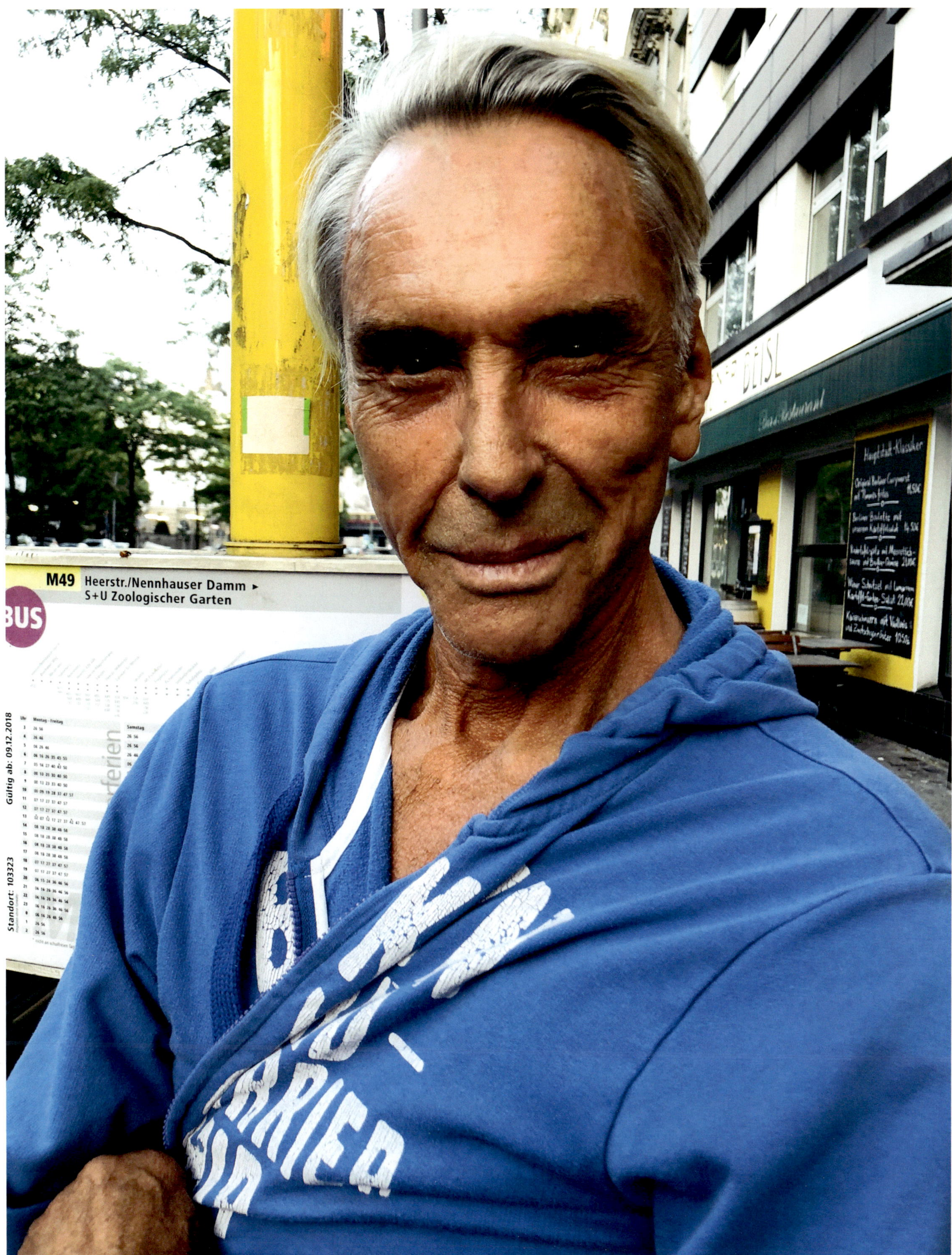
M49
Heerstr./Nennhauser Damm
S+U Zoologischer Garten
BUS
Gültig ab: 09.12.2018
Standort: 103323

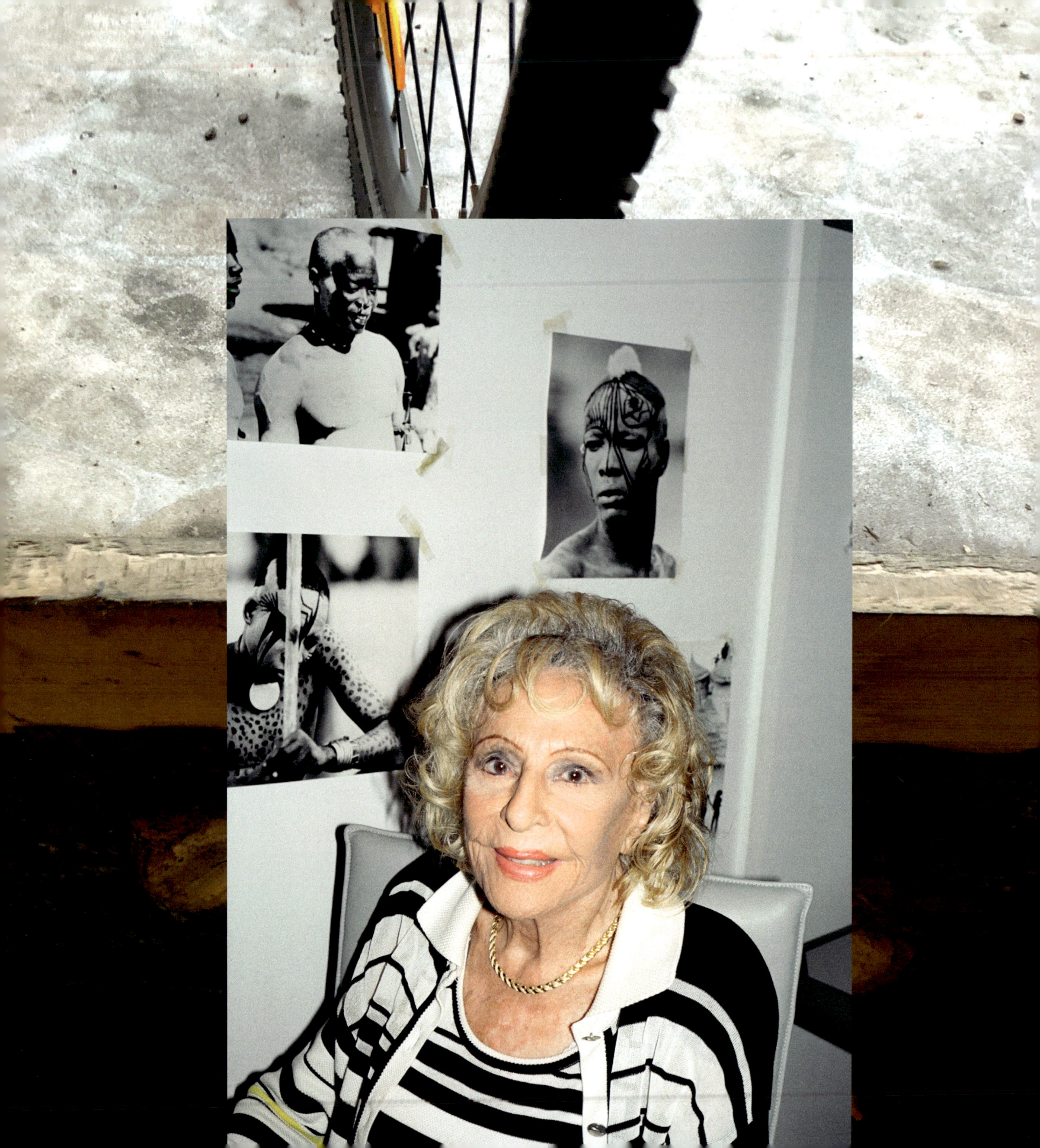

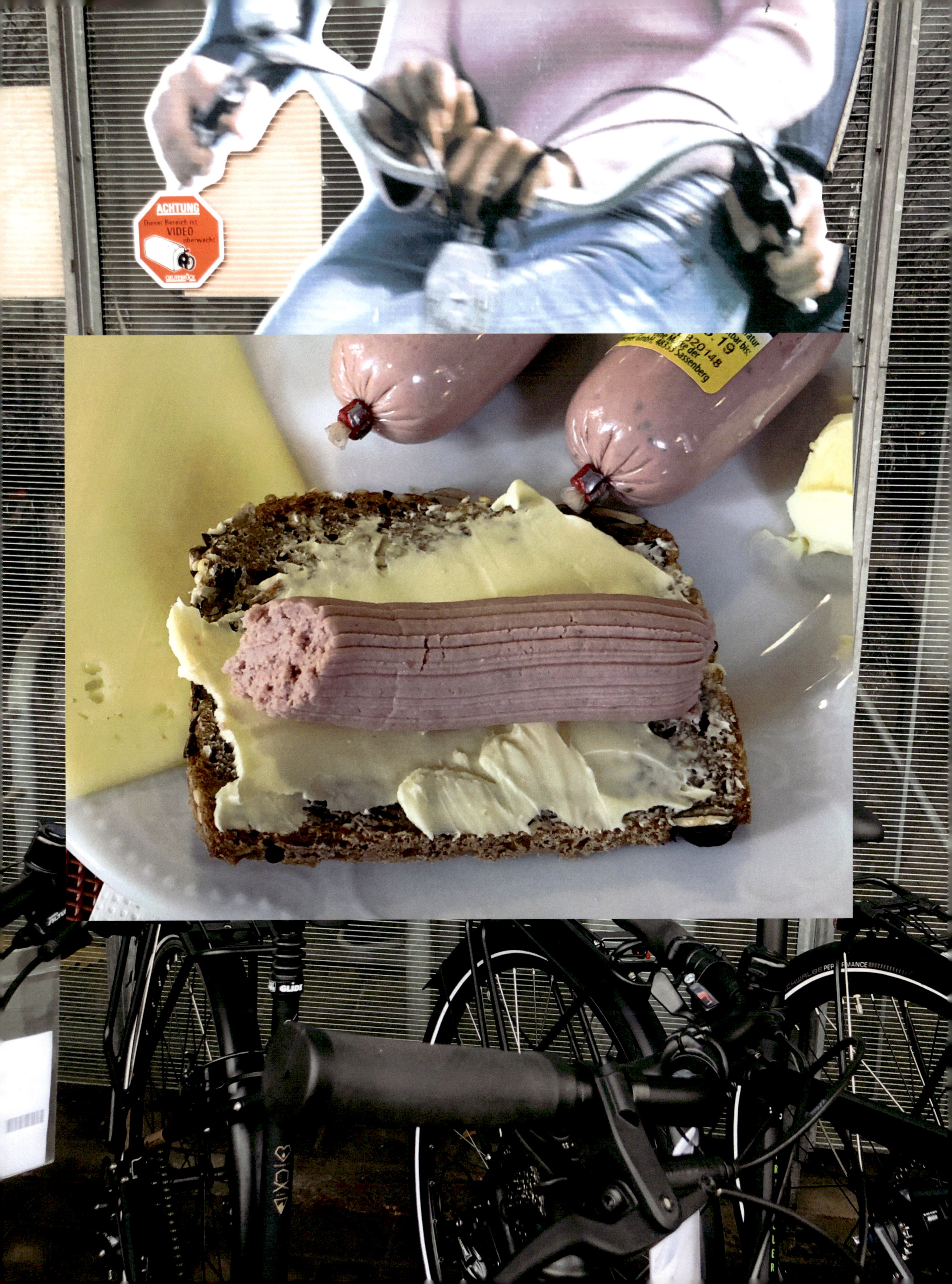
ACHTUNG
Dieser Bereich ist
VIDEO
überwacht!

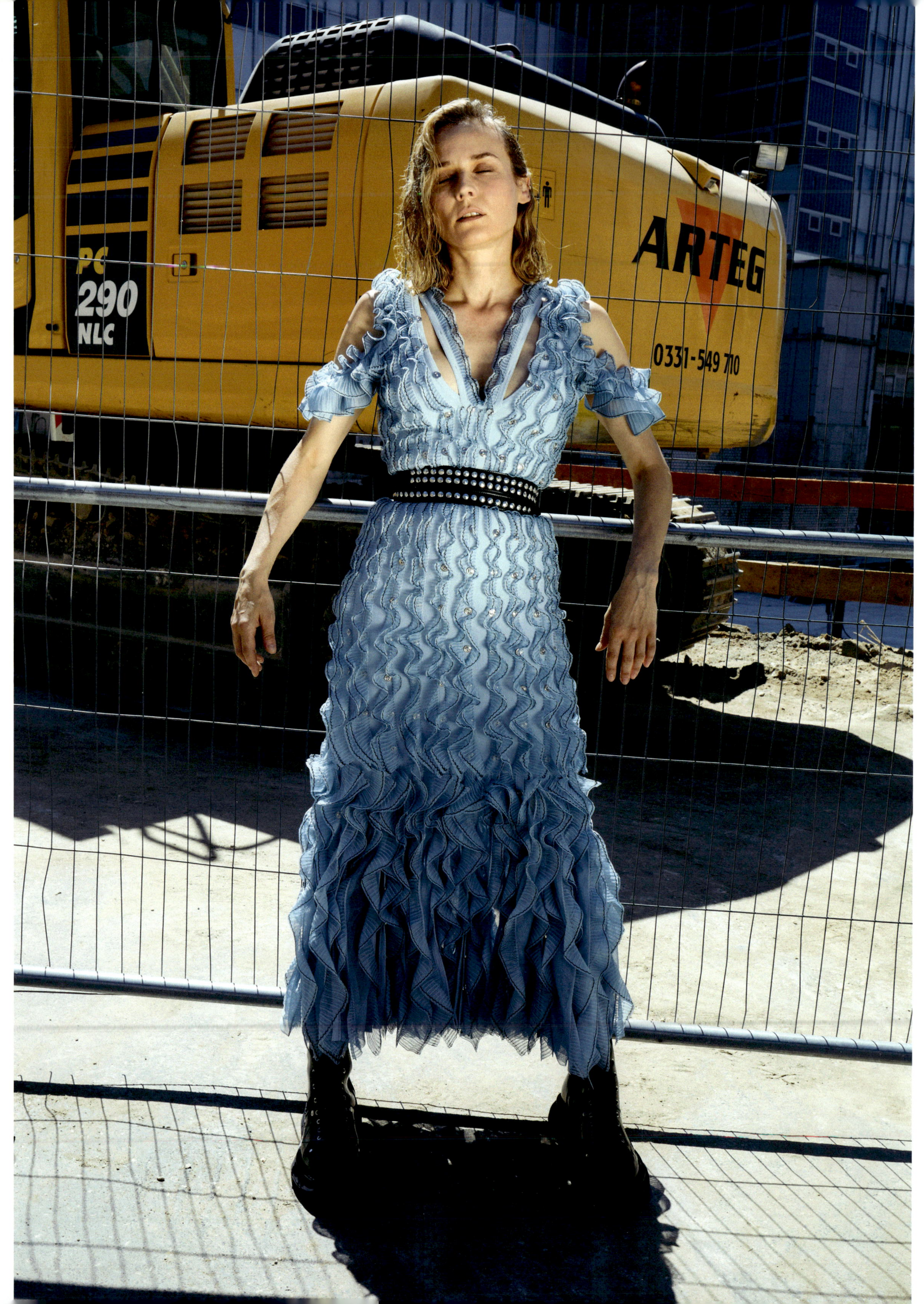
290
NLC
ARTEG
0331-549 710

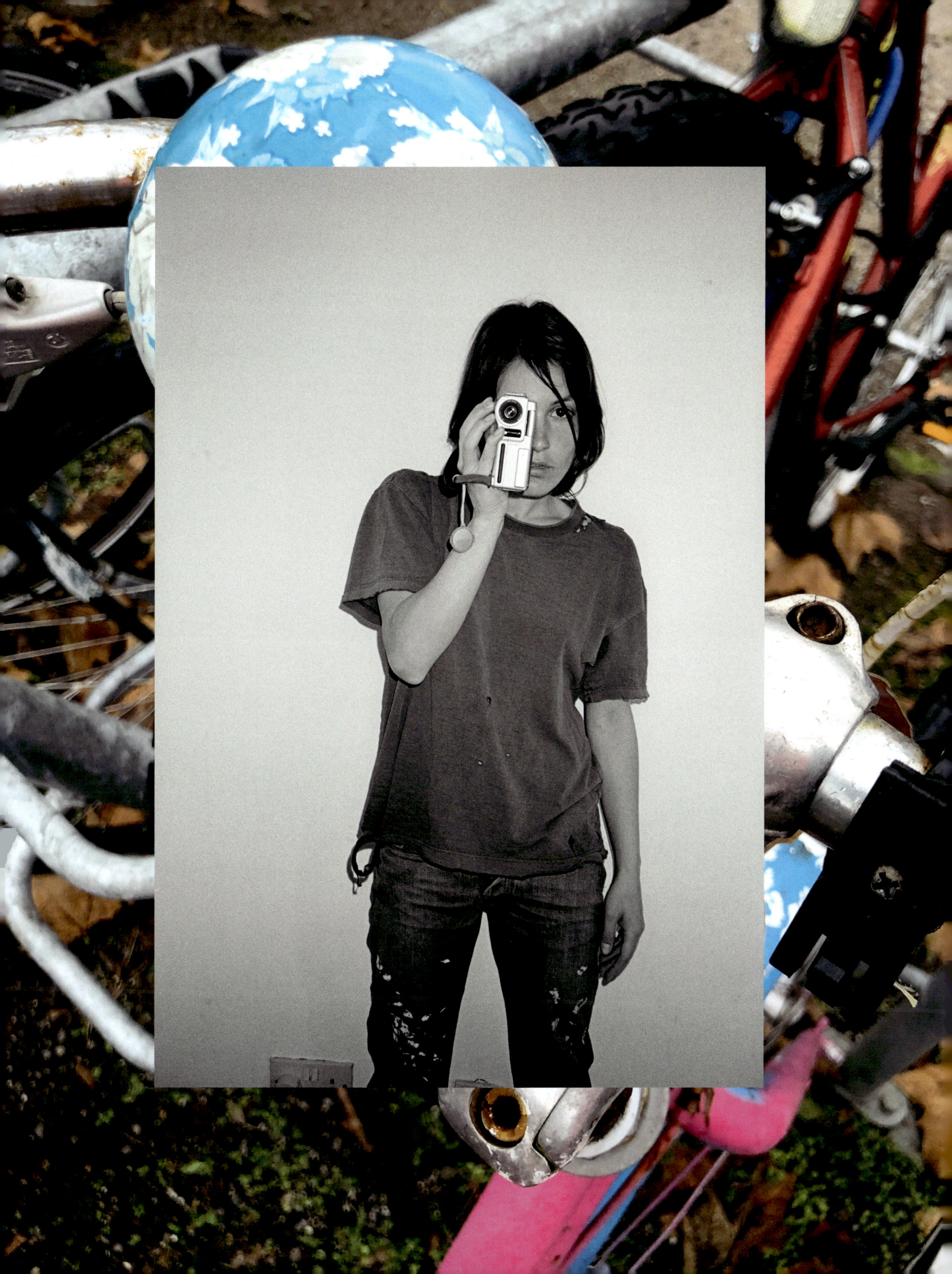

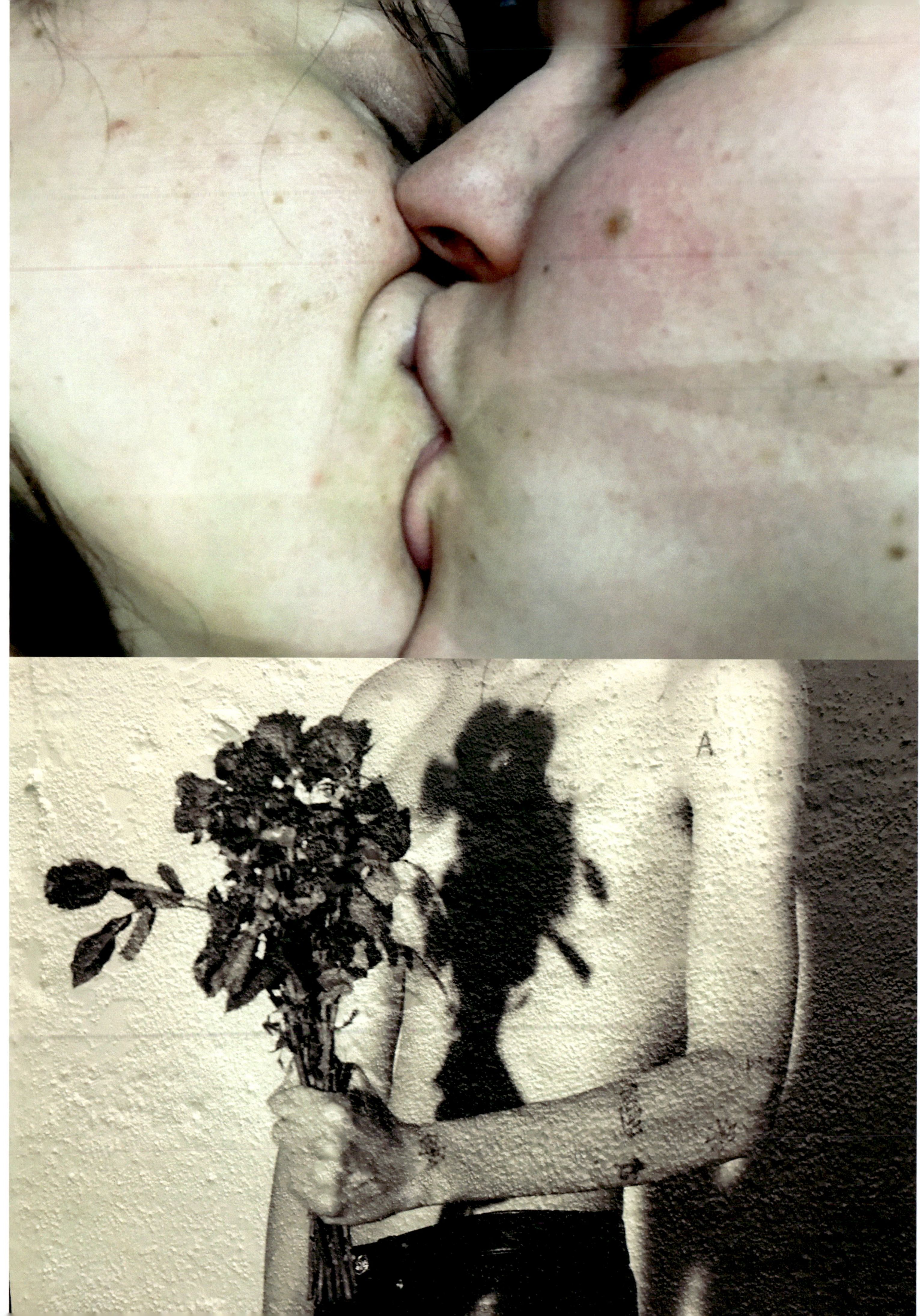
A

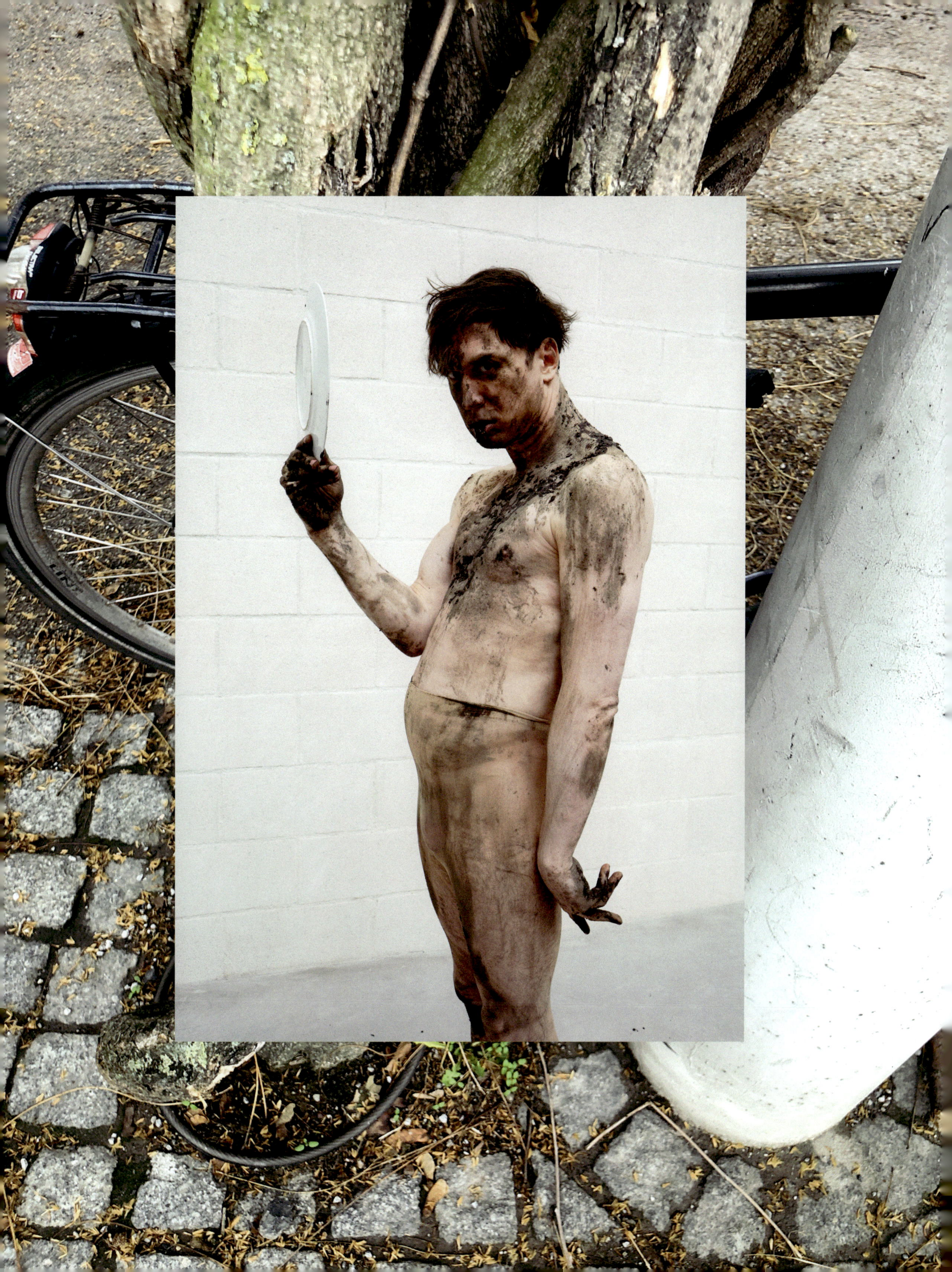

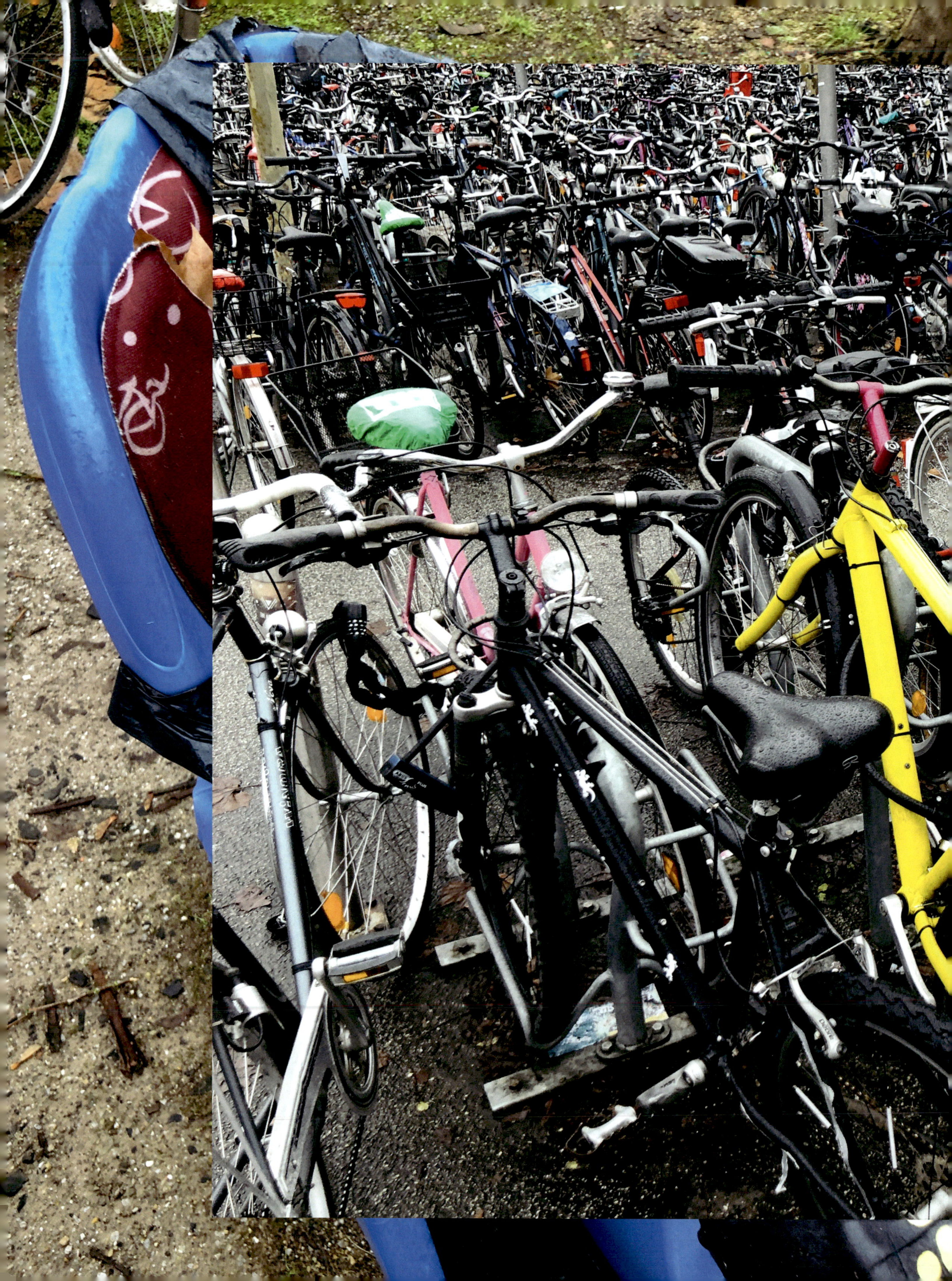

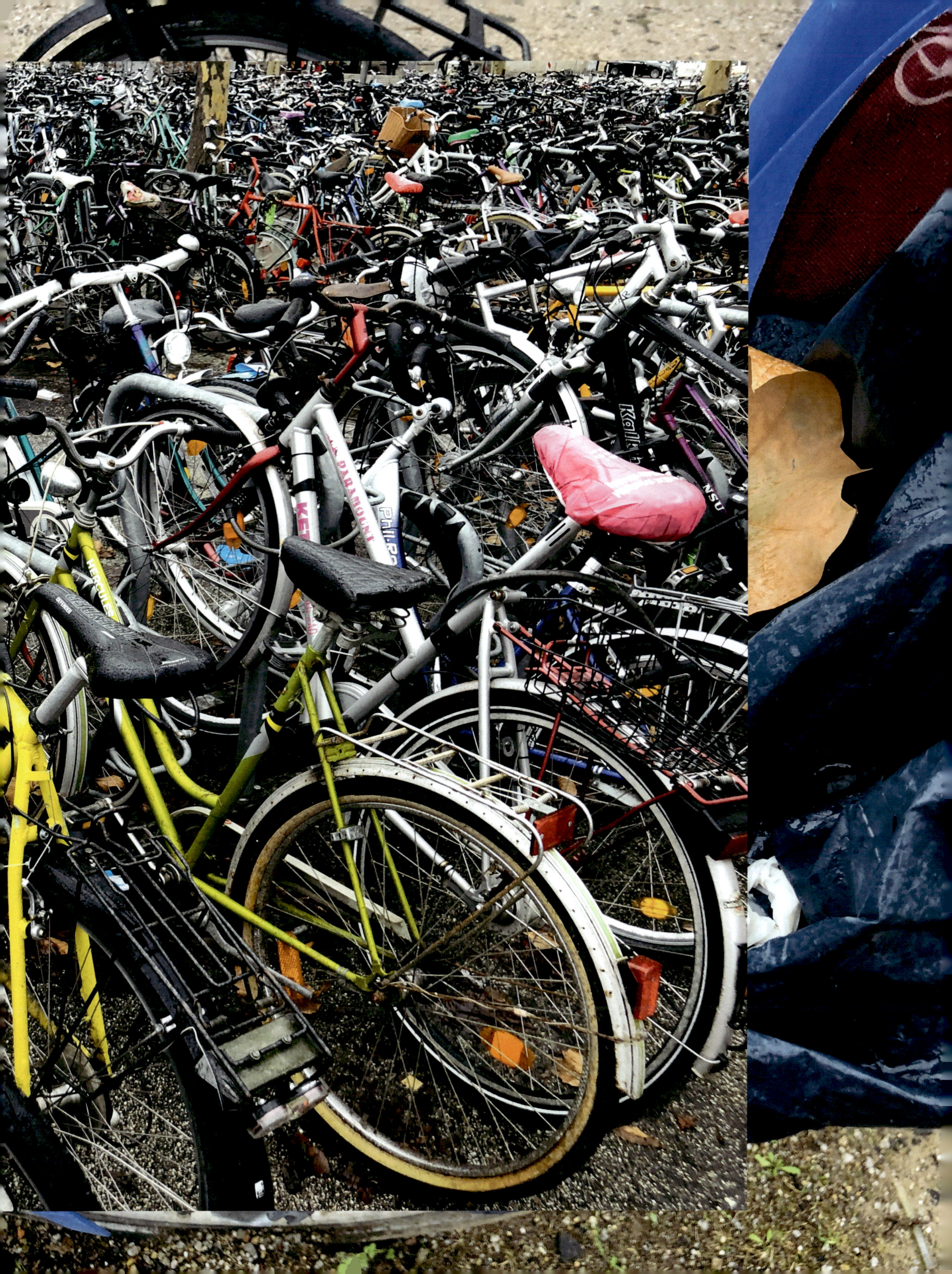
HERCULES
NSU

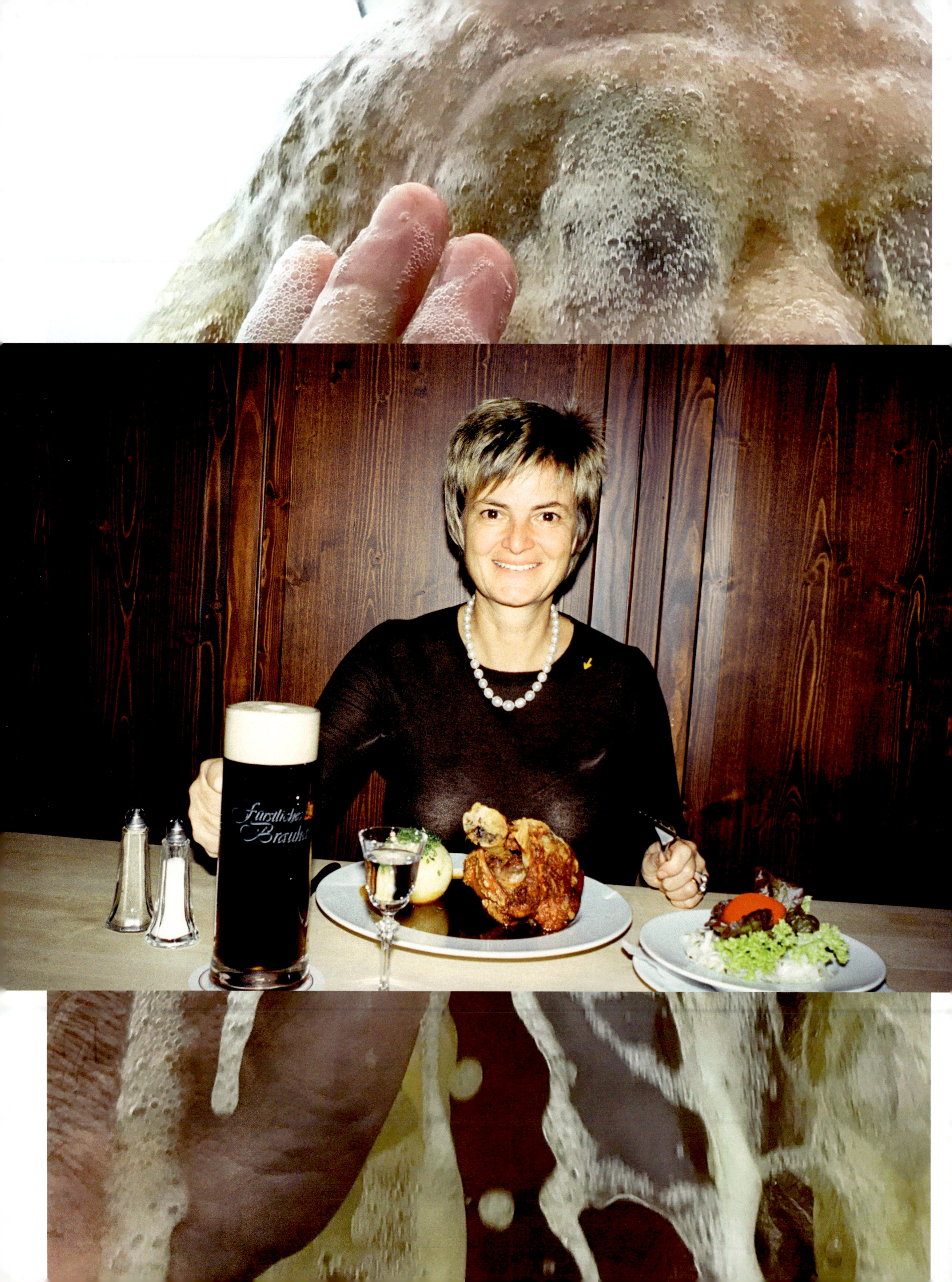

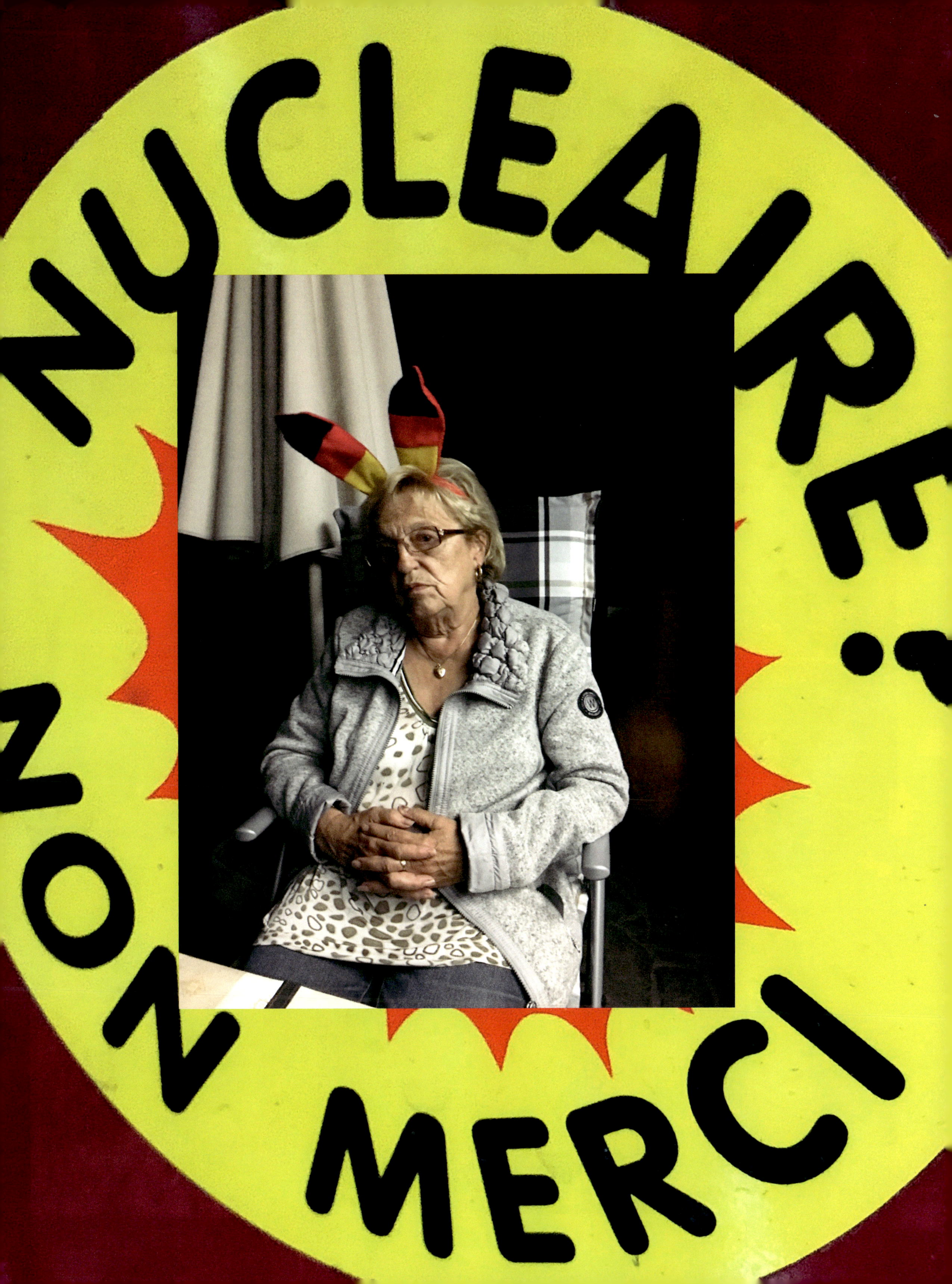
NUCLEAIRE?
NON MERCI

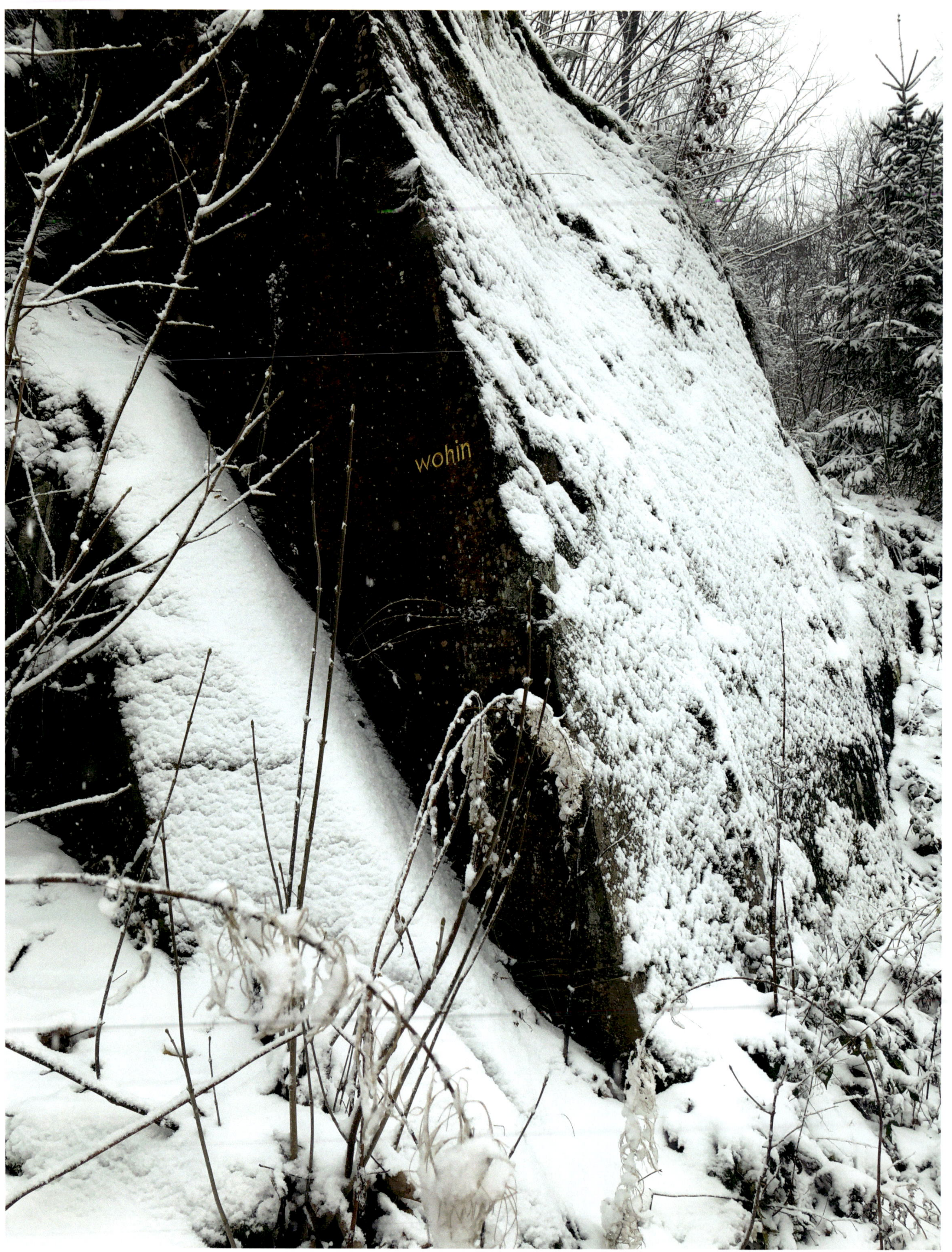
wohin

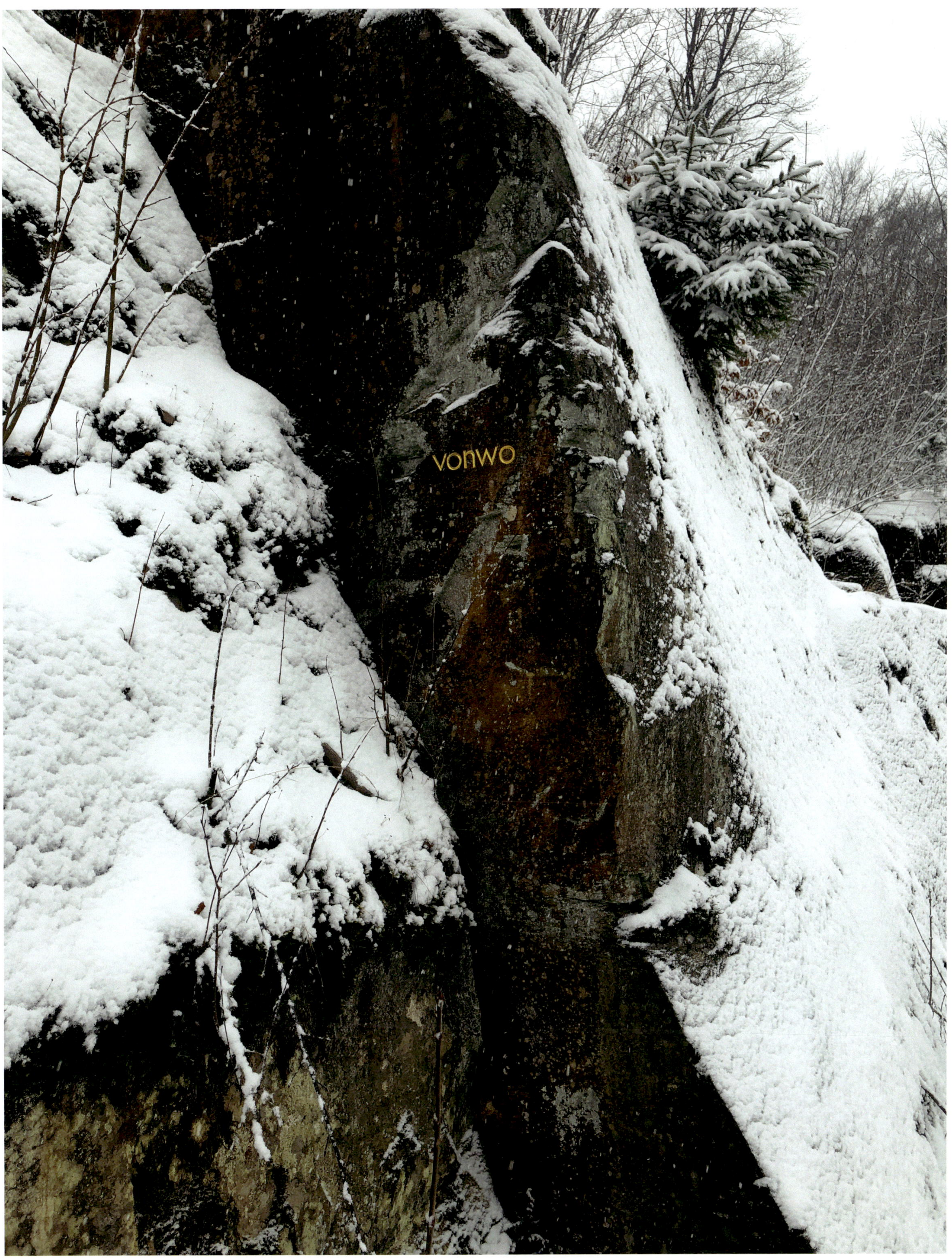
vonwo

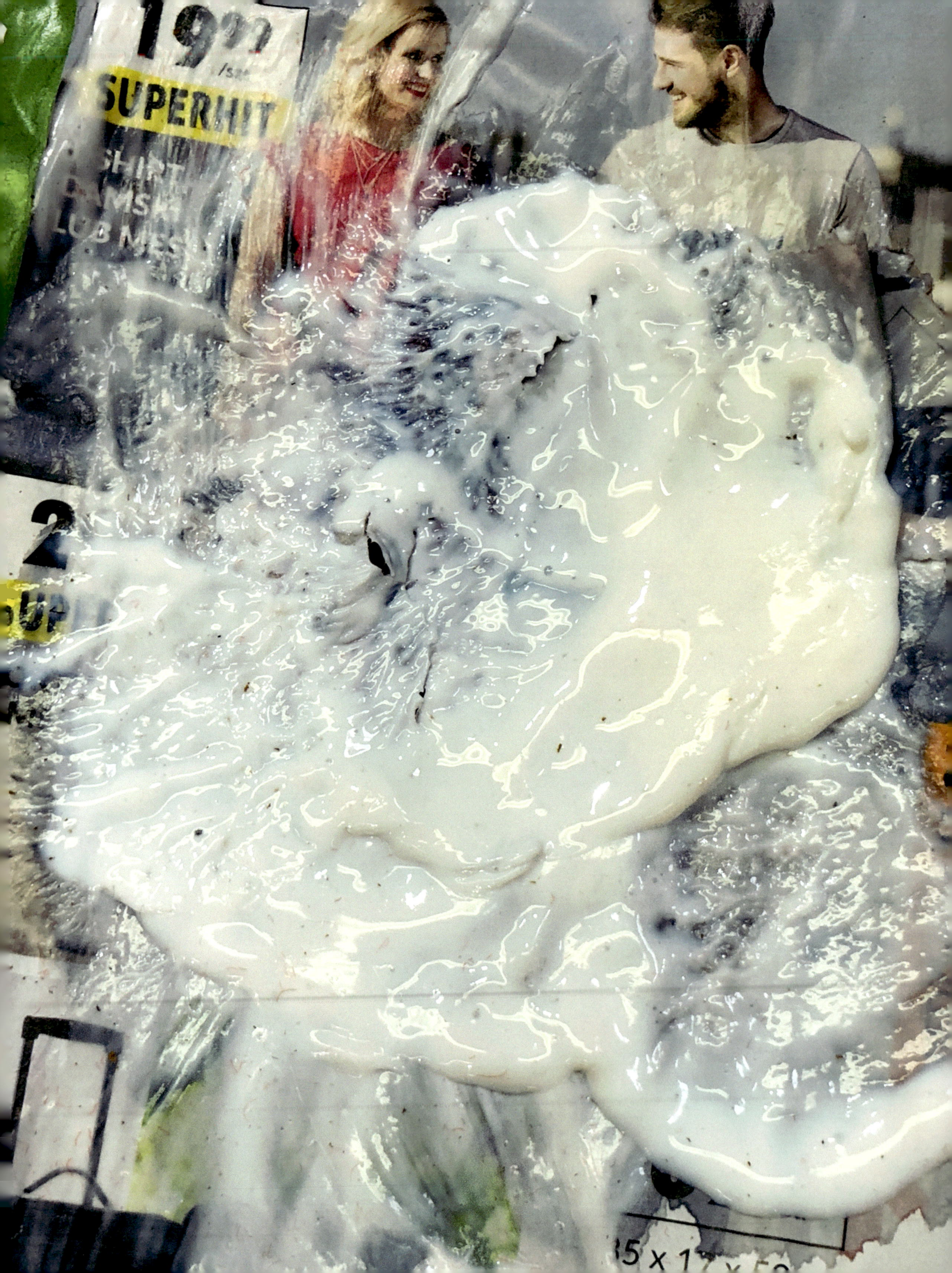
SUPERHIT

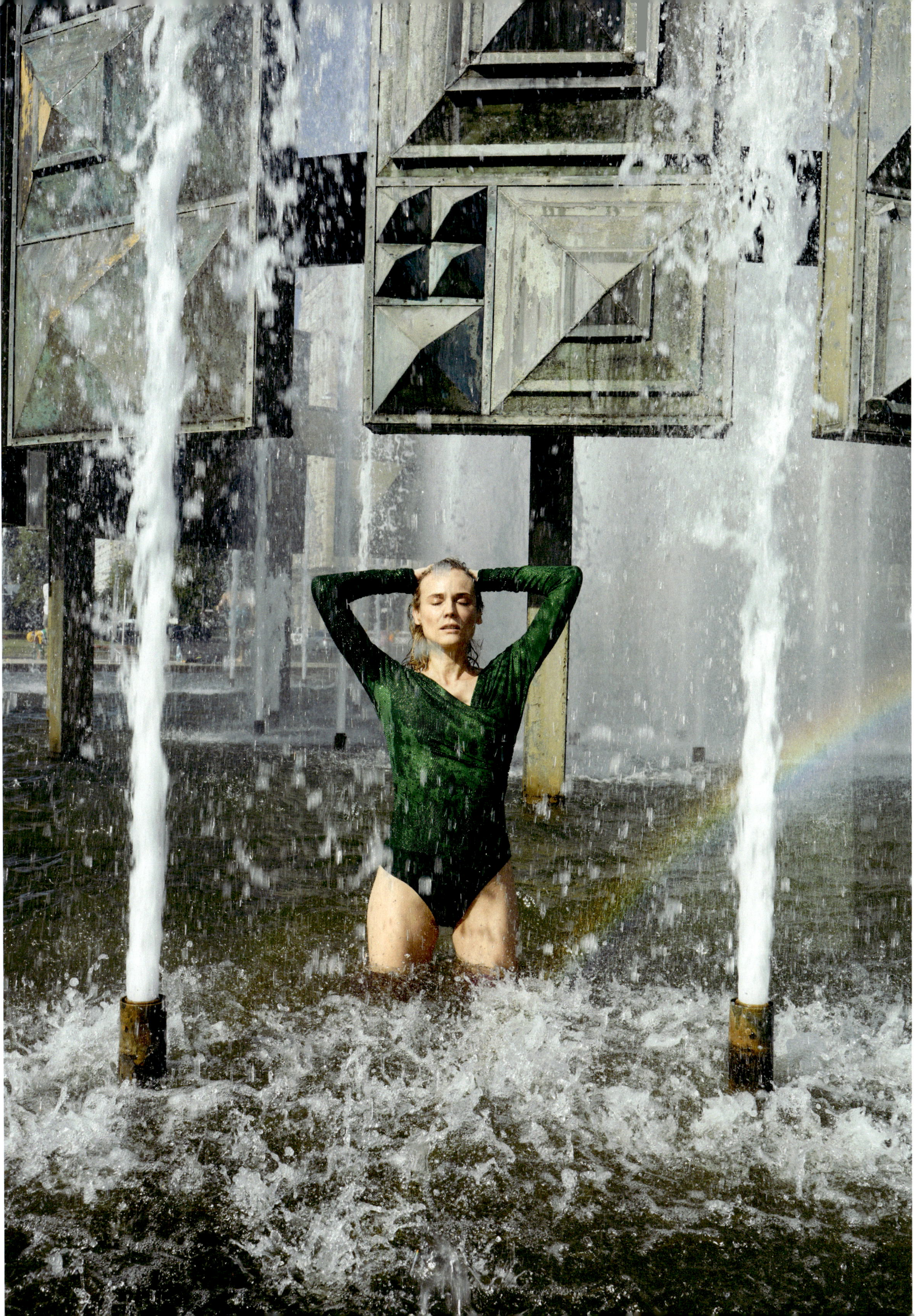

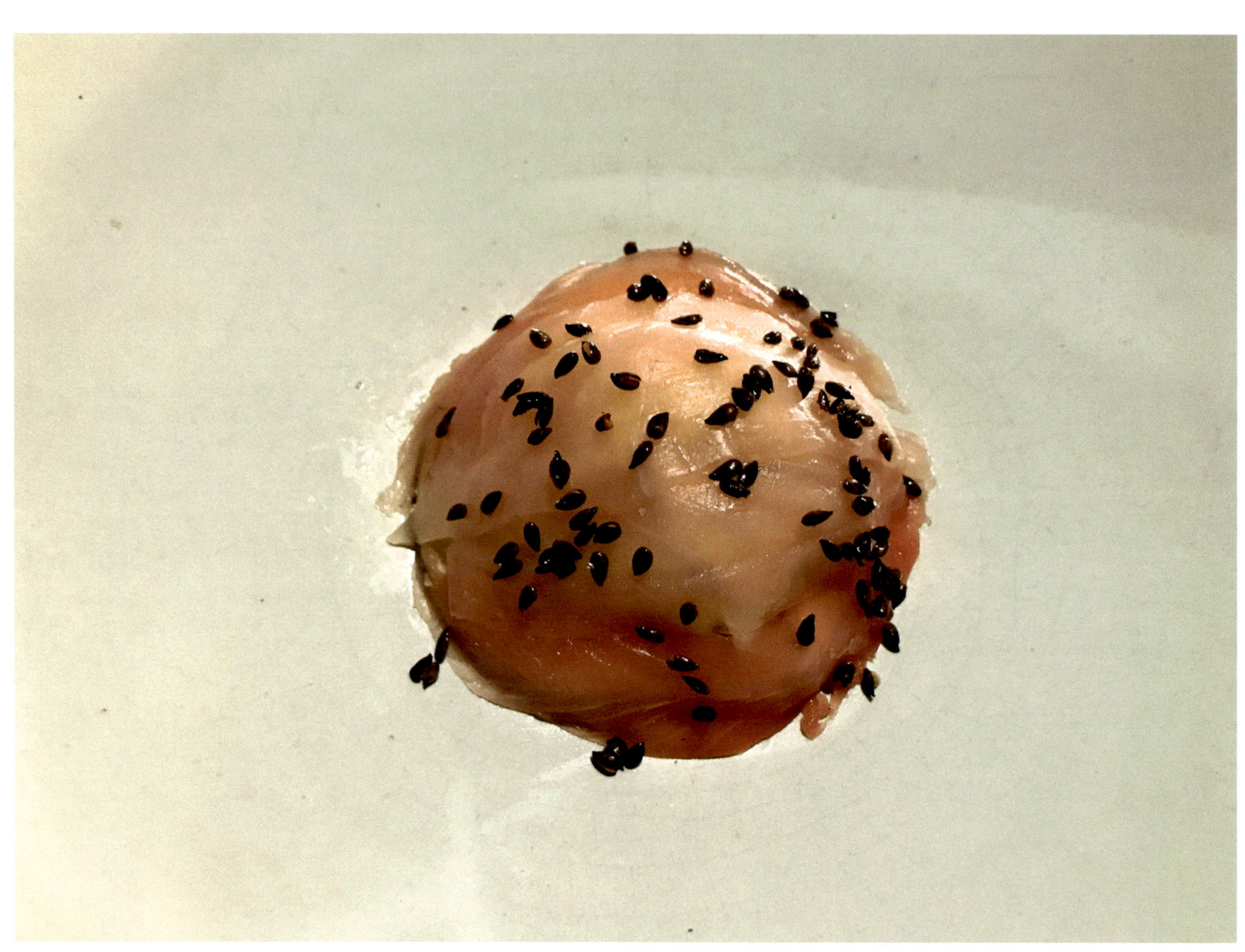

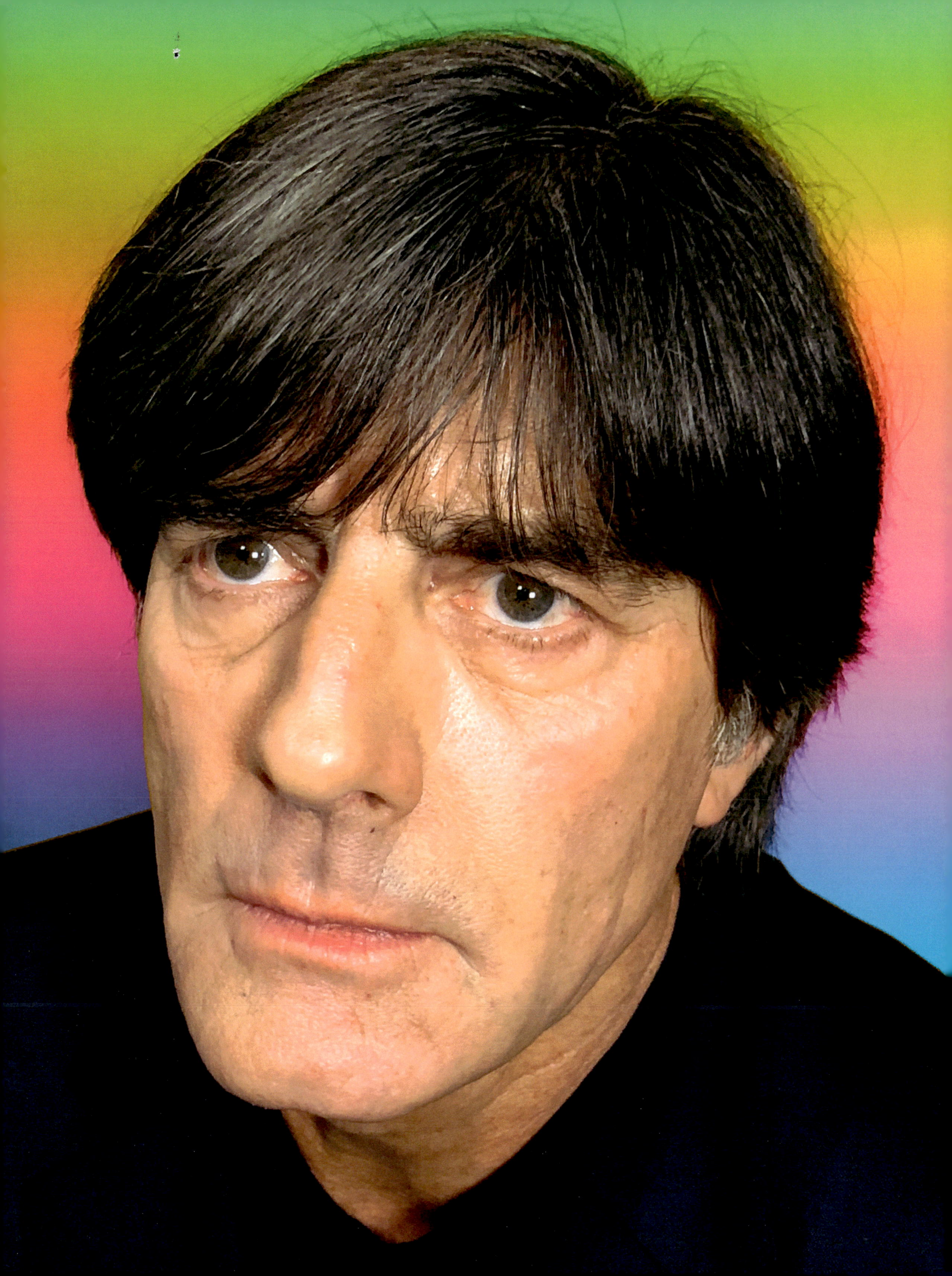

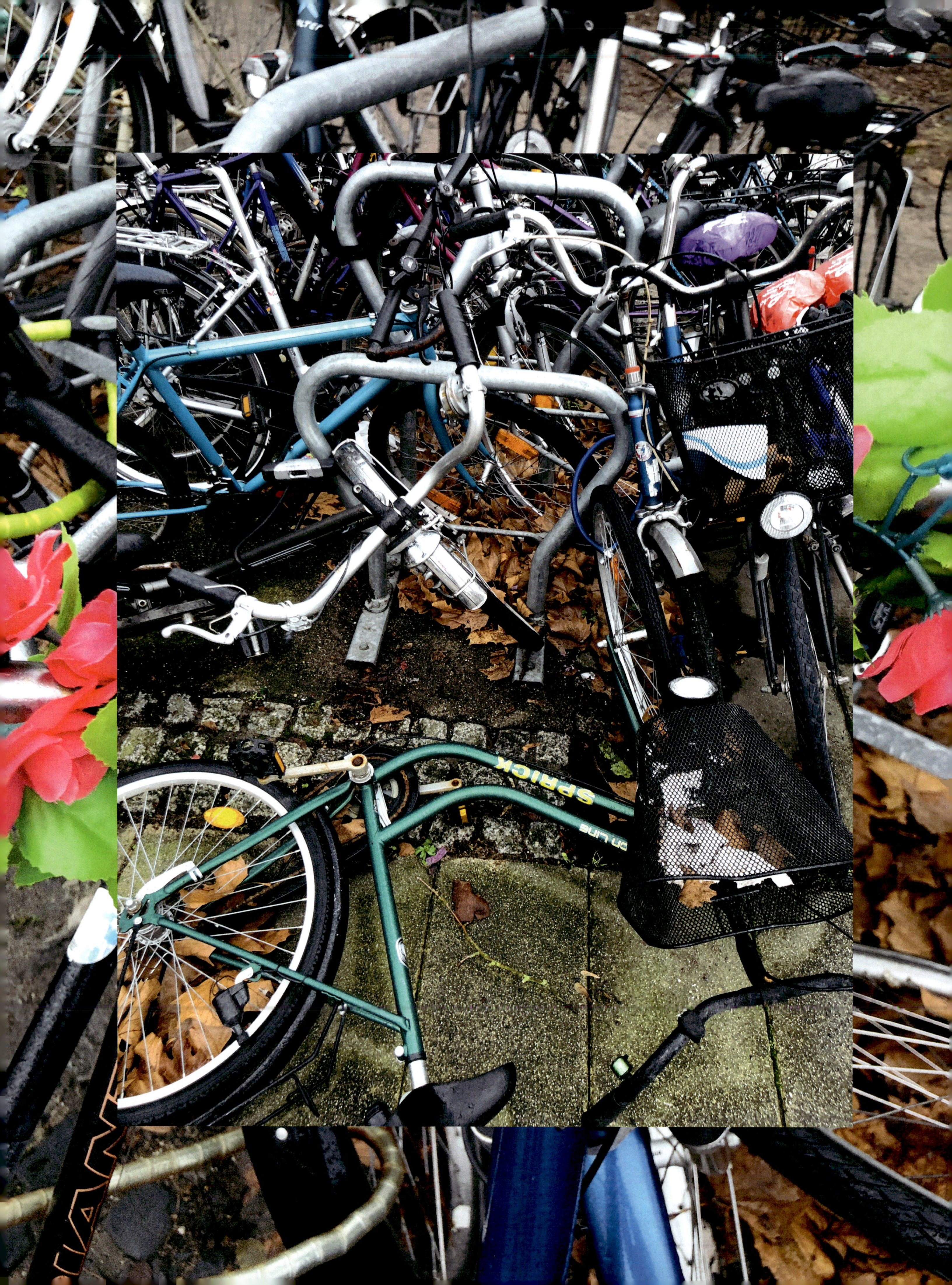
SPRICK

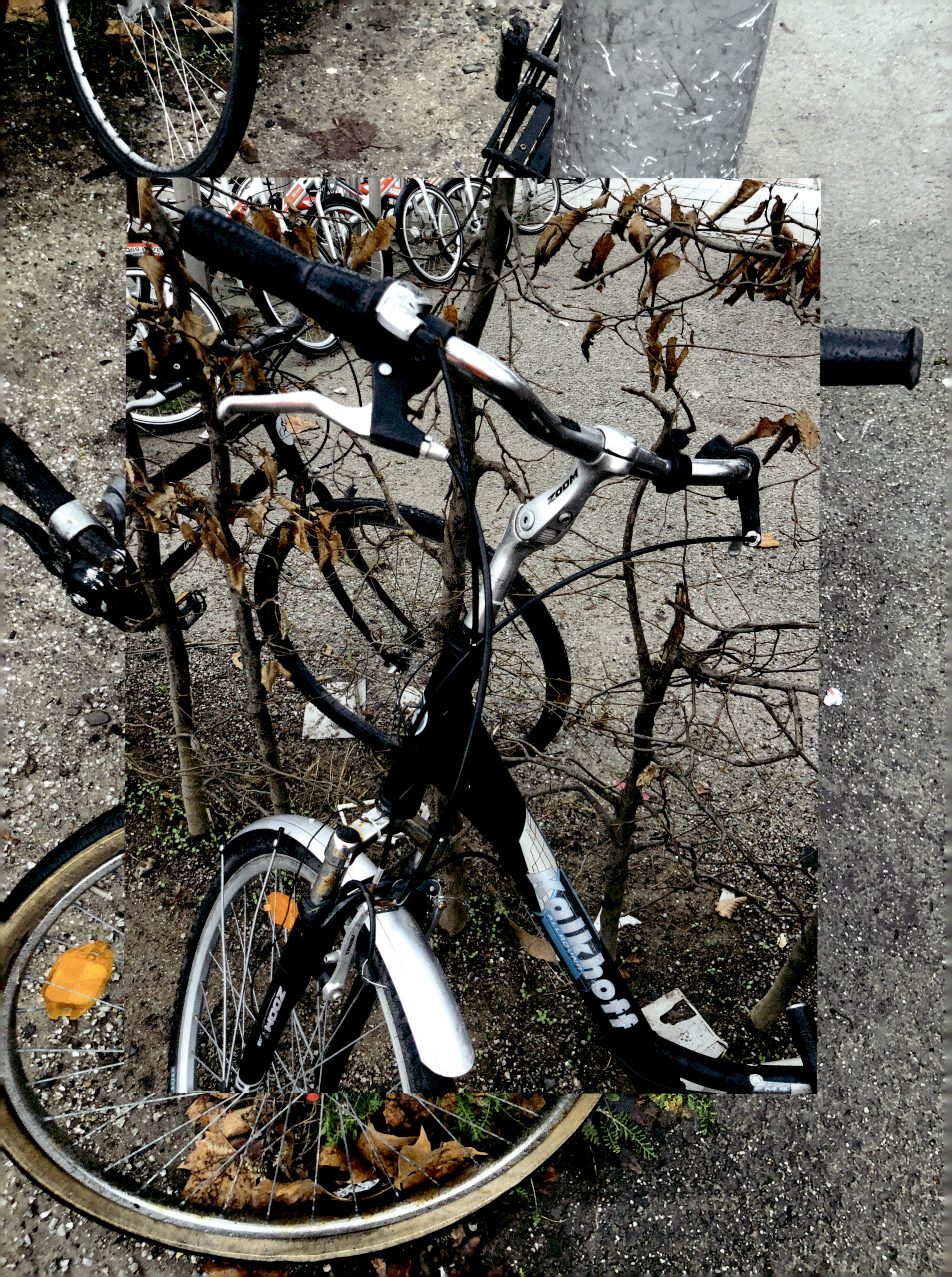
ZOOM
Kalkhoff
ZOOM

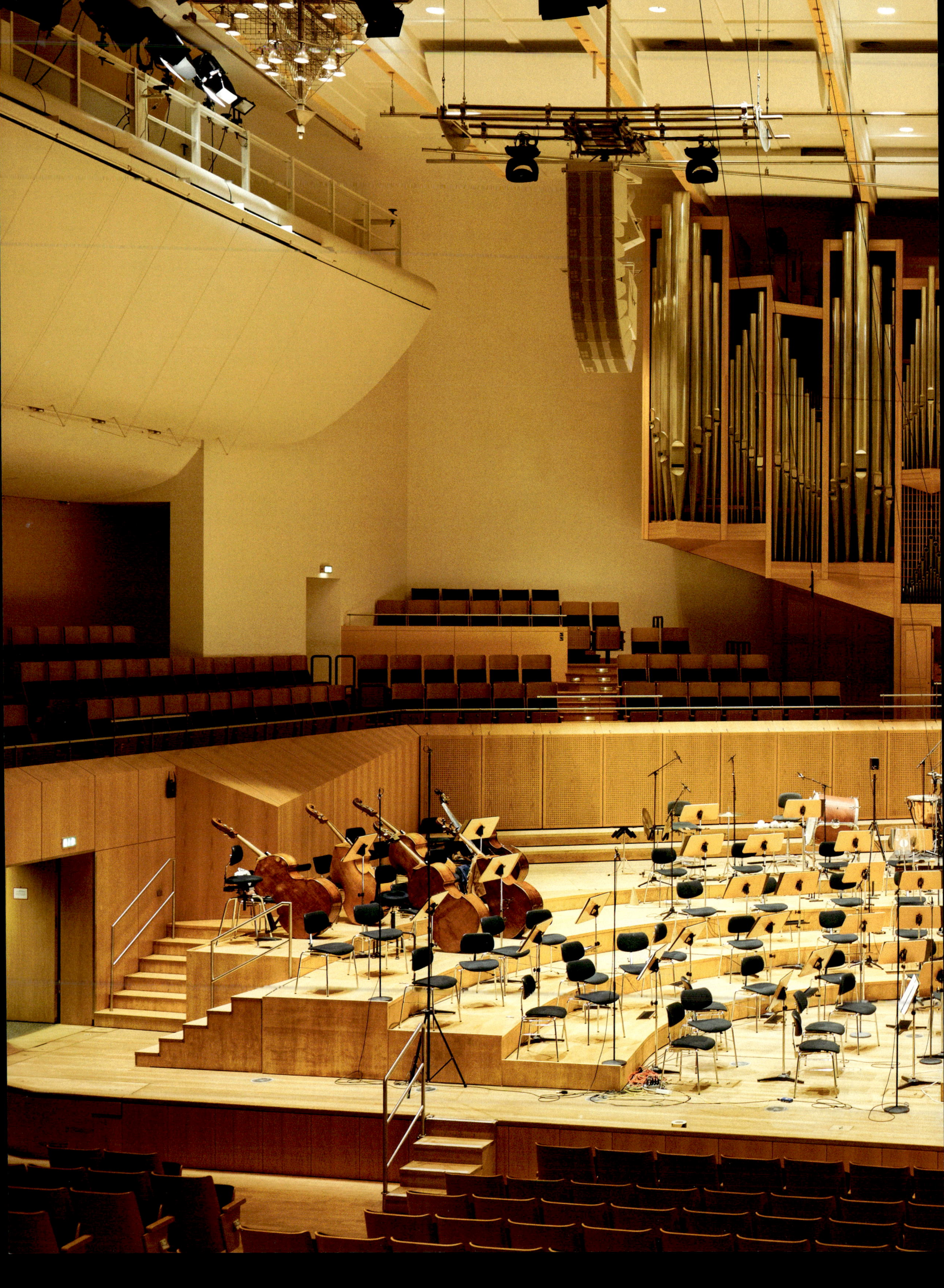

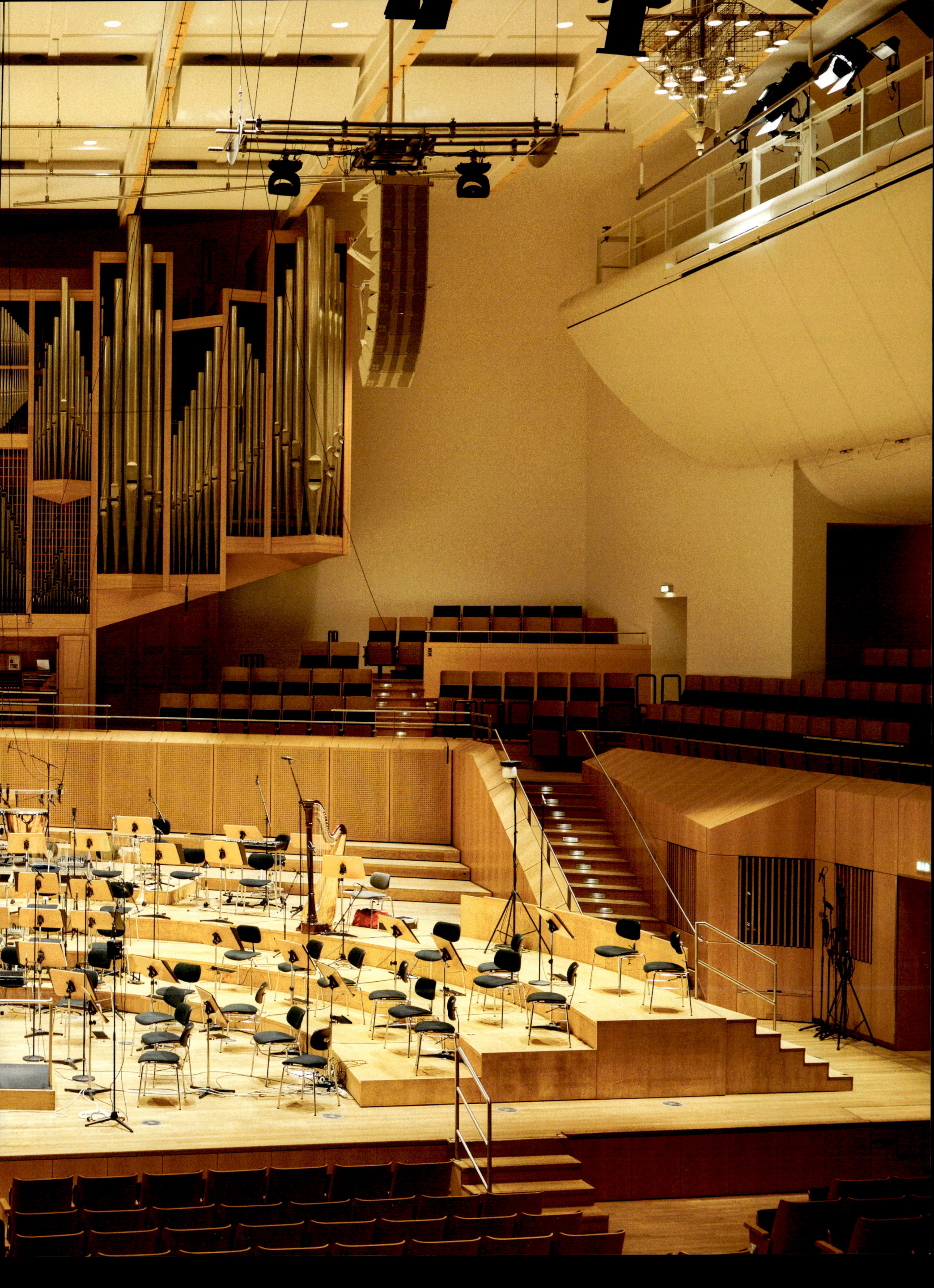

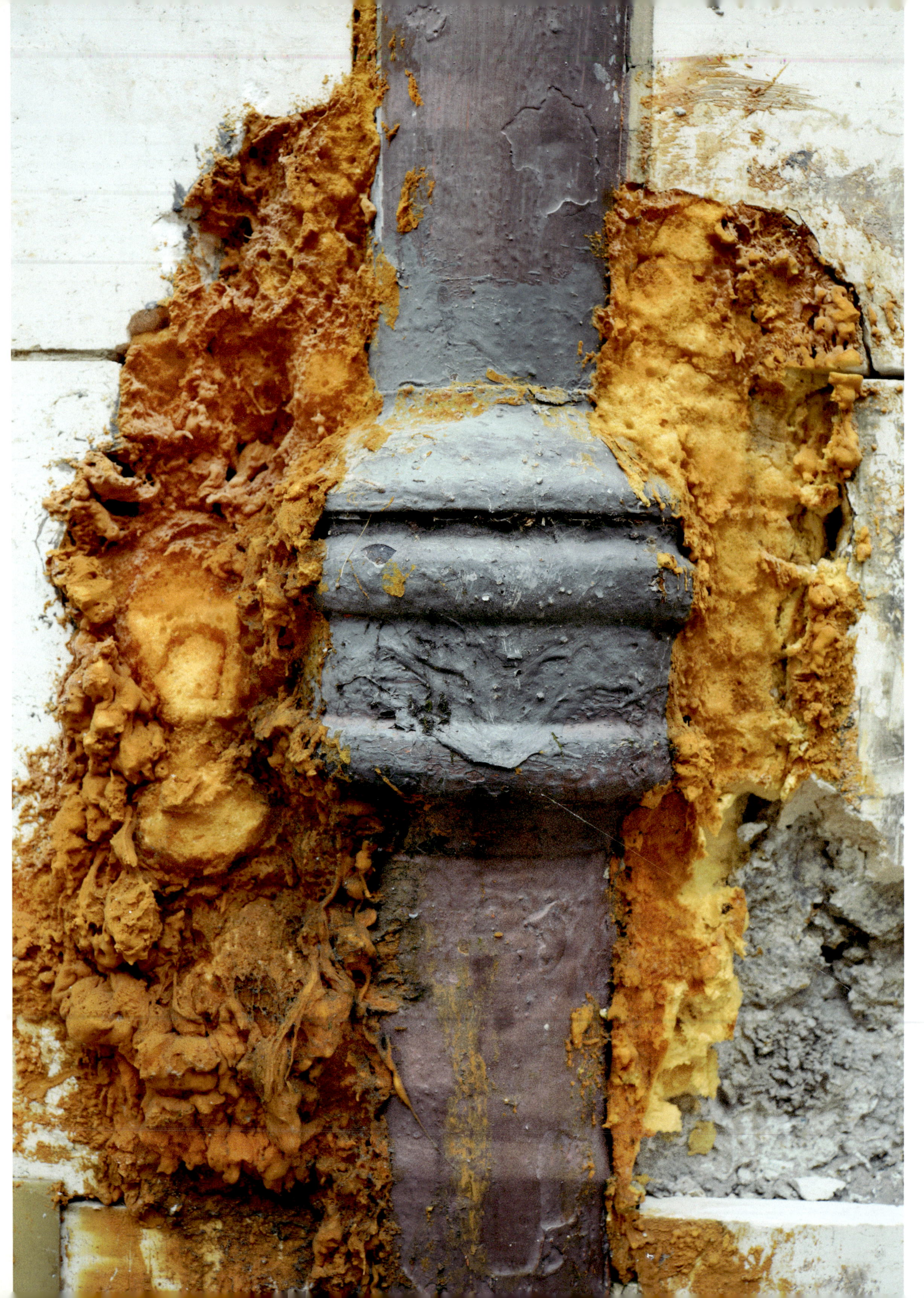

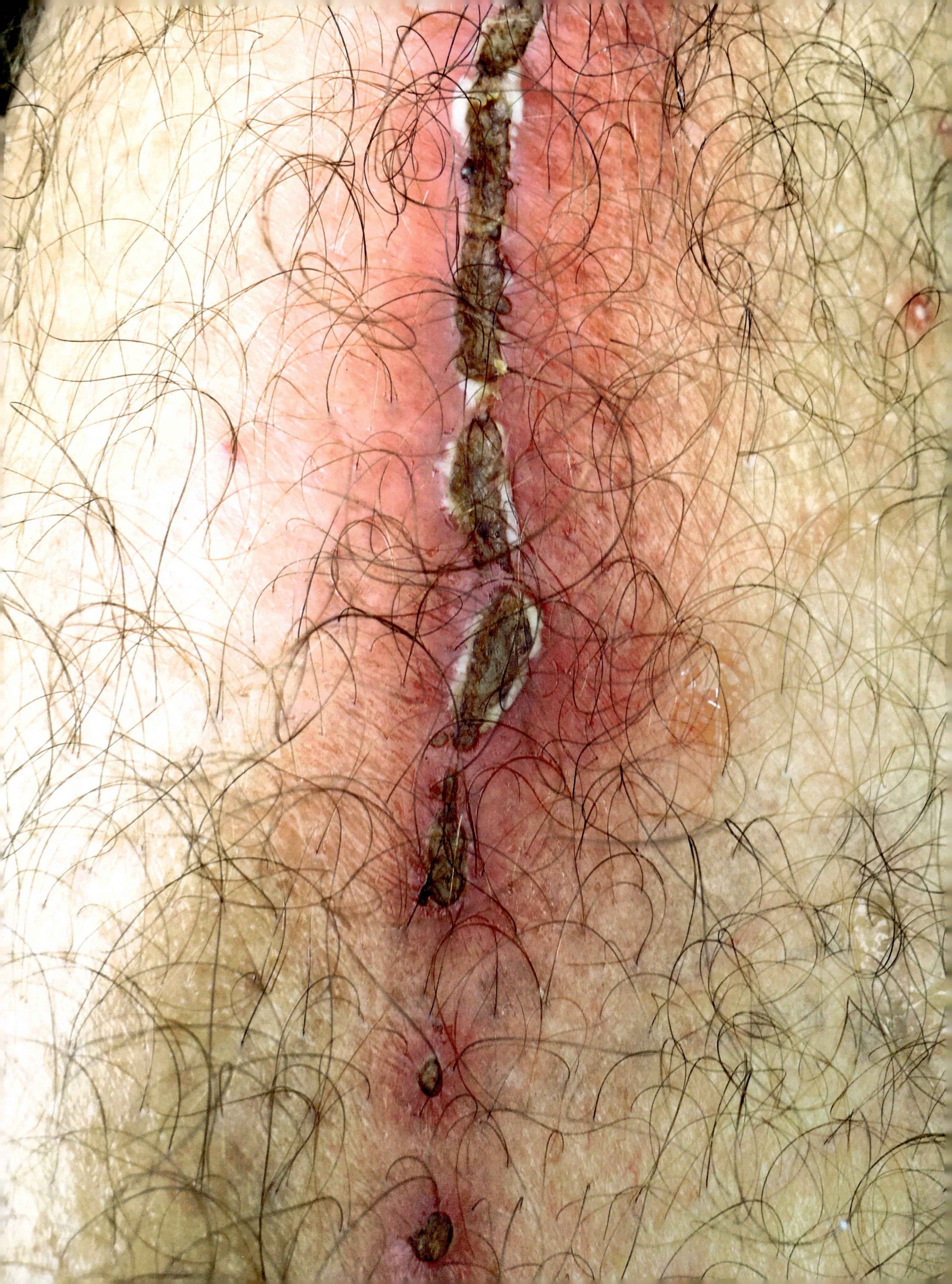

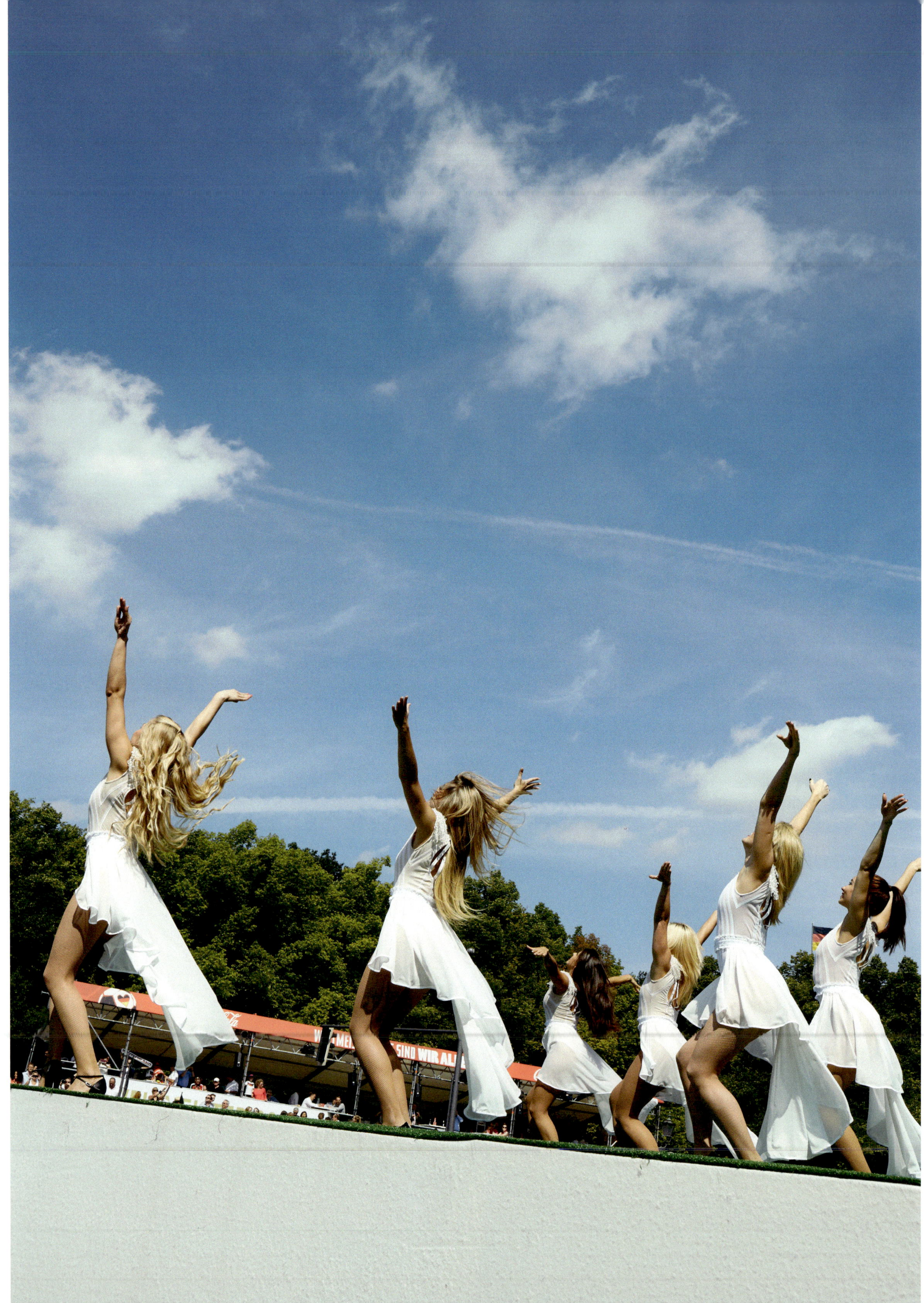
SIND WIR

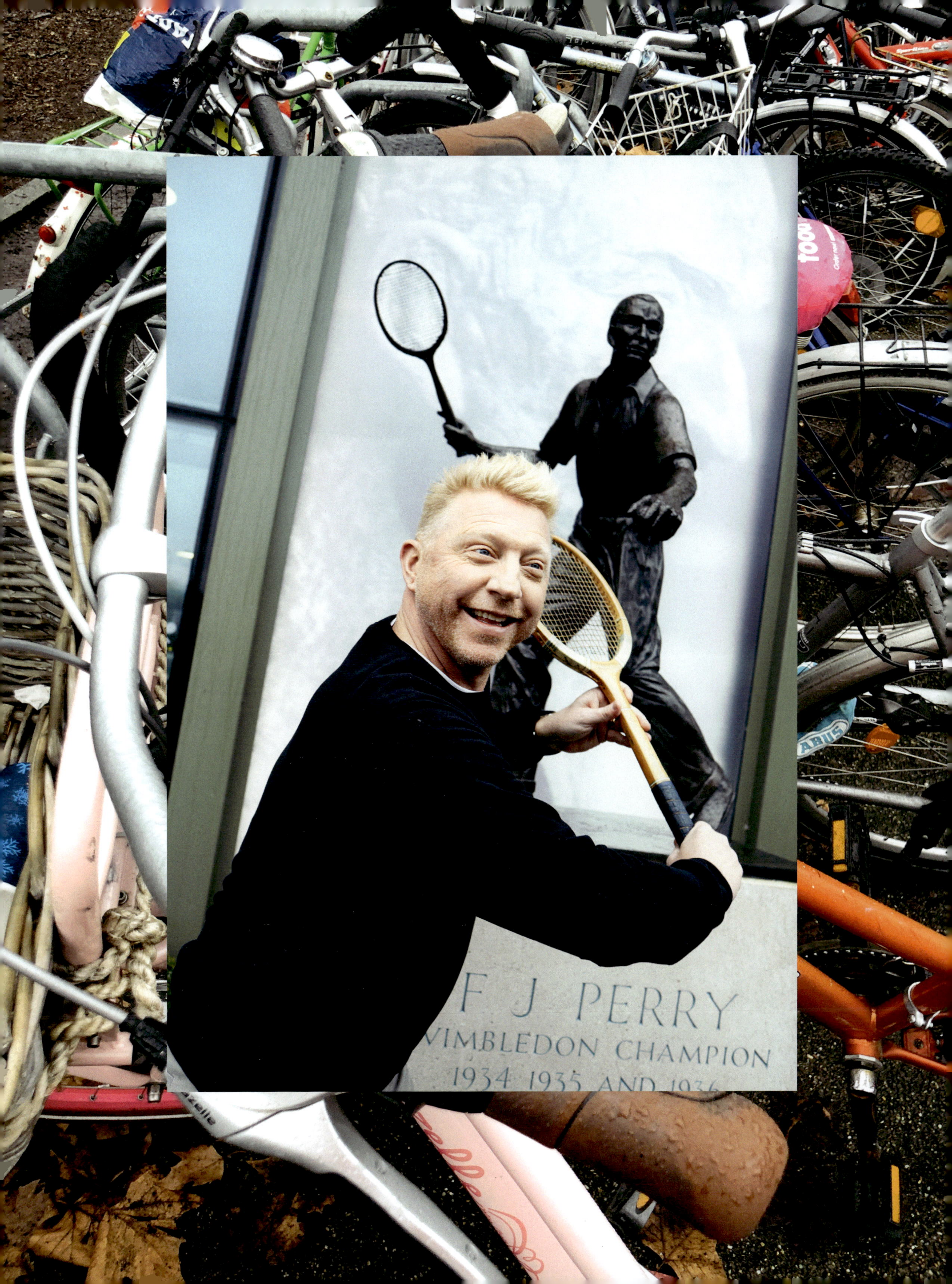
F J PERRY
WIMBLEDON CHAMPION

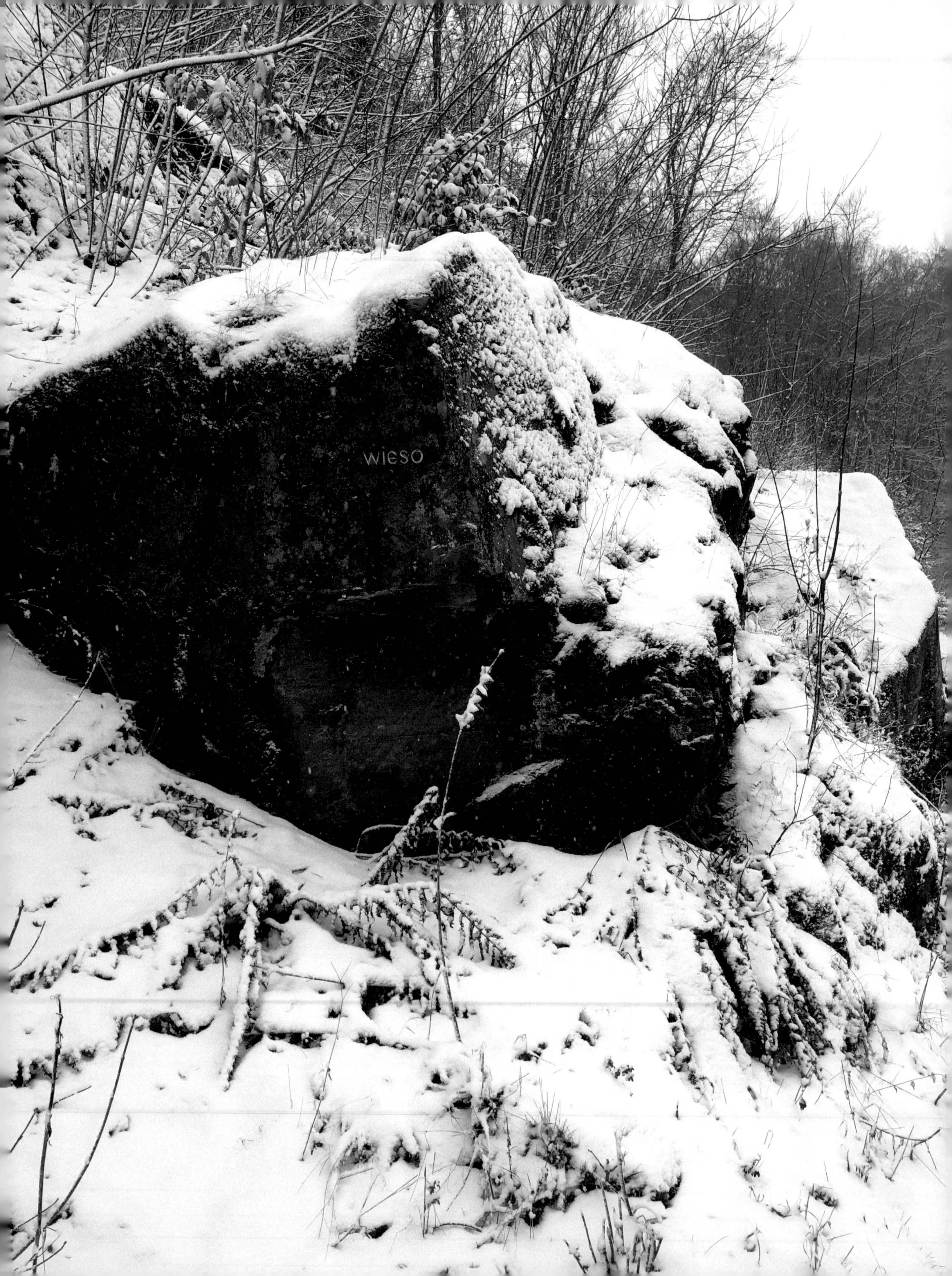
wieso

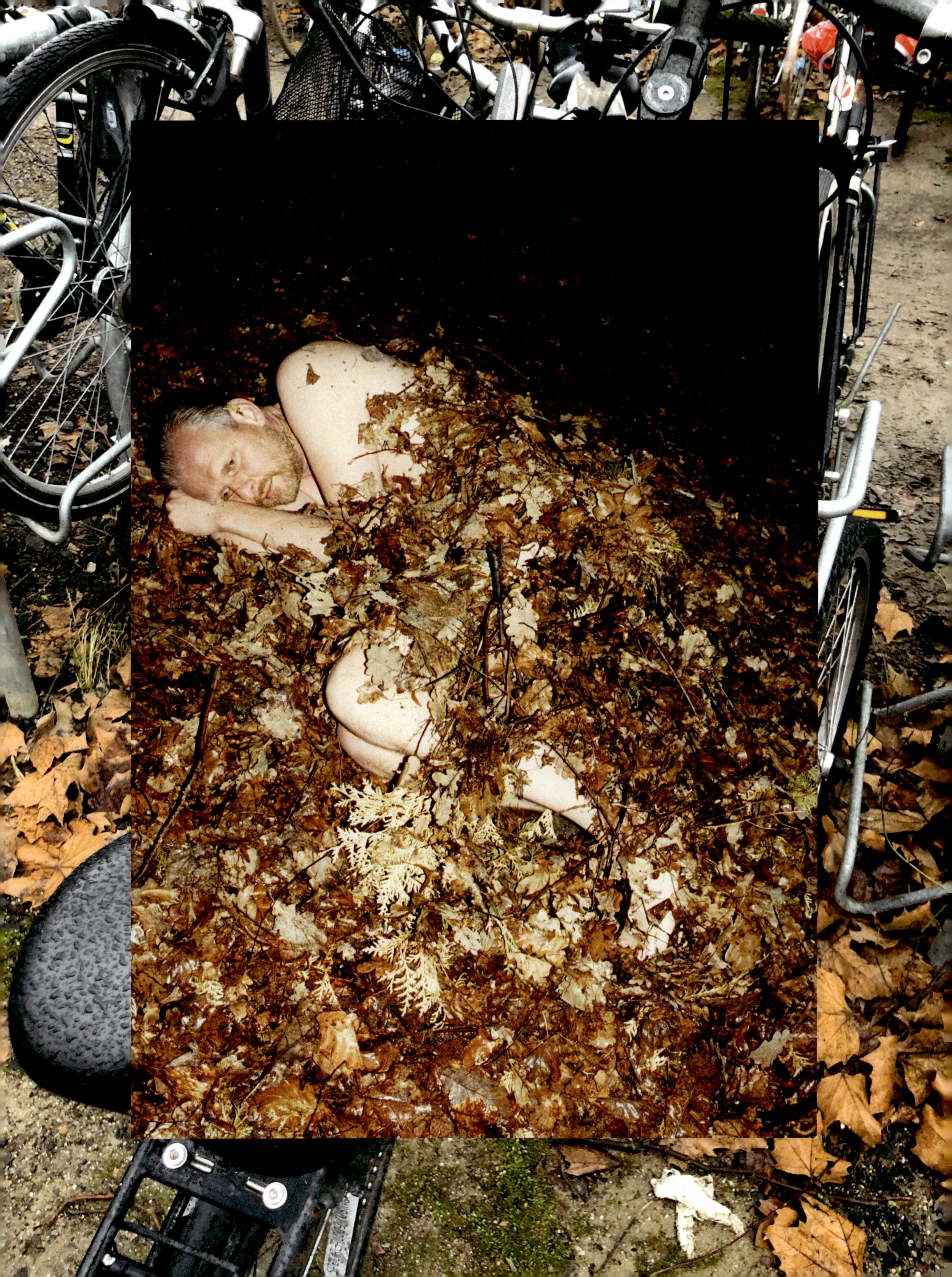

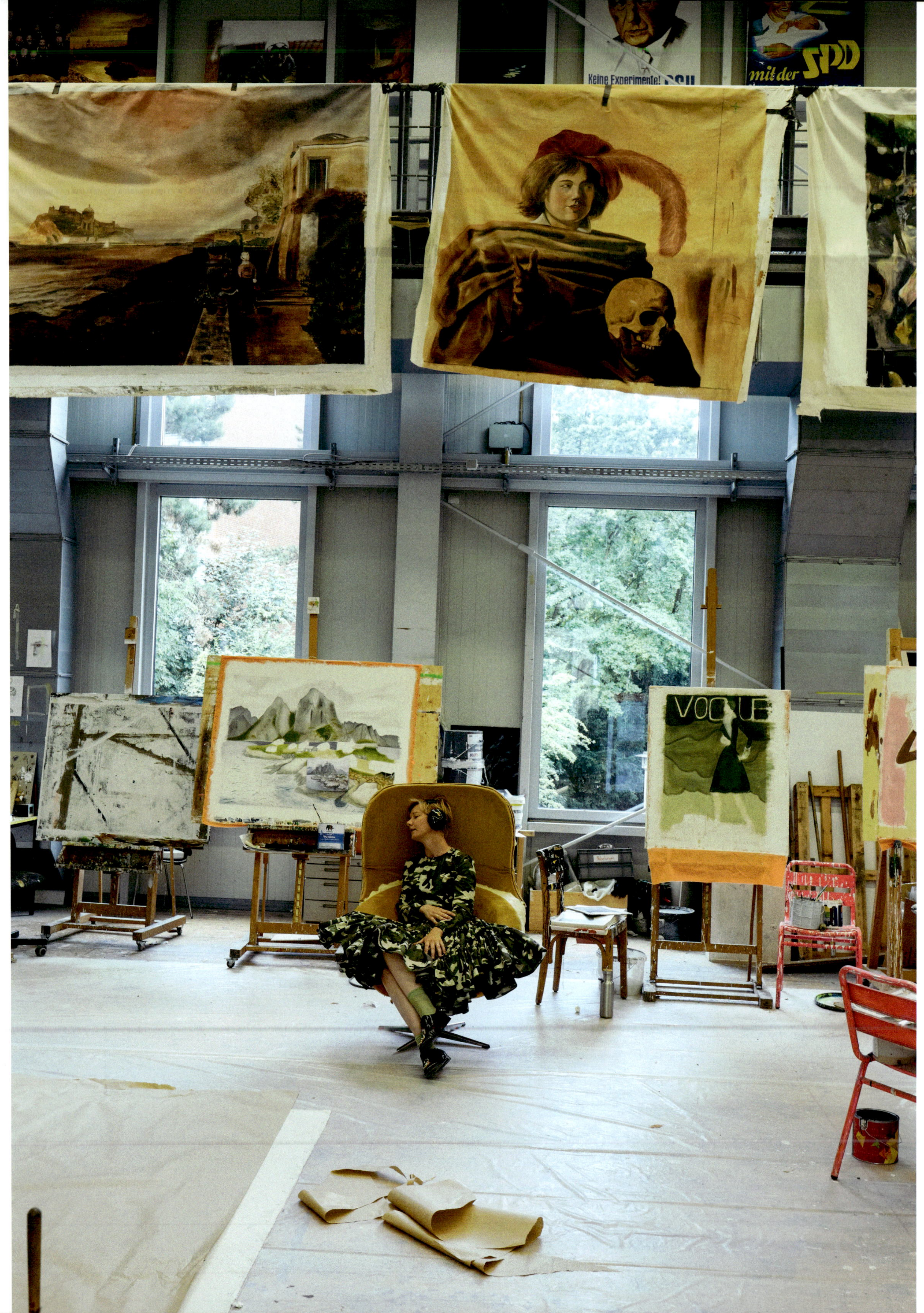
Keine Experimente!
mit der SPD
VOGUE

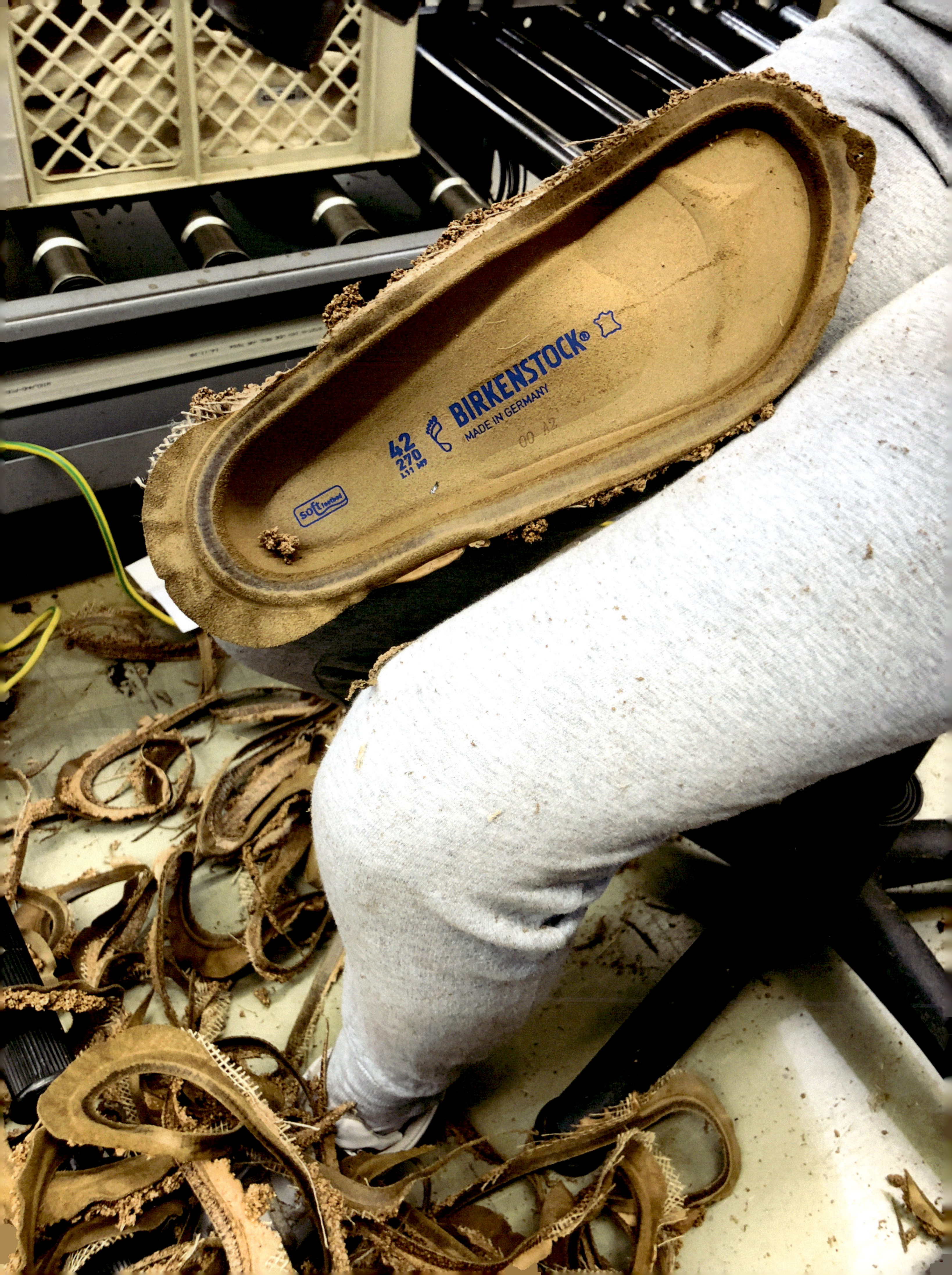
BIRKENSTOCK®
MADE IN GERMANY
42
270
soft

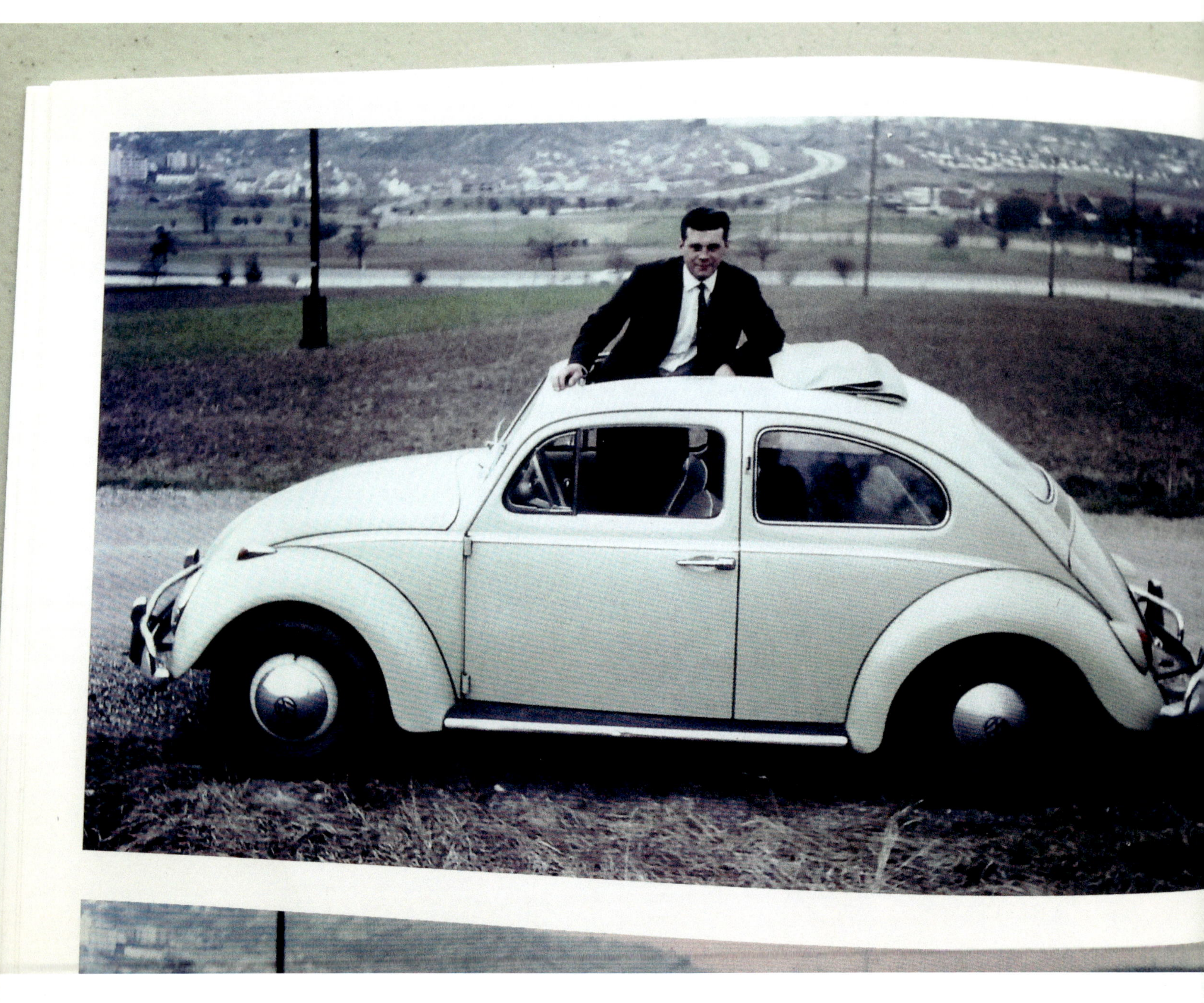

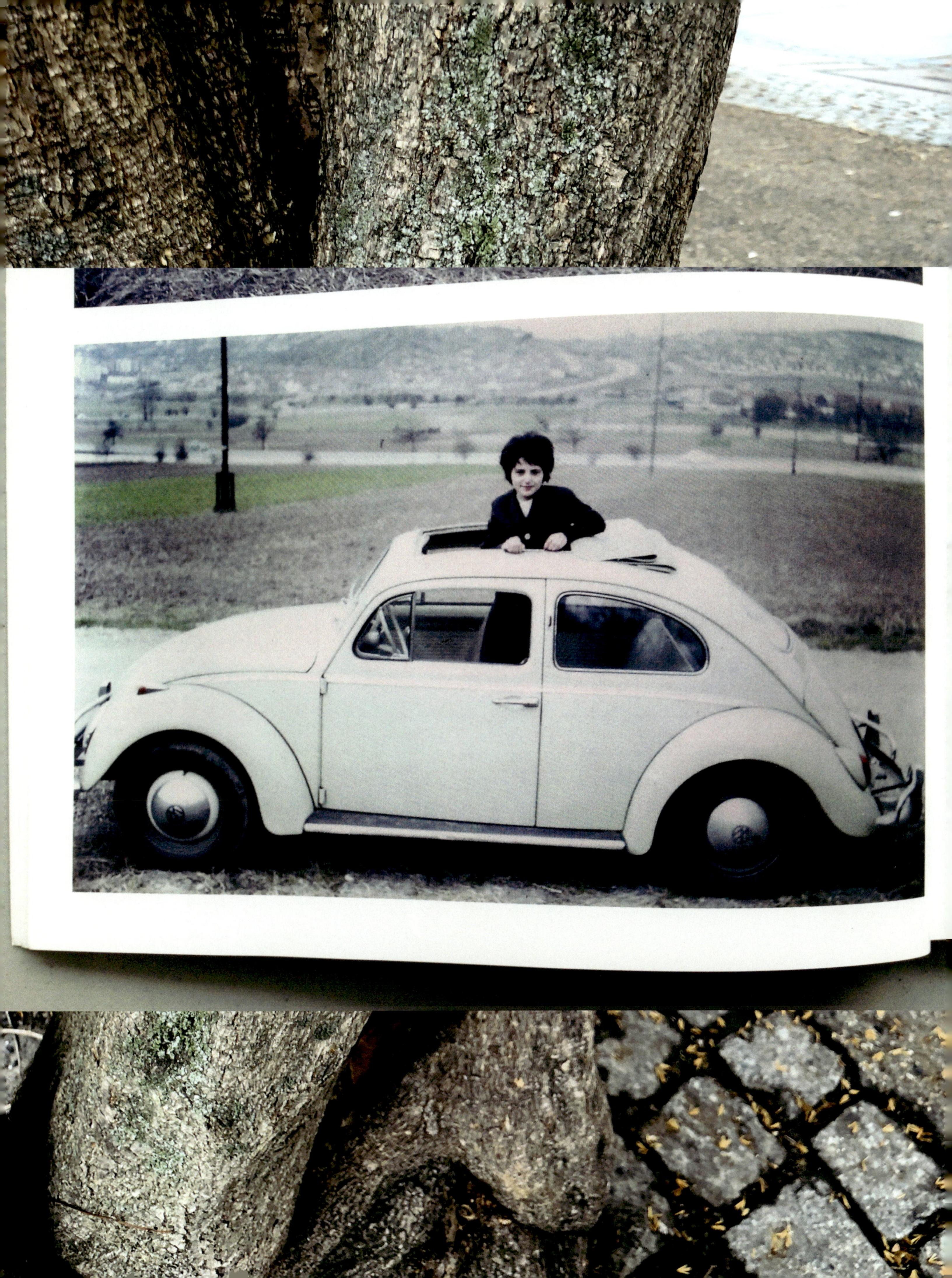

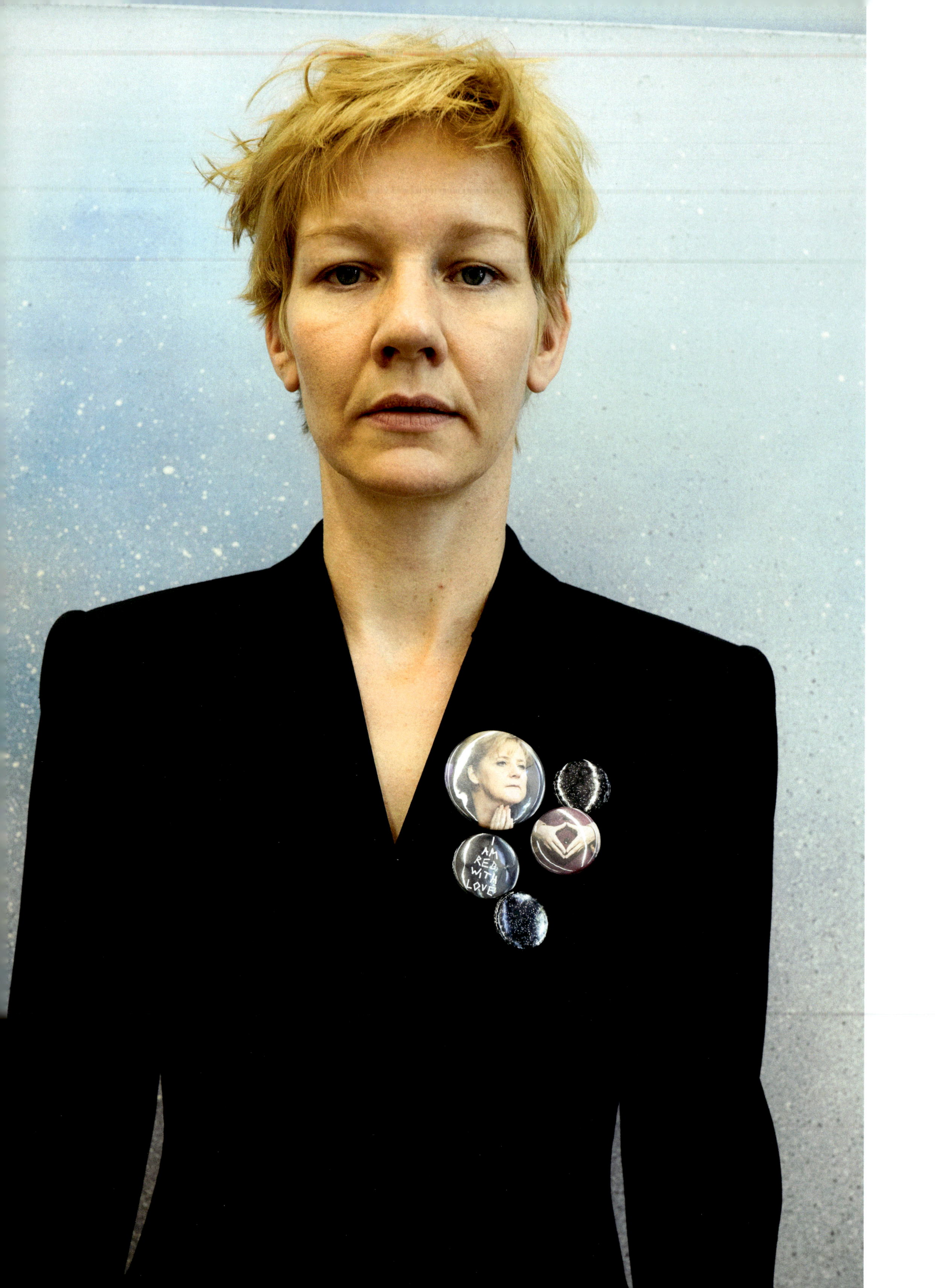
I AM RED WITH LOVE

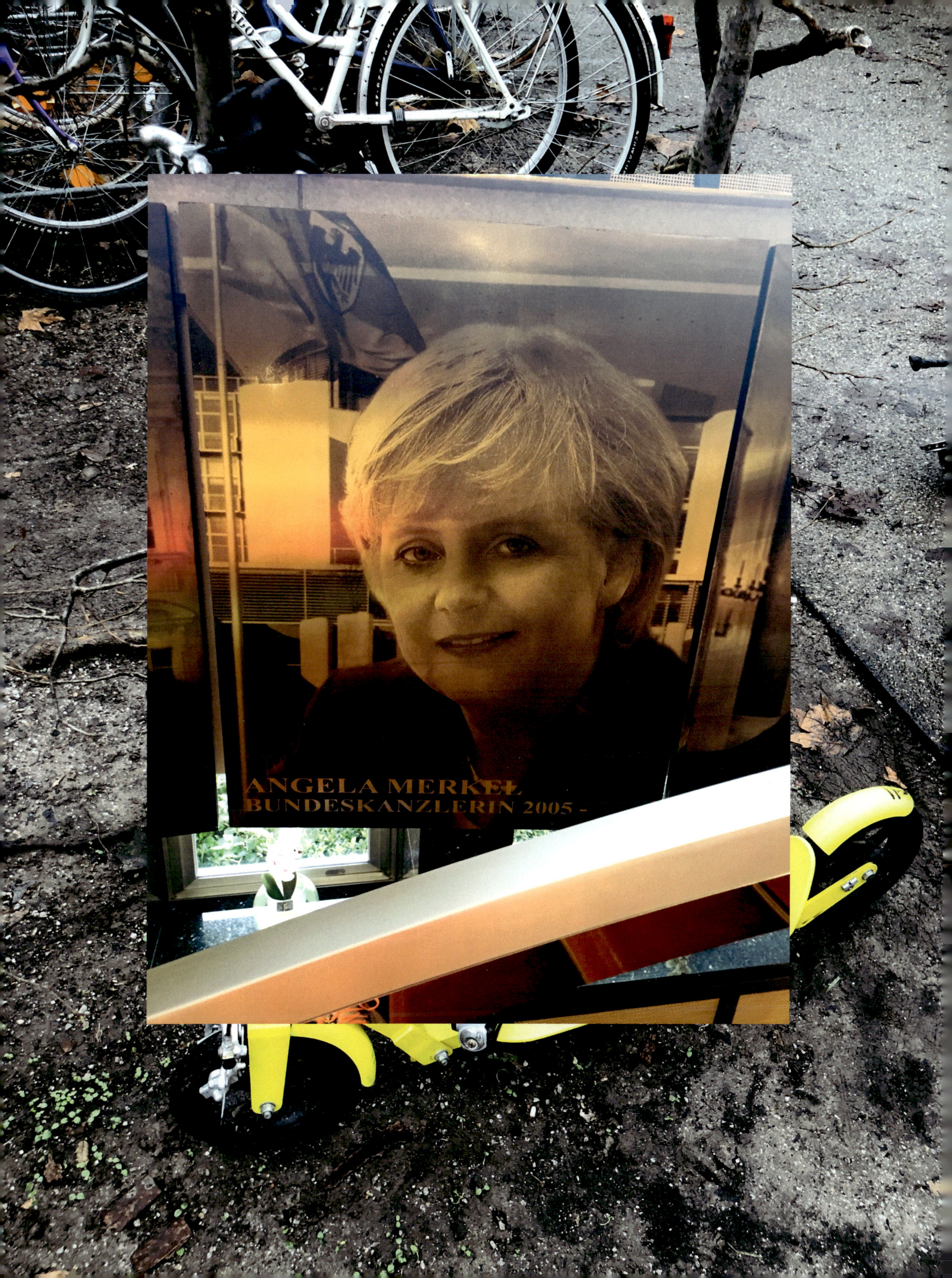
ANGELA MERKEL
BUNDESKANZLERIN 2005 -

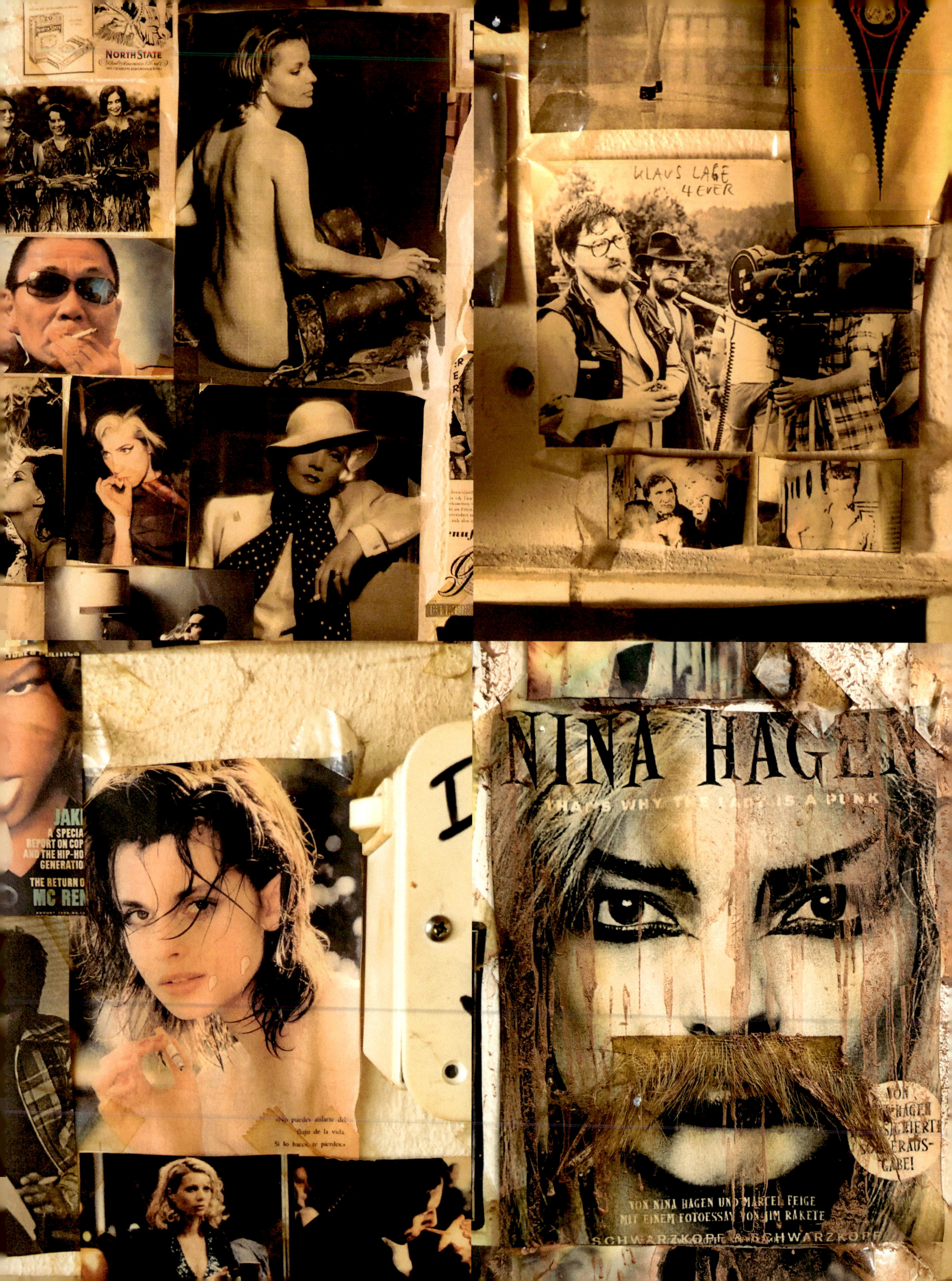
NORTH STATE
KLAUS LAGE
4EVER
«No puedes aislarte del
flujo de la vida
Si lo haces, te pierdes.»
NINA HAGEN
VON NINA HAGEN UND MARCEL FEIGE
MIT EINEM FOTOESSAY VON JIM RAKETE

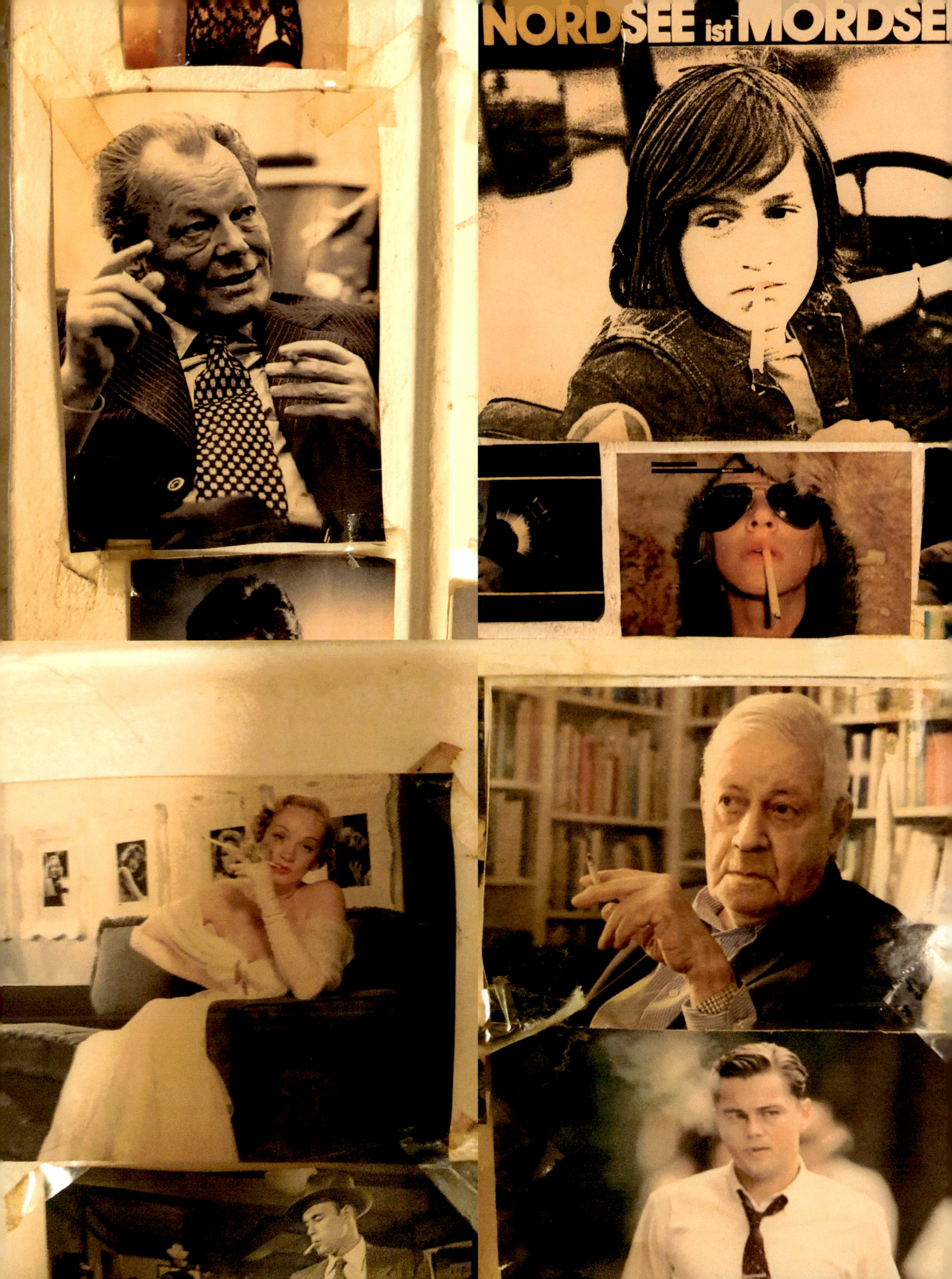
NORDSEE ist MORDSE

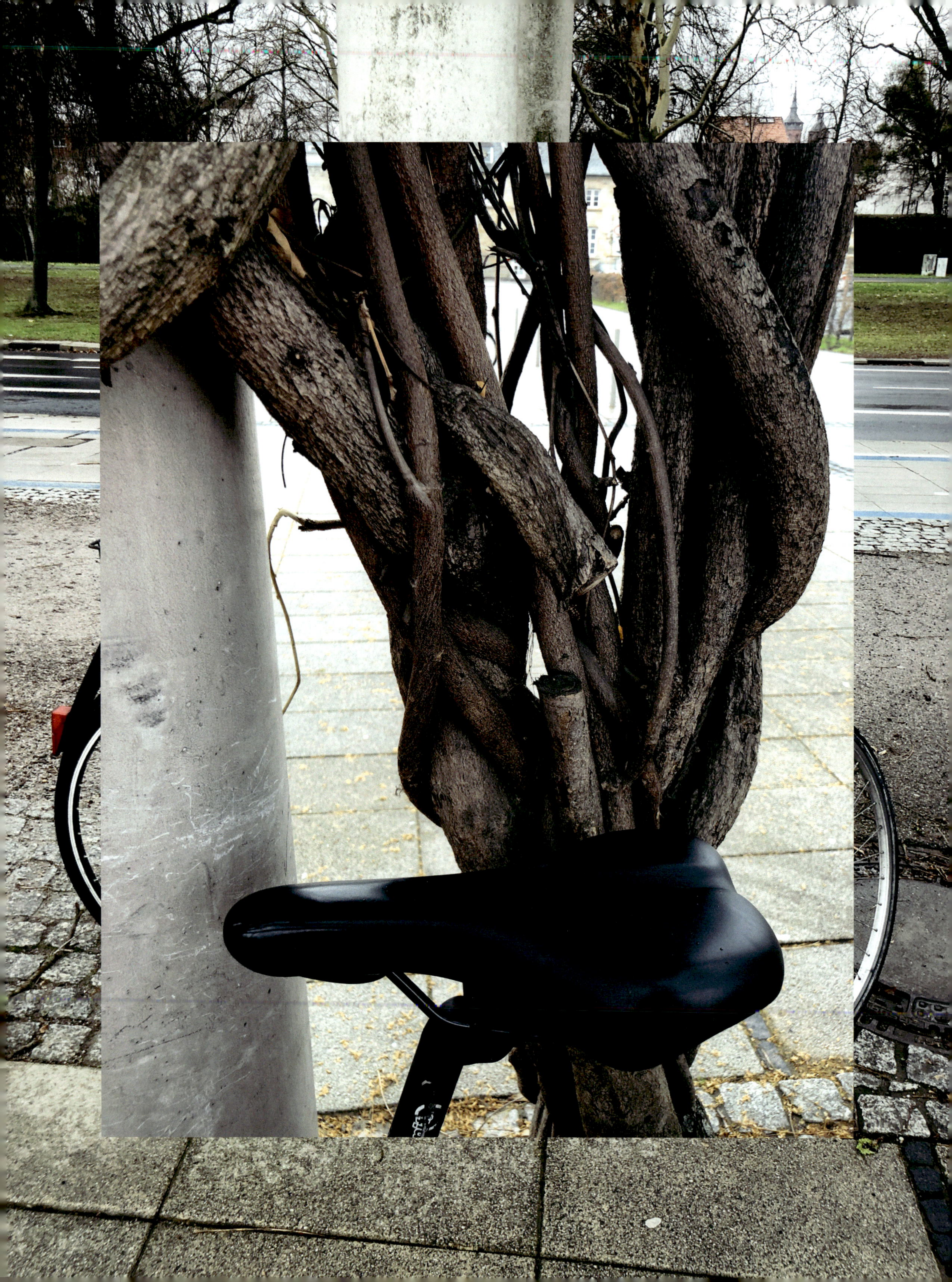

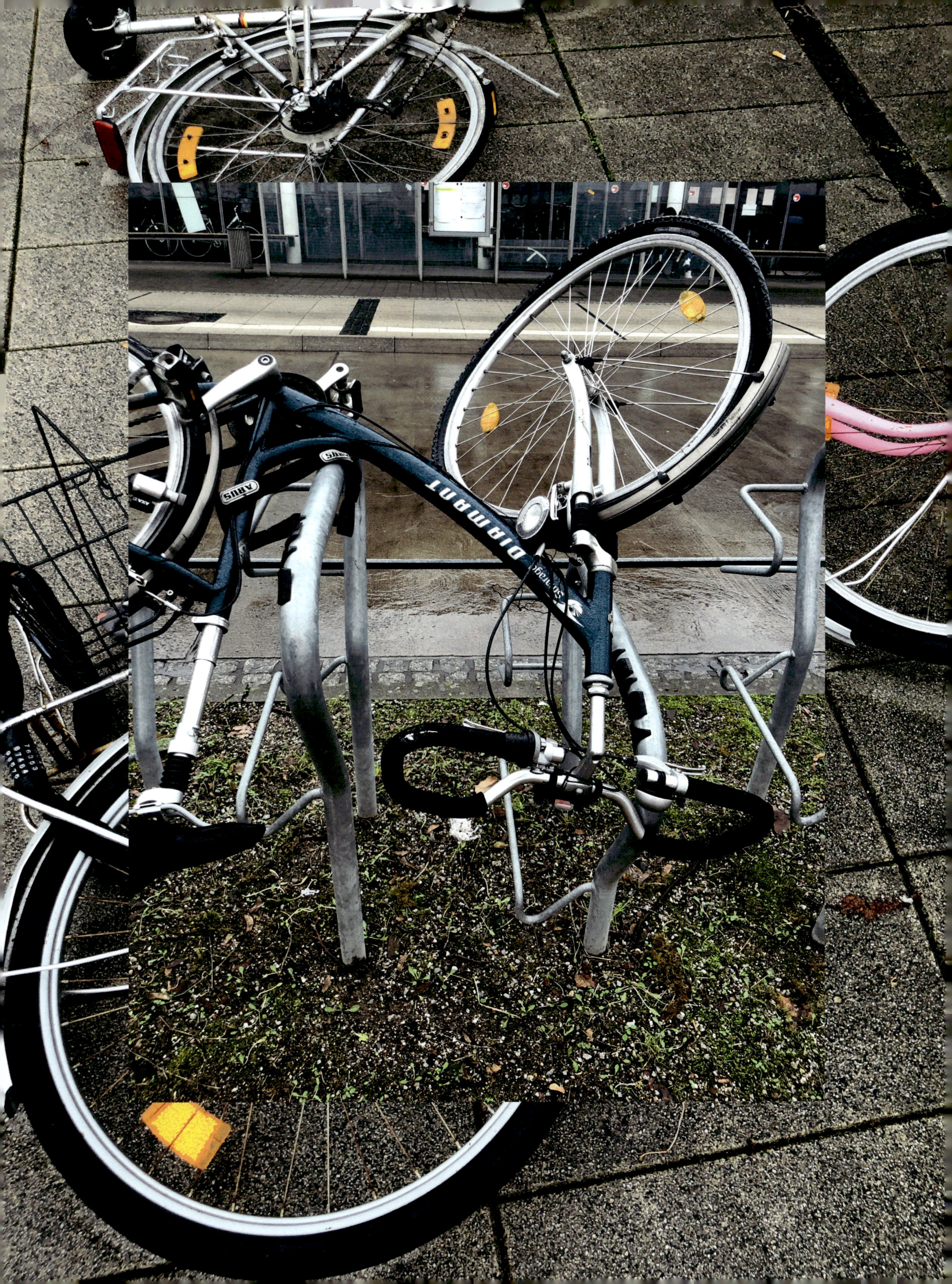
DIAMANT
ABUS

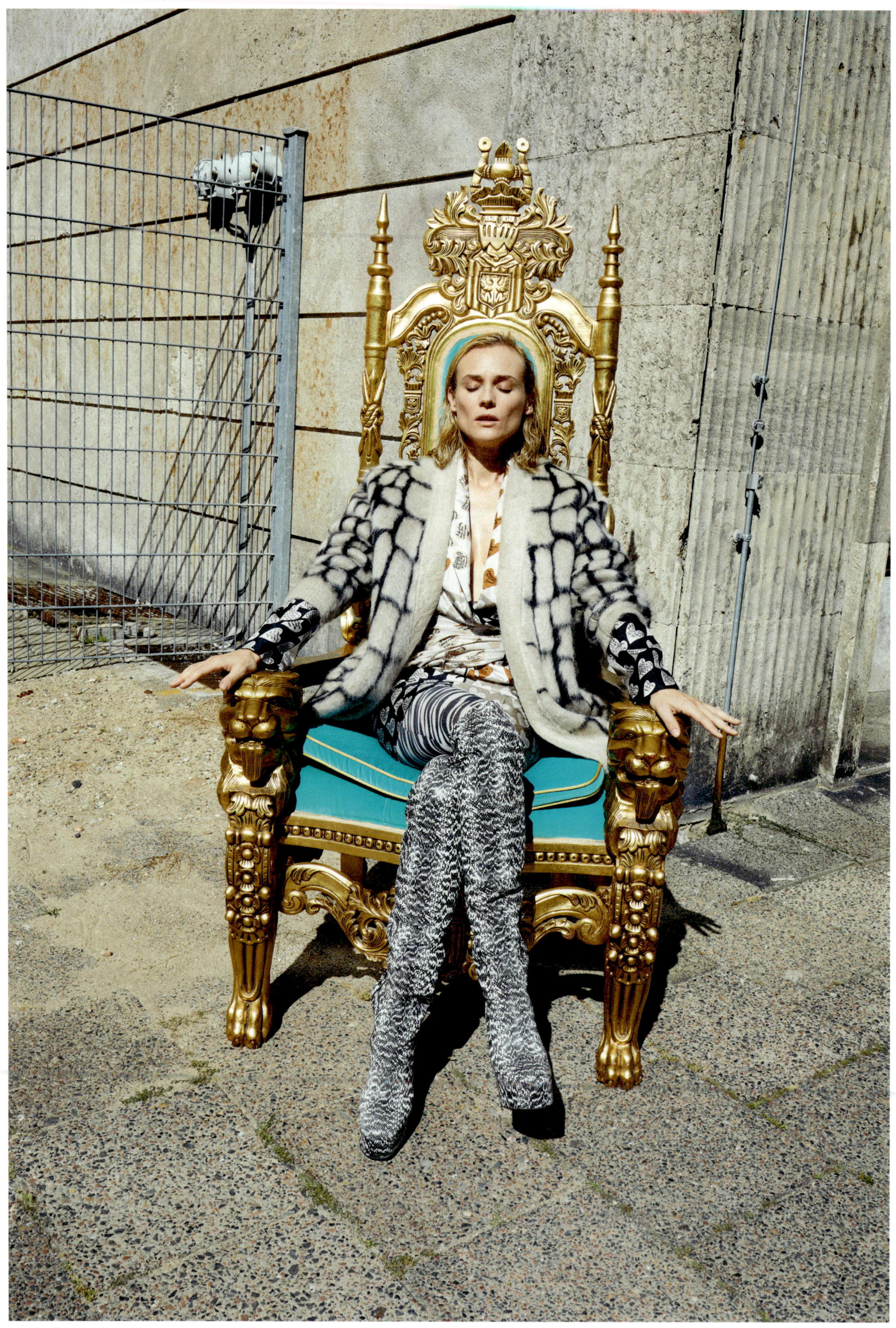

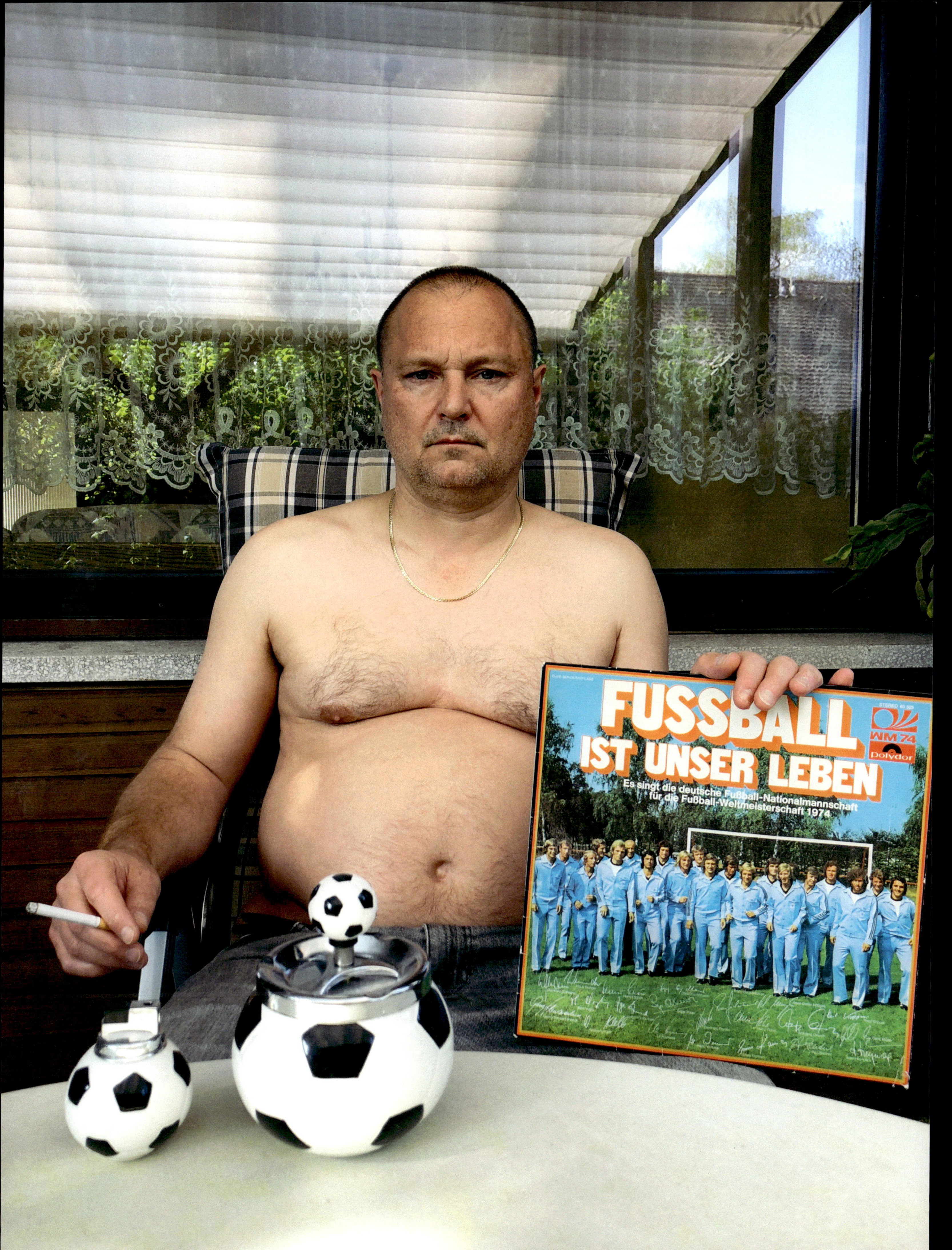
FUSSBALL
IST UNSER LEBEN
Es singt die deutsche Fußball-Nationalmannschaft
für die Fußball-Weltmeisterschaft 1974
WM 74
Polydor

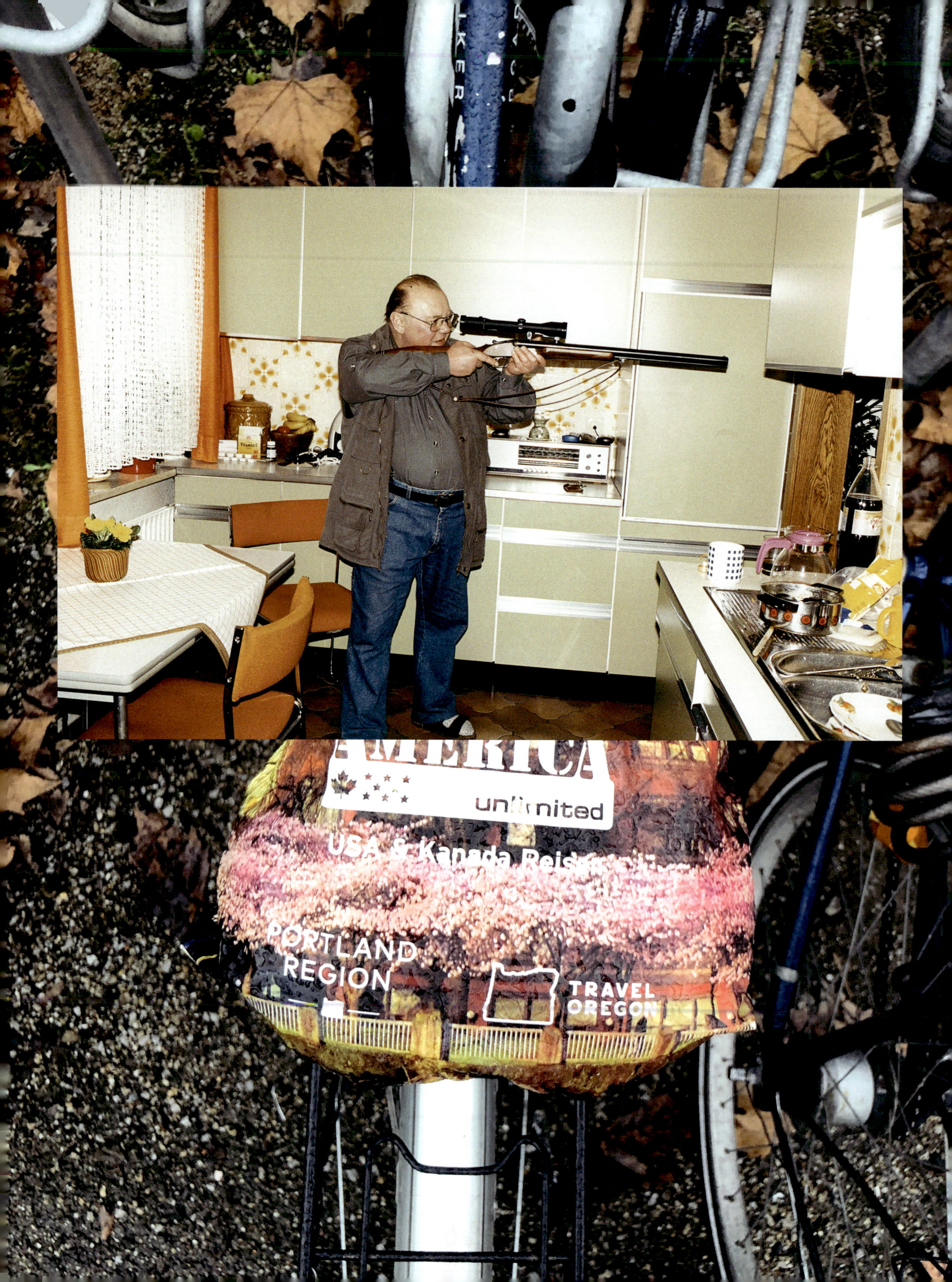
AMERICA
unlimited
USA & Kanada Reisen
PORTLAND
REGION
TRAVEL
OREGON

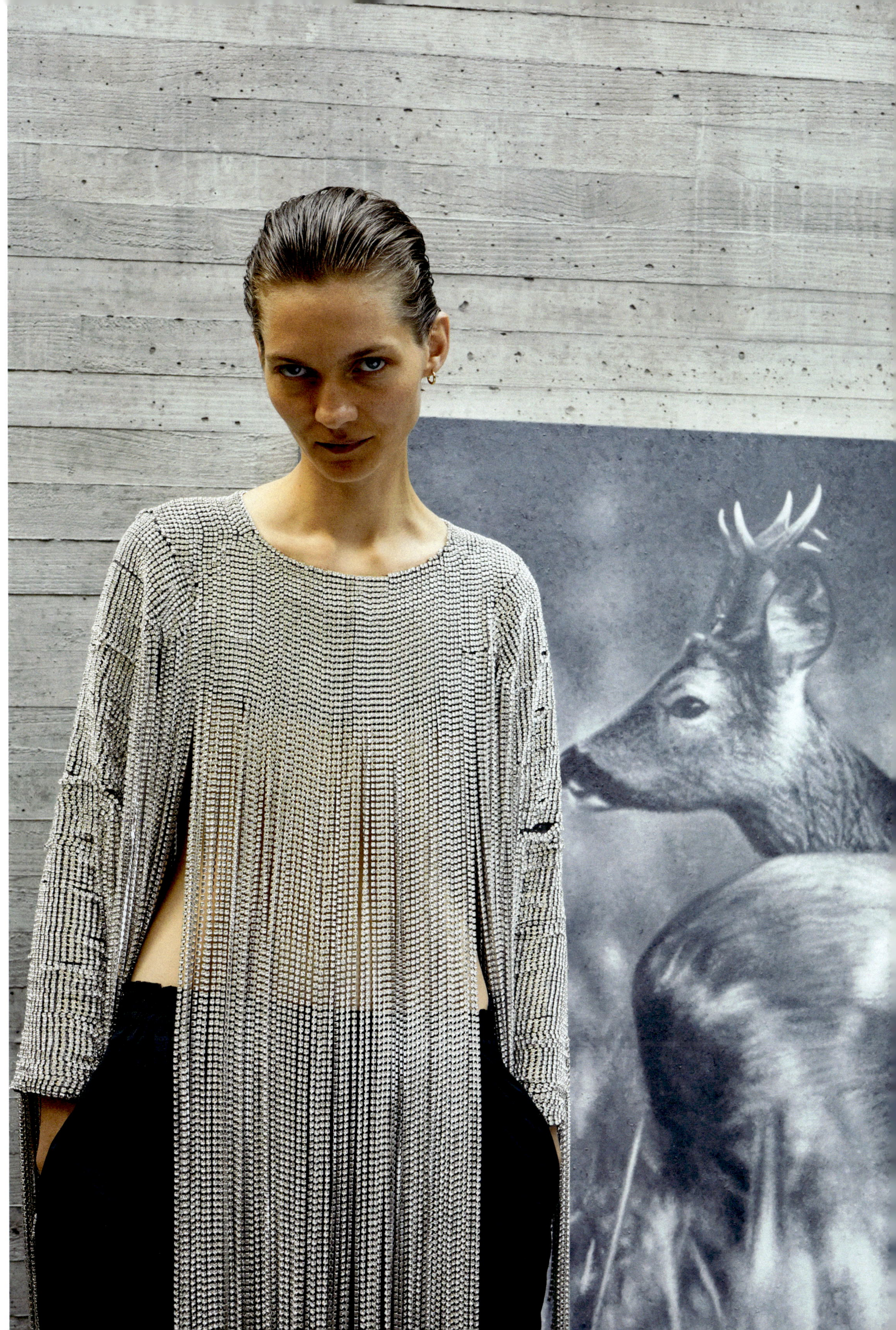

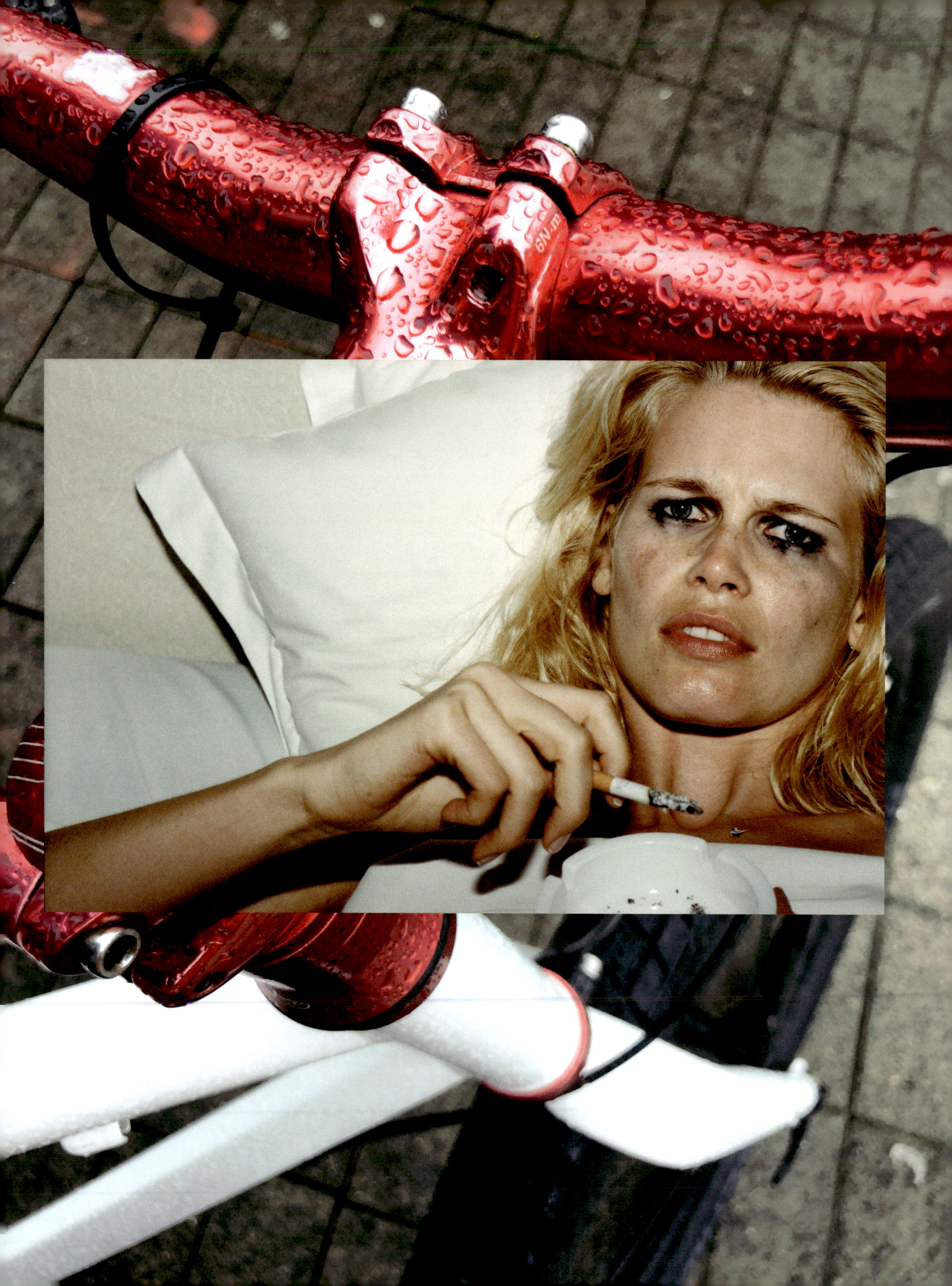
6N.m

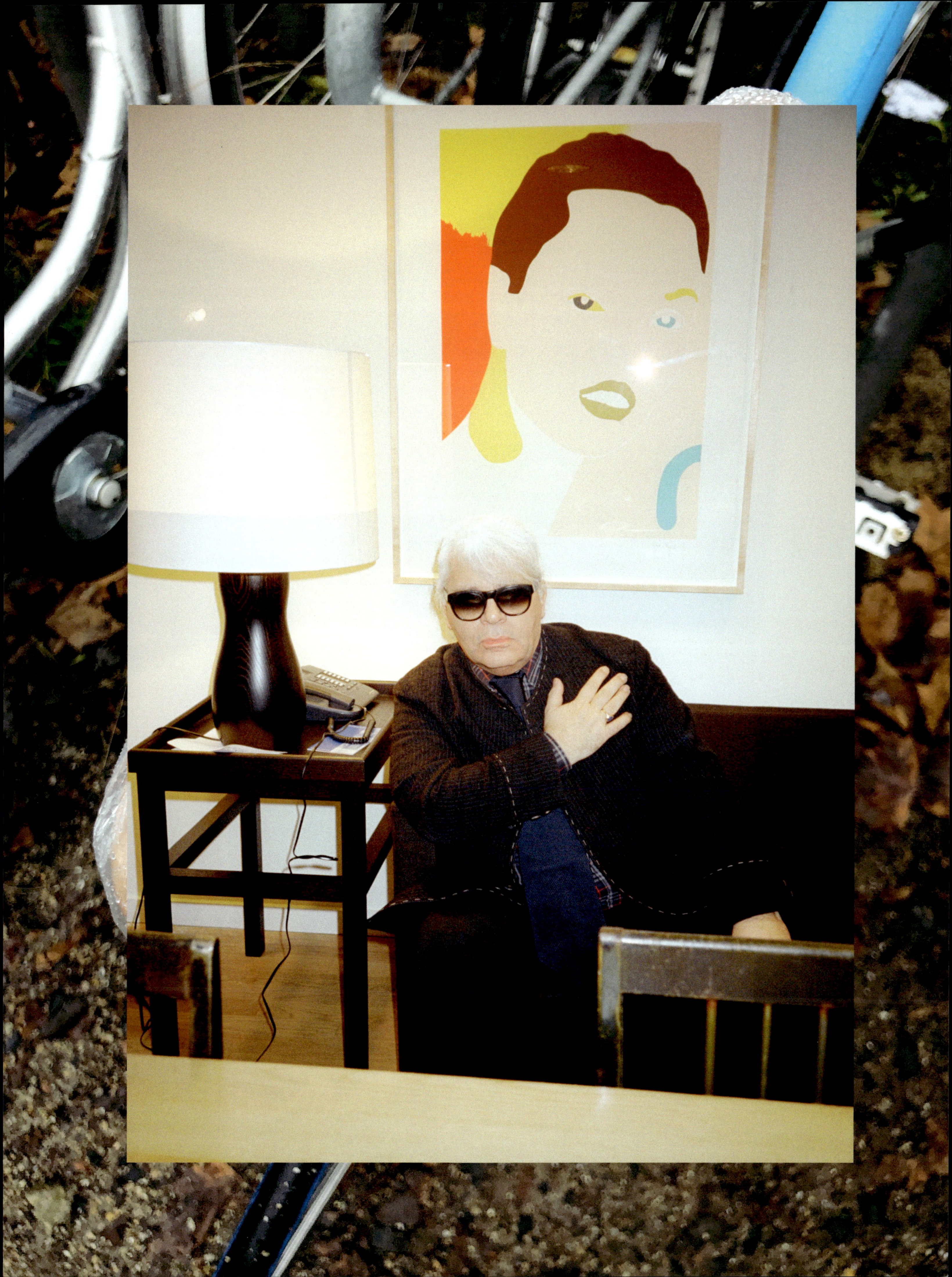

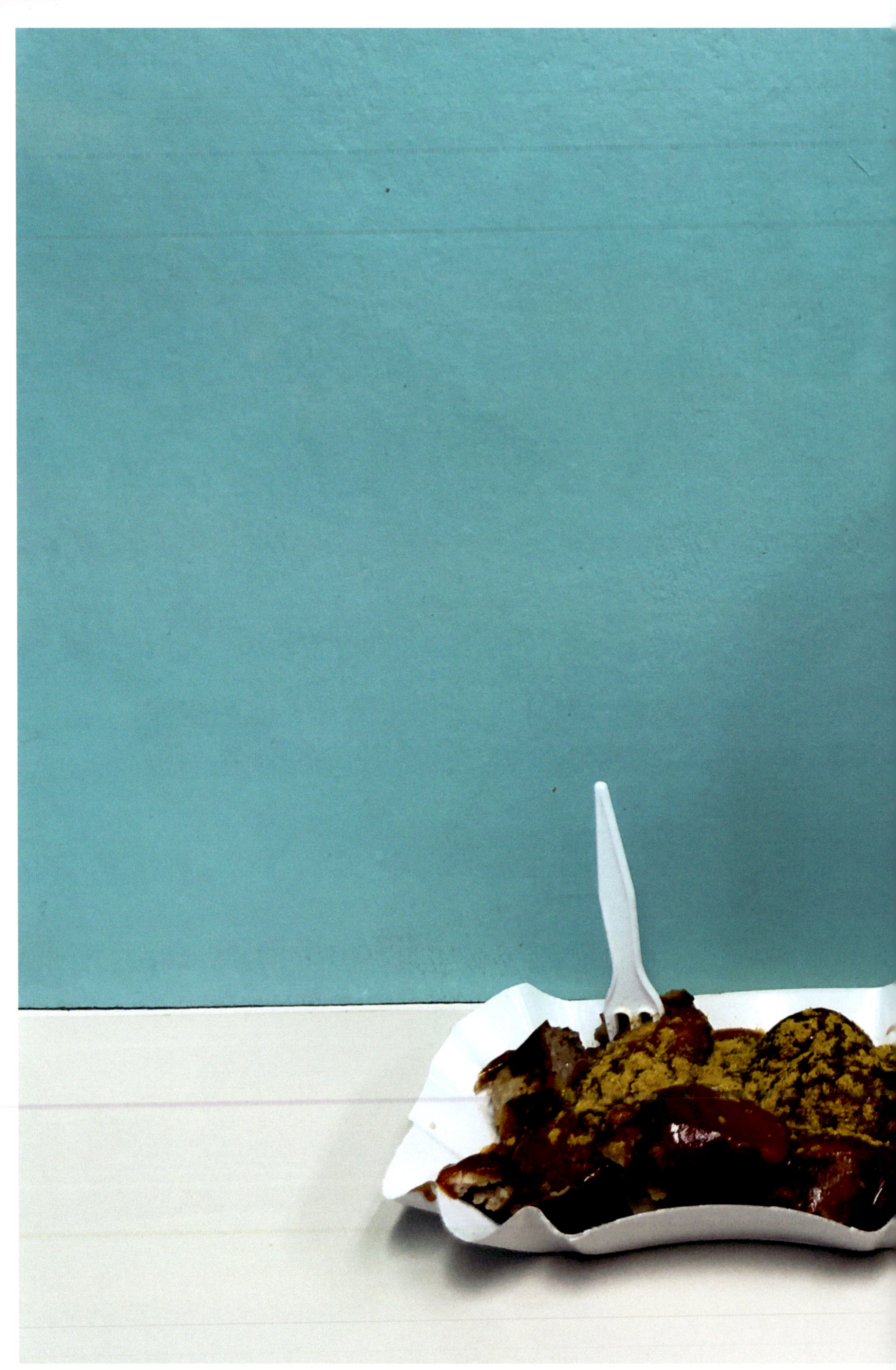

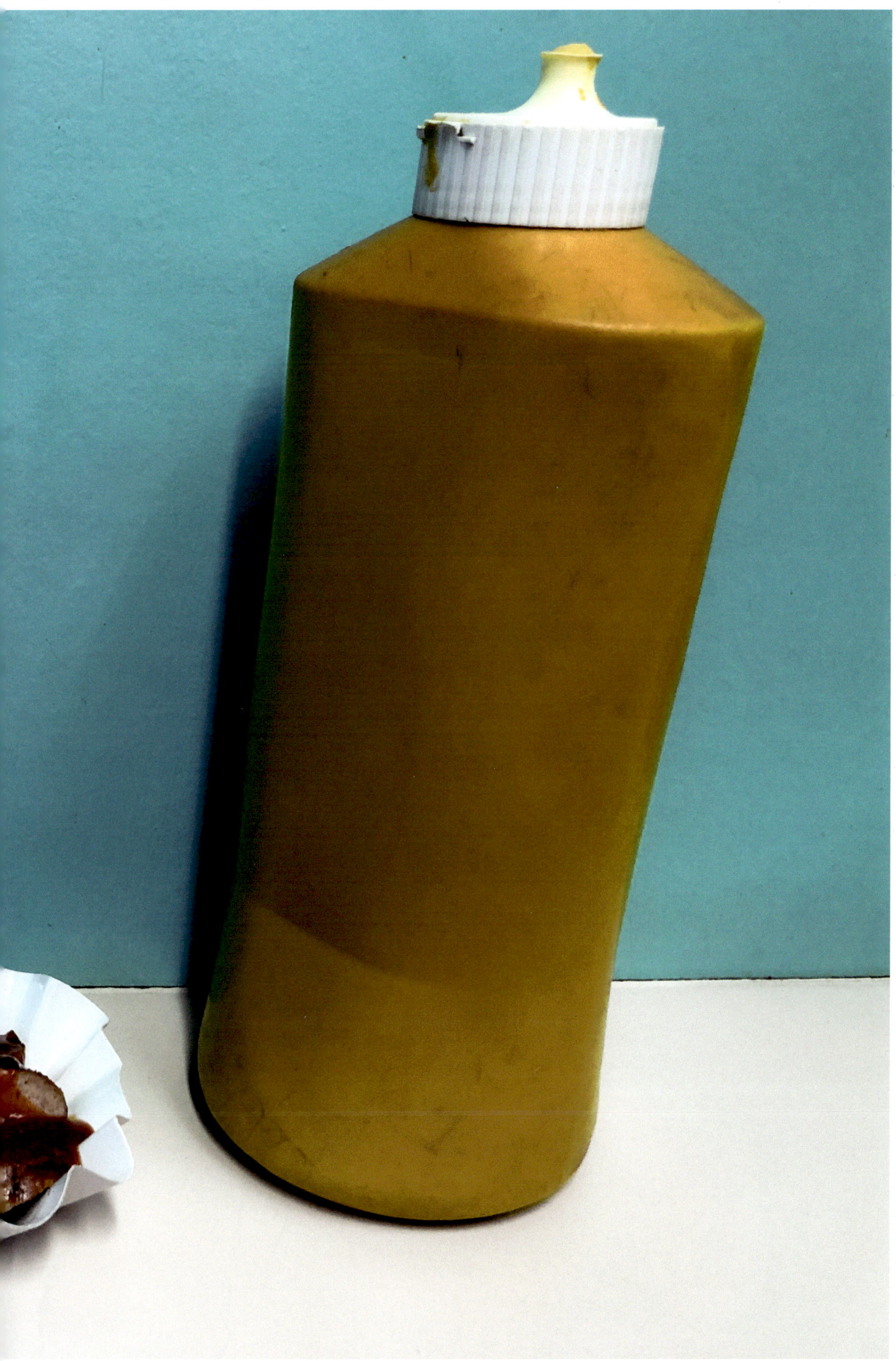

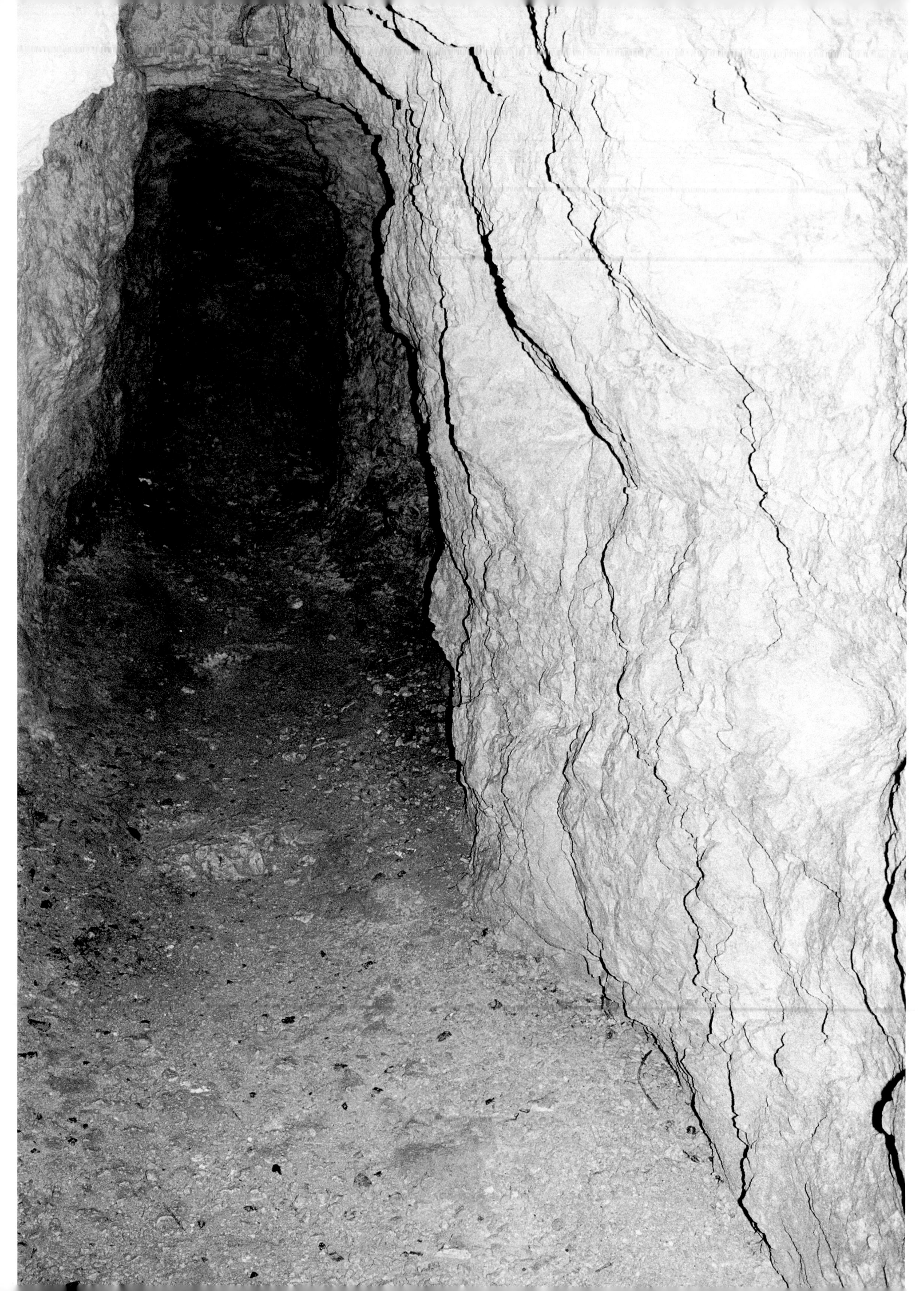

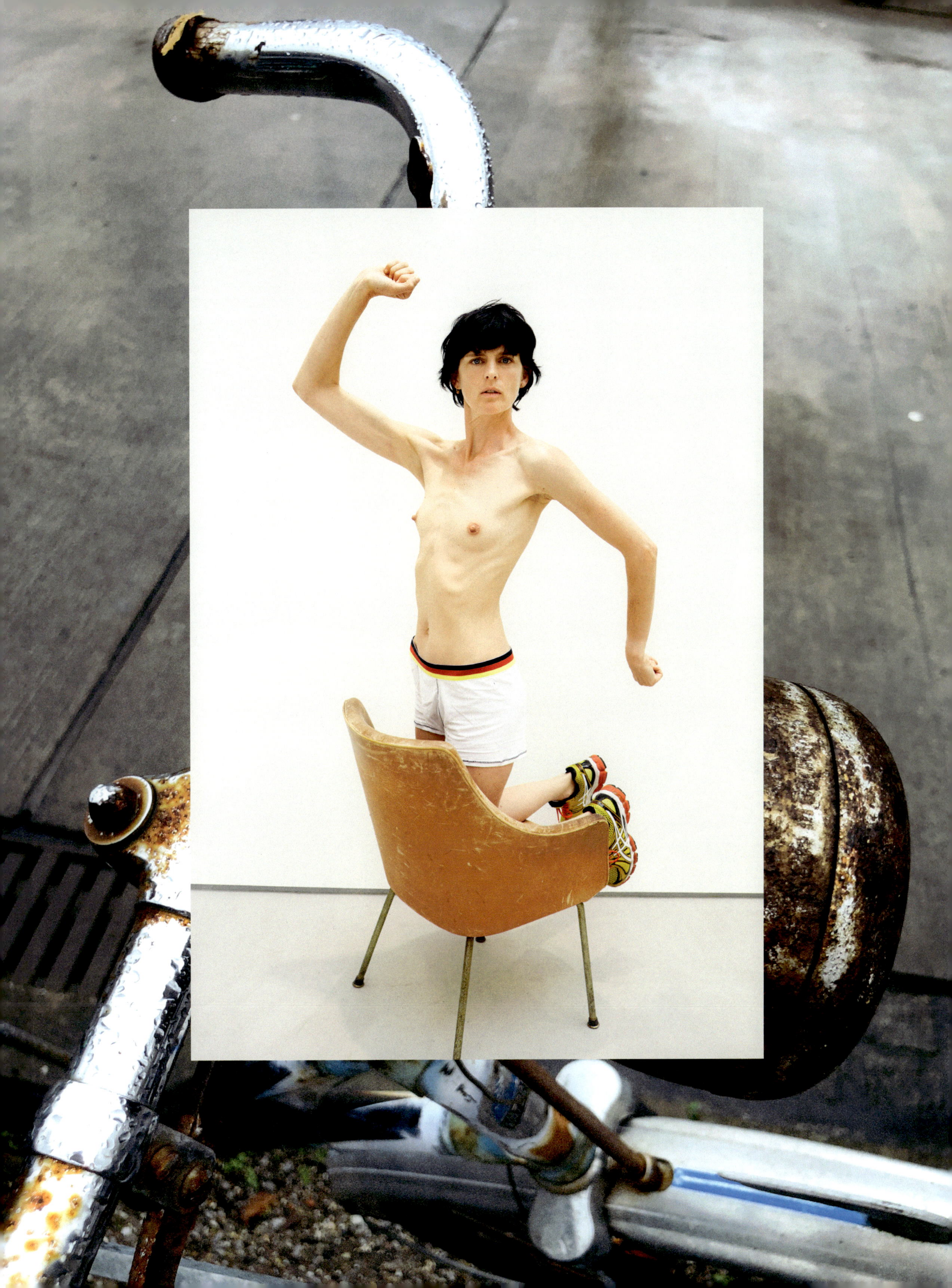

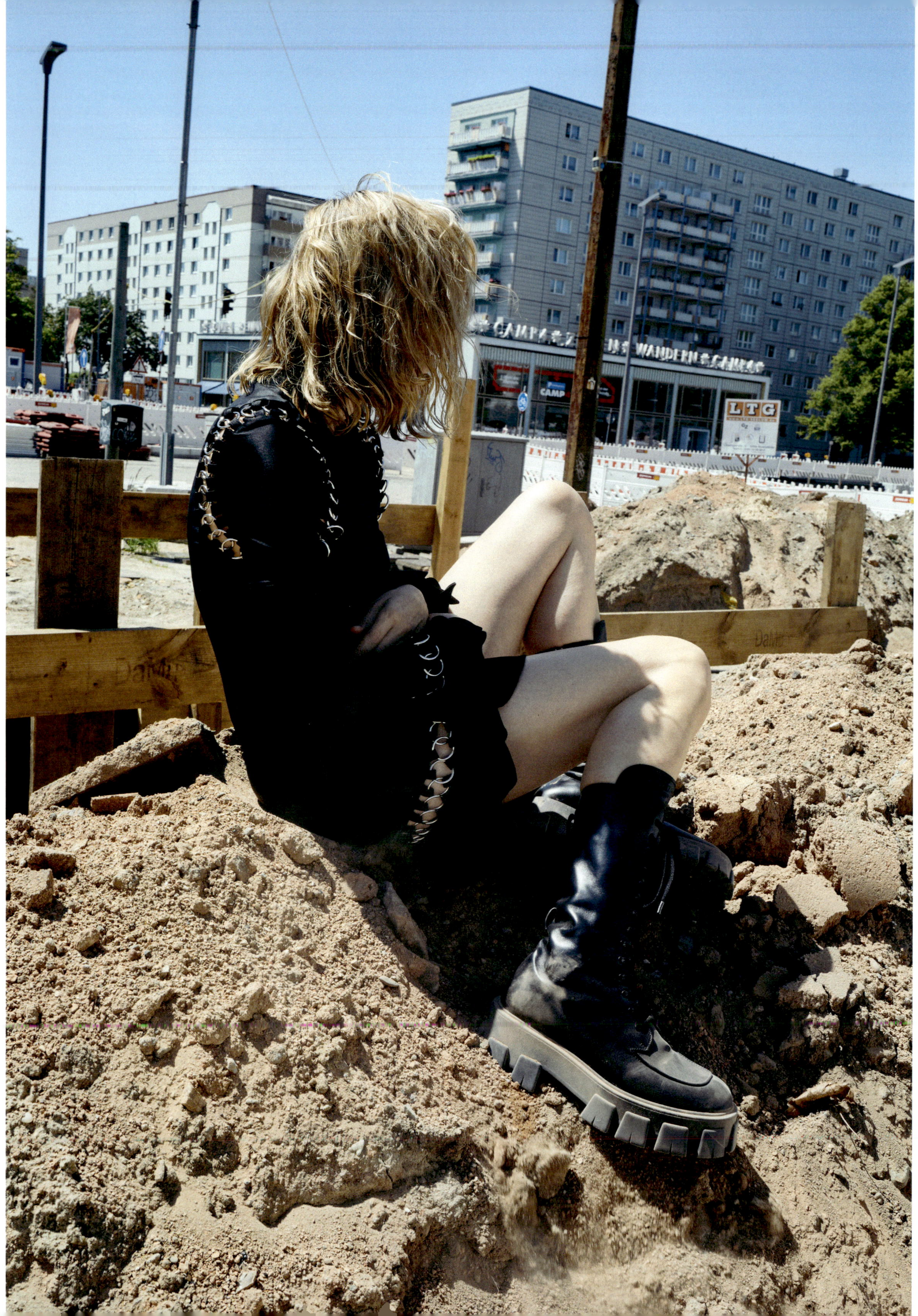
LTG
CAMP

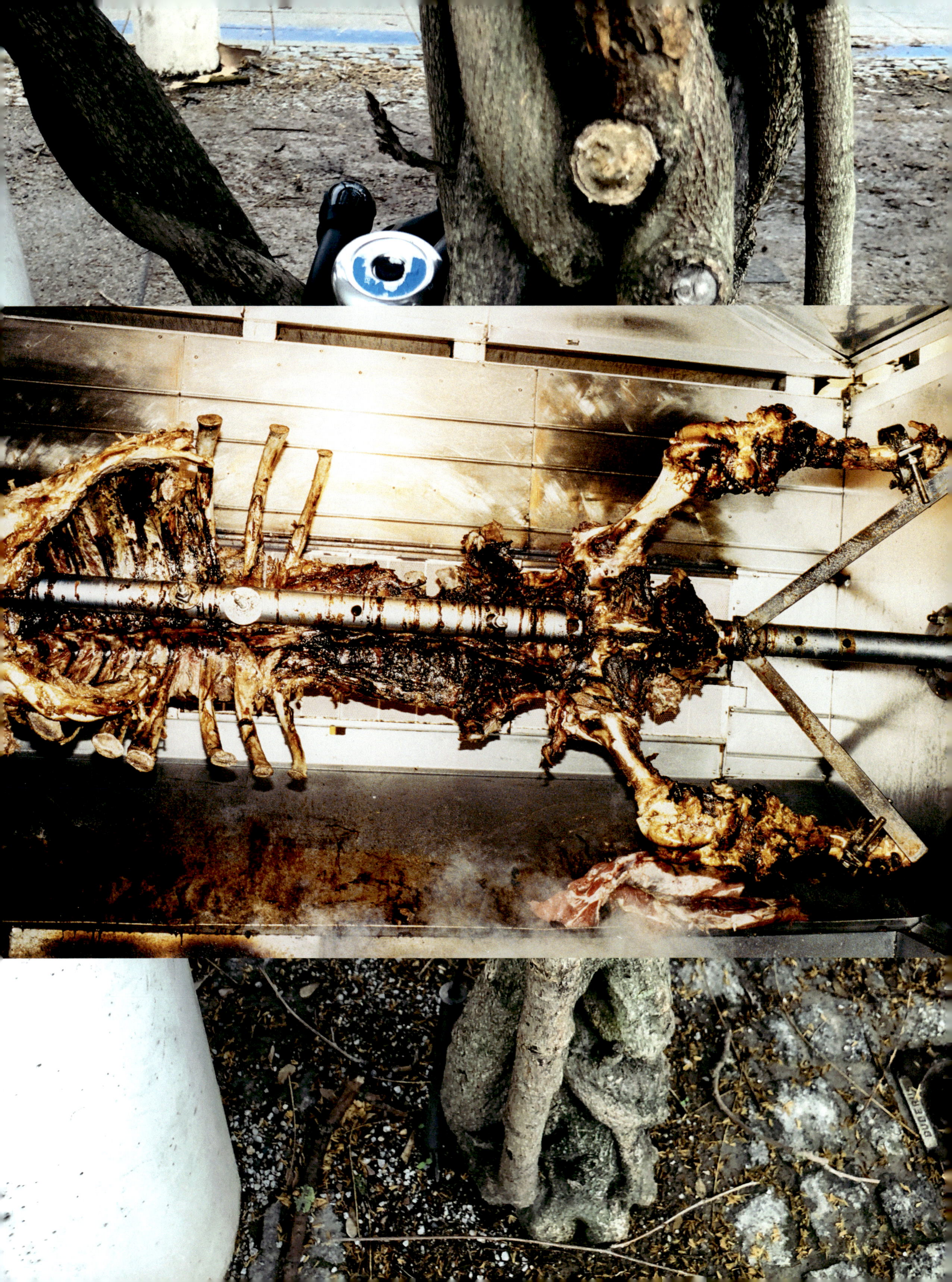

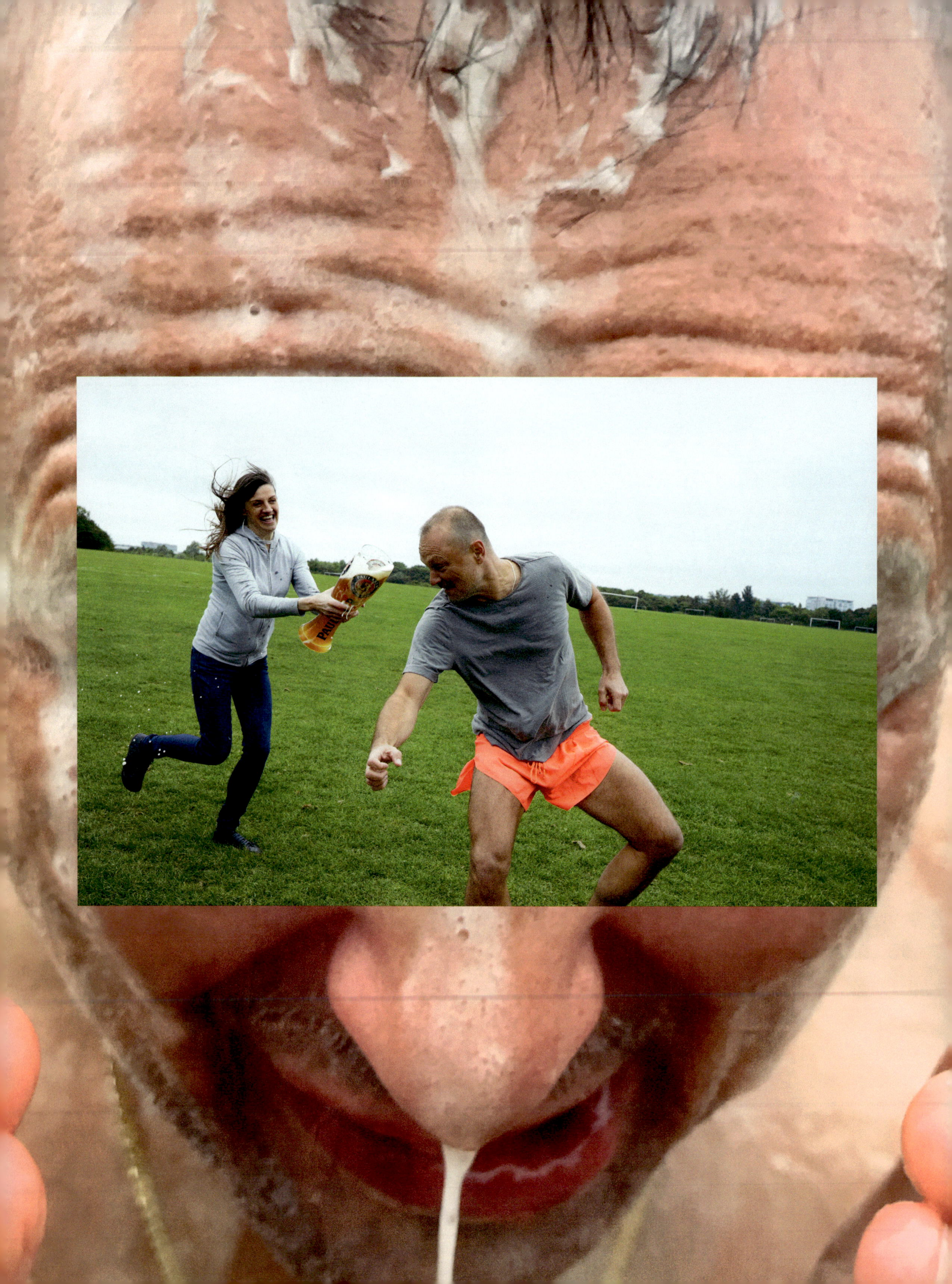

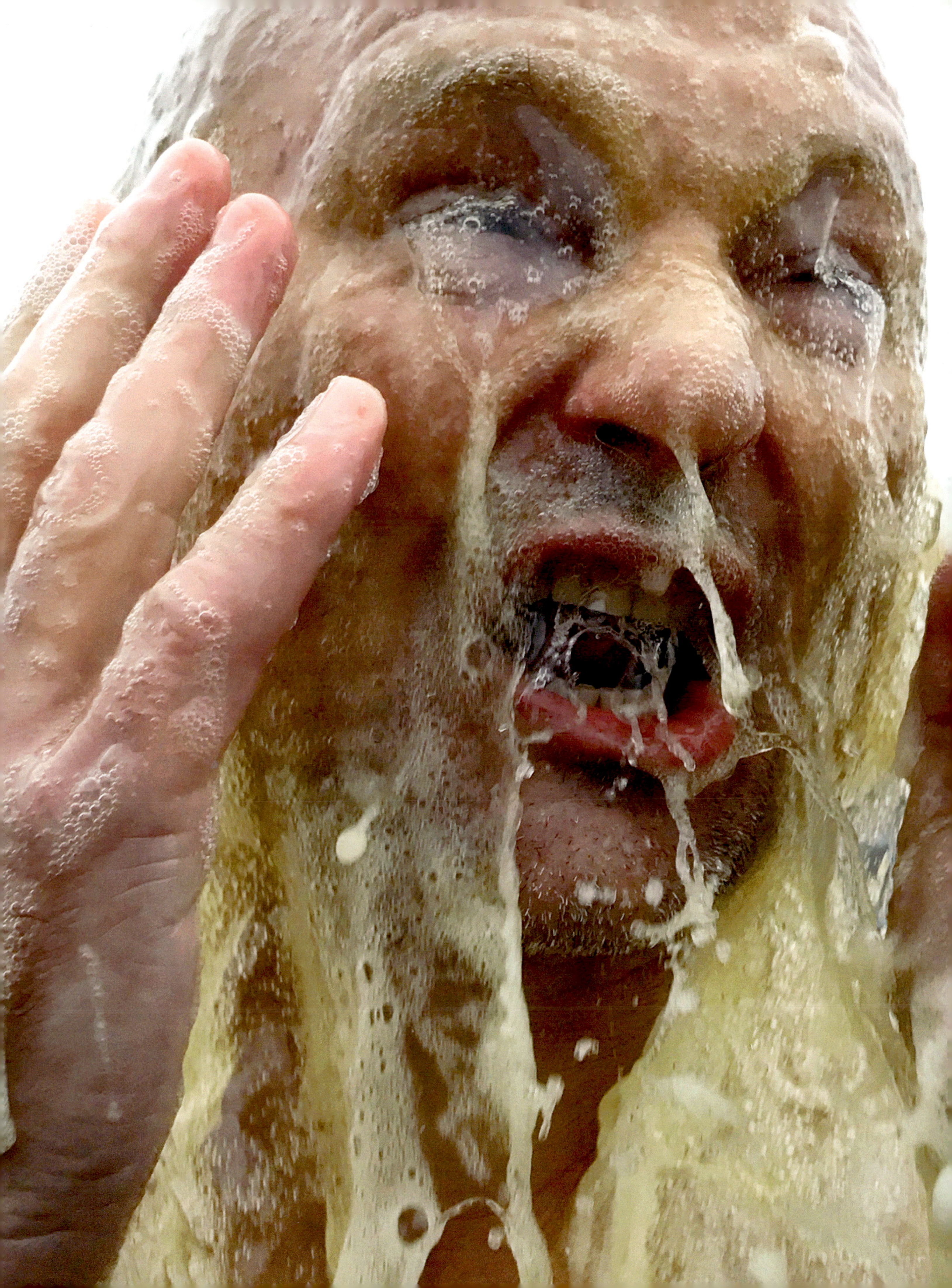

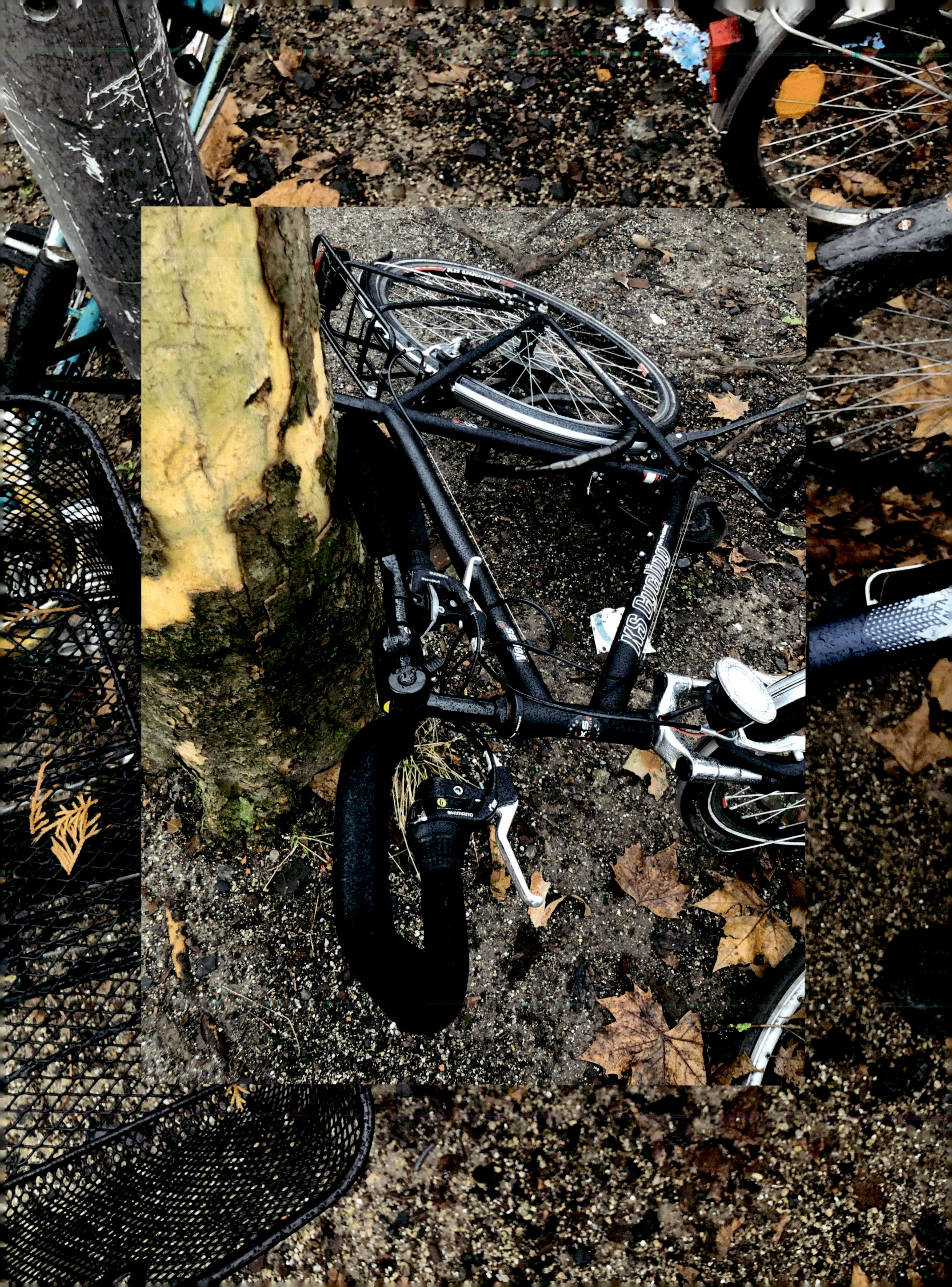

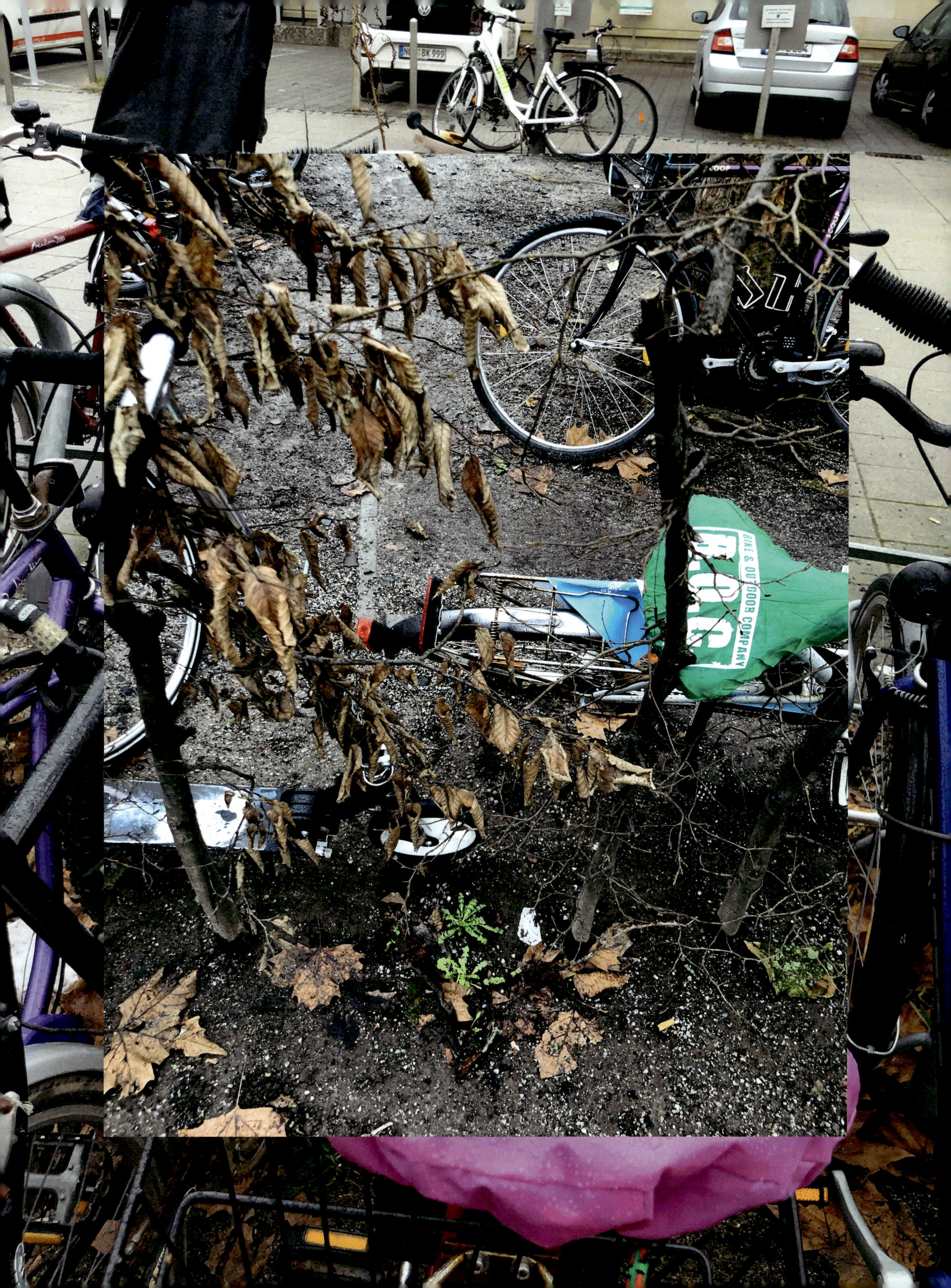
BIKE & OUTDOOR COMPANY

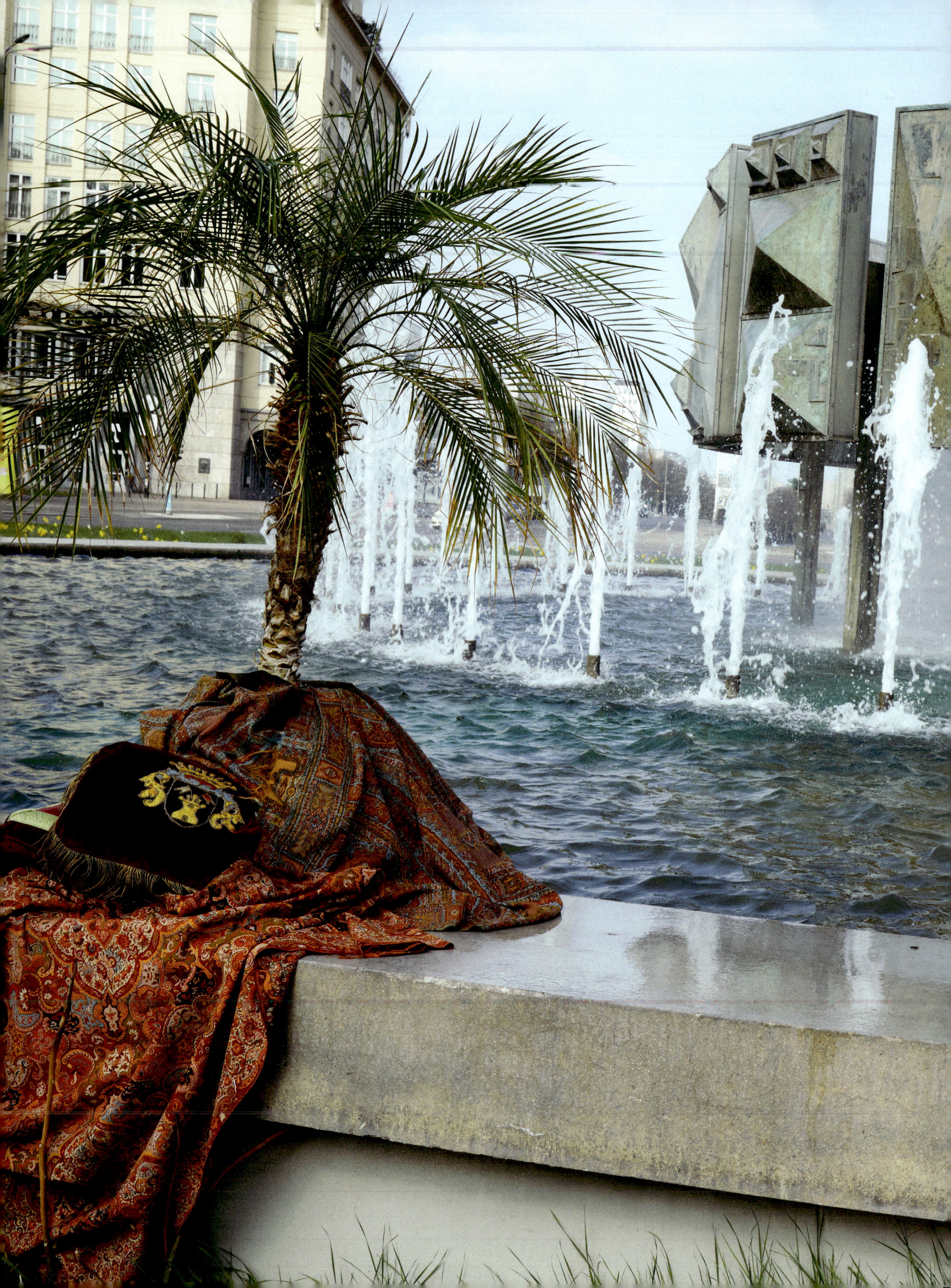

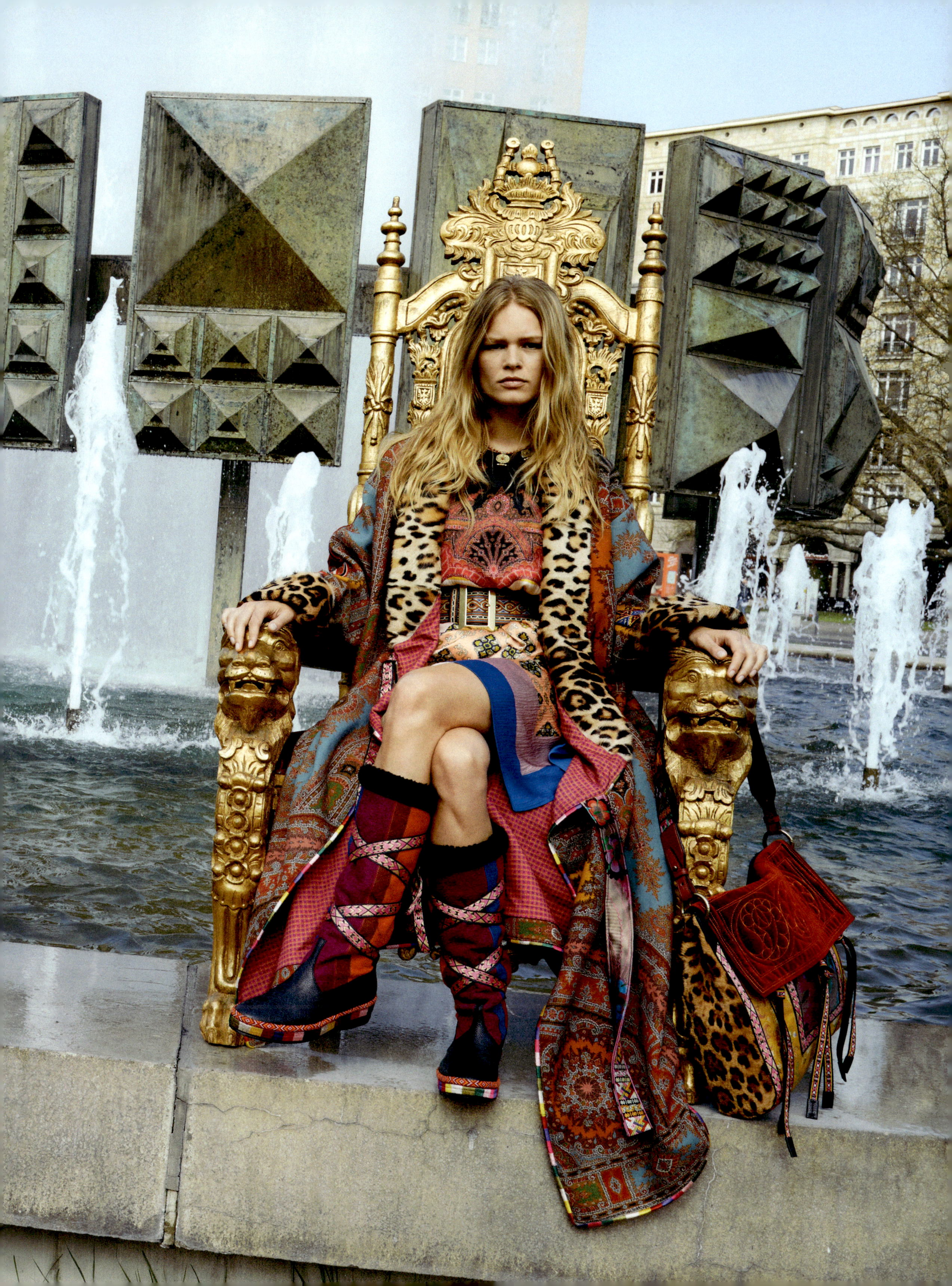

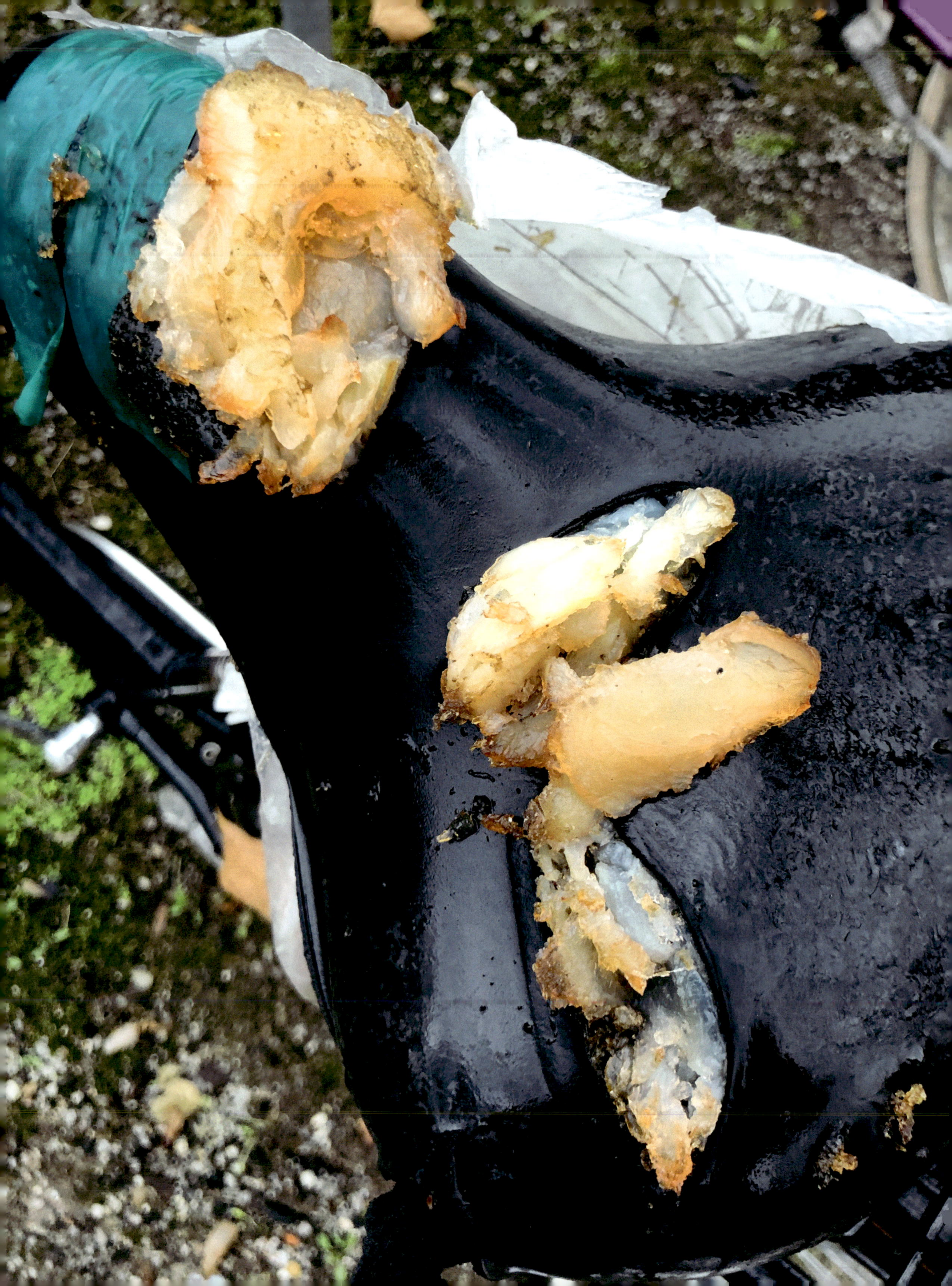

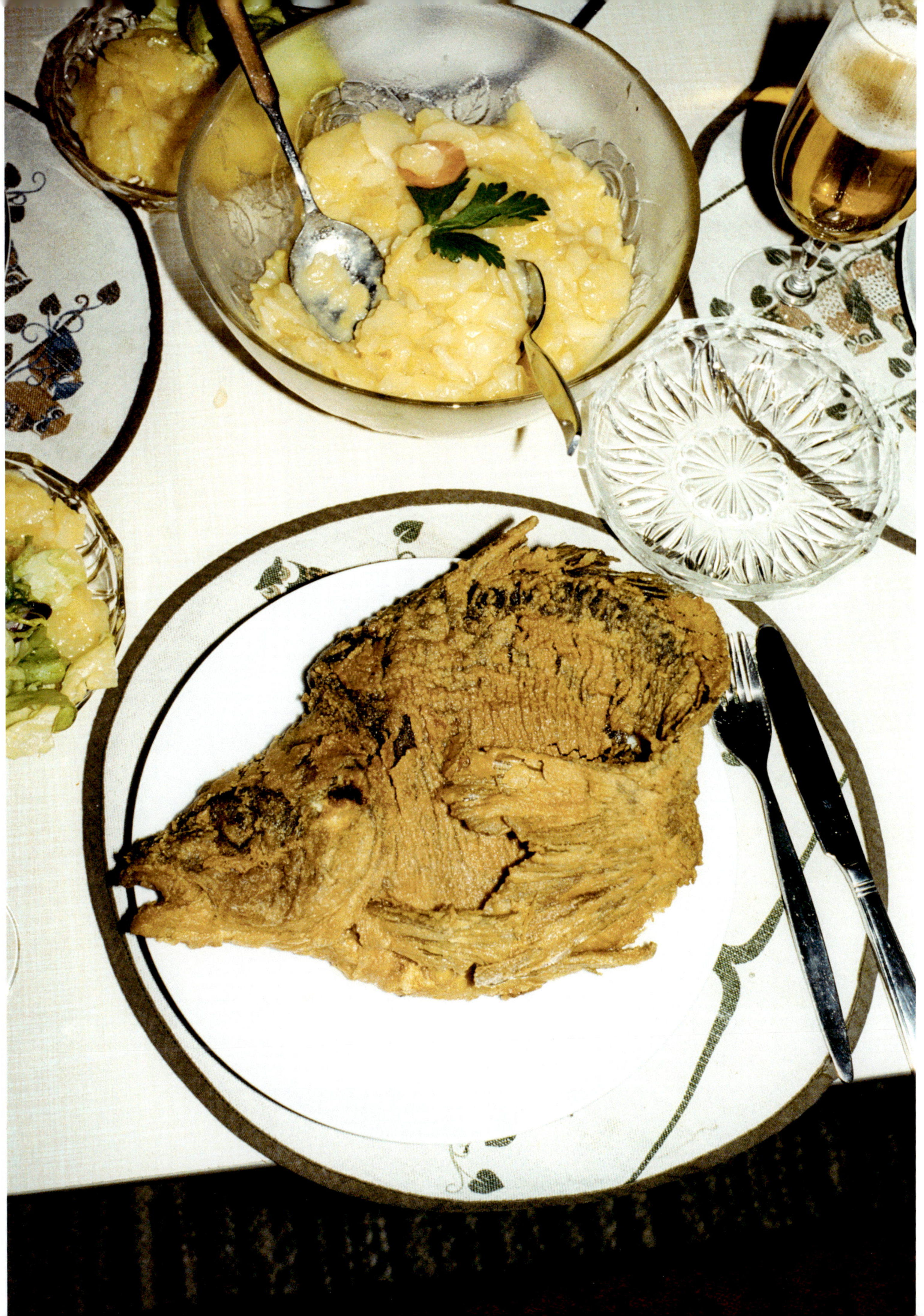

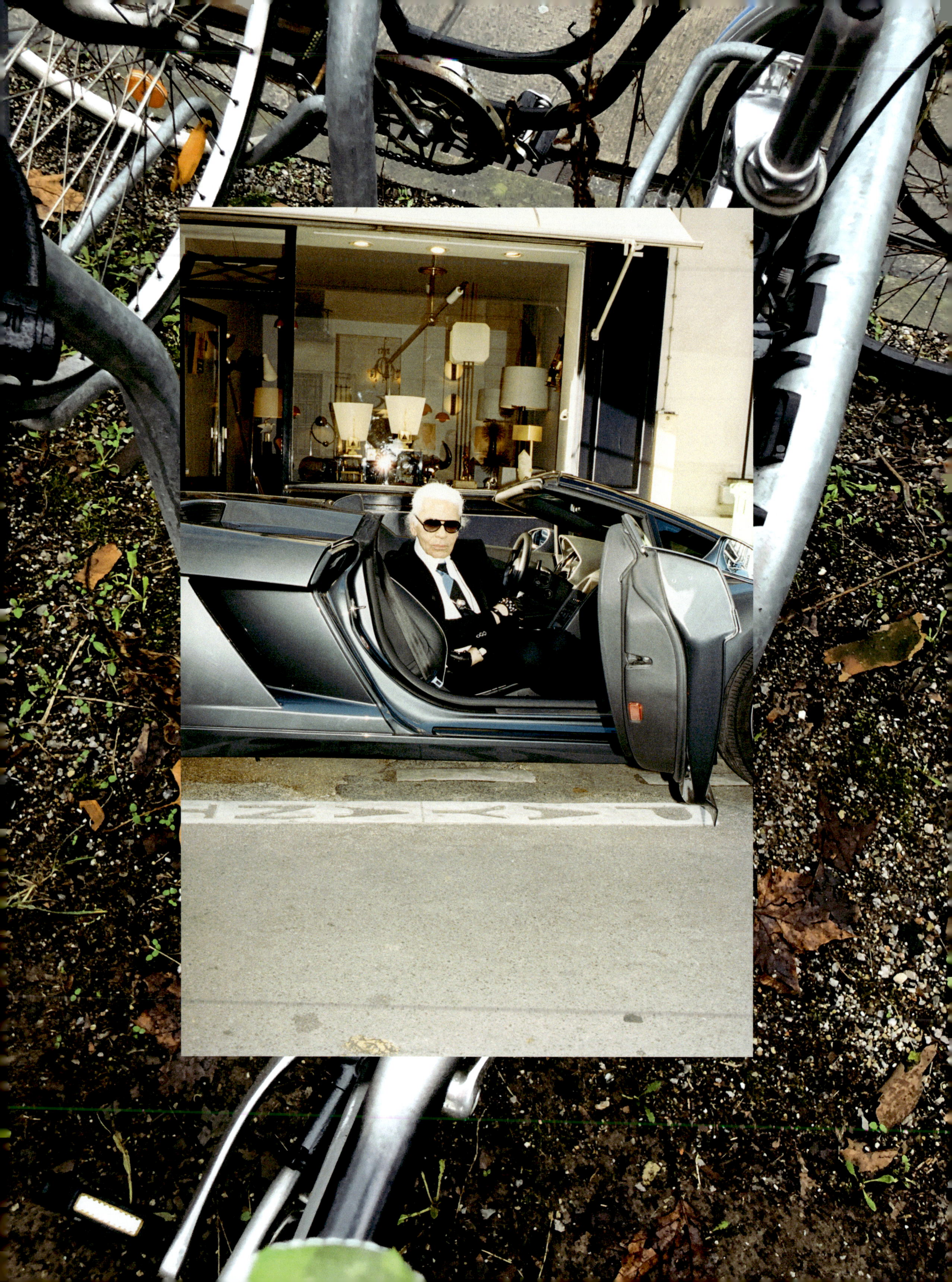

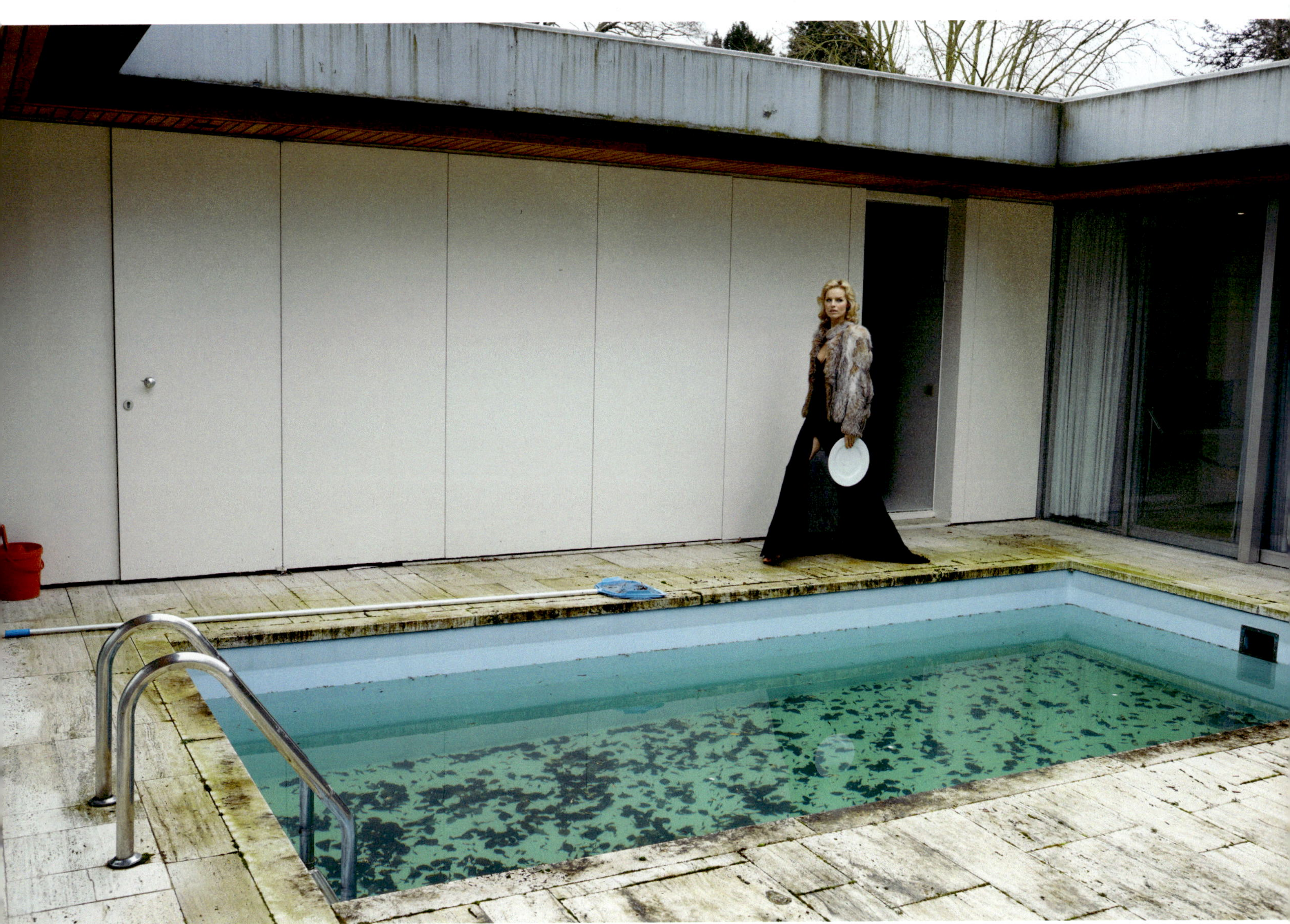

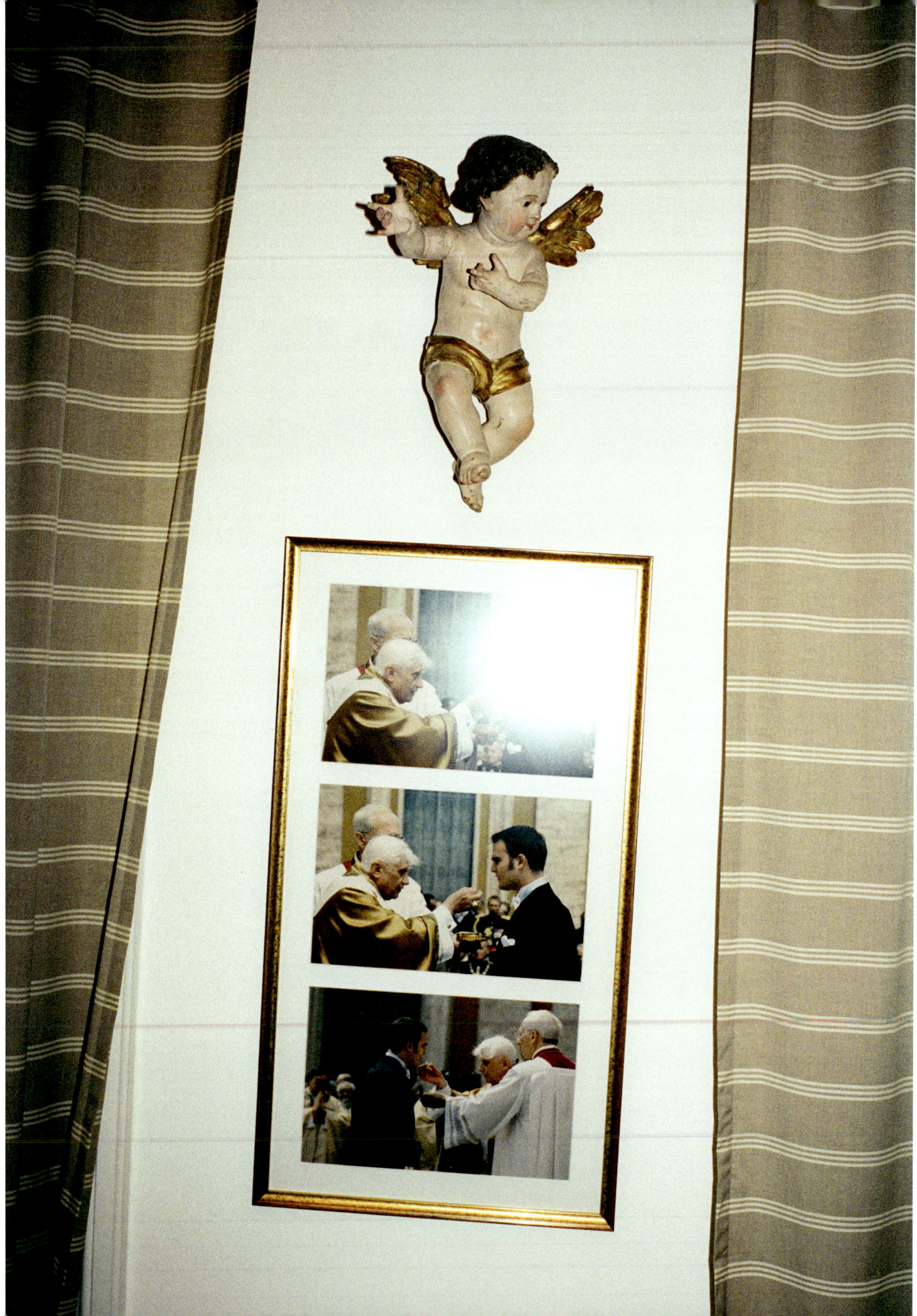

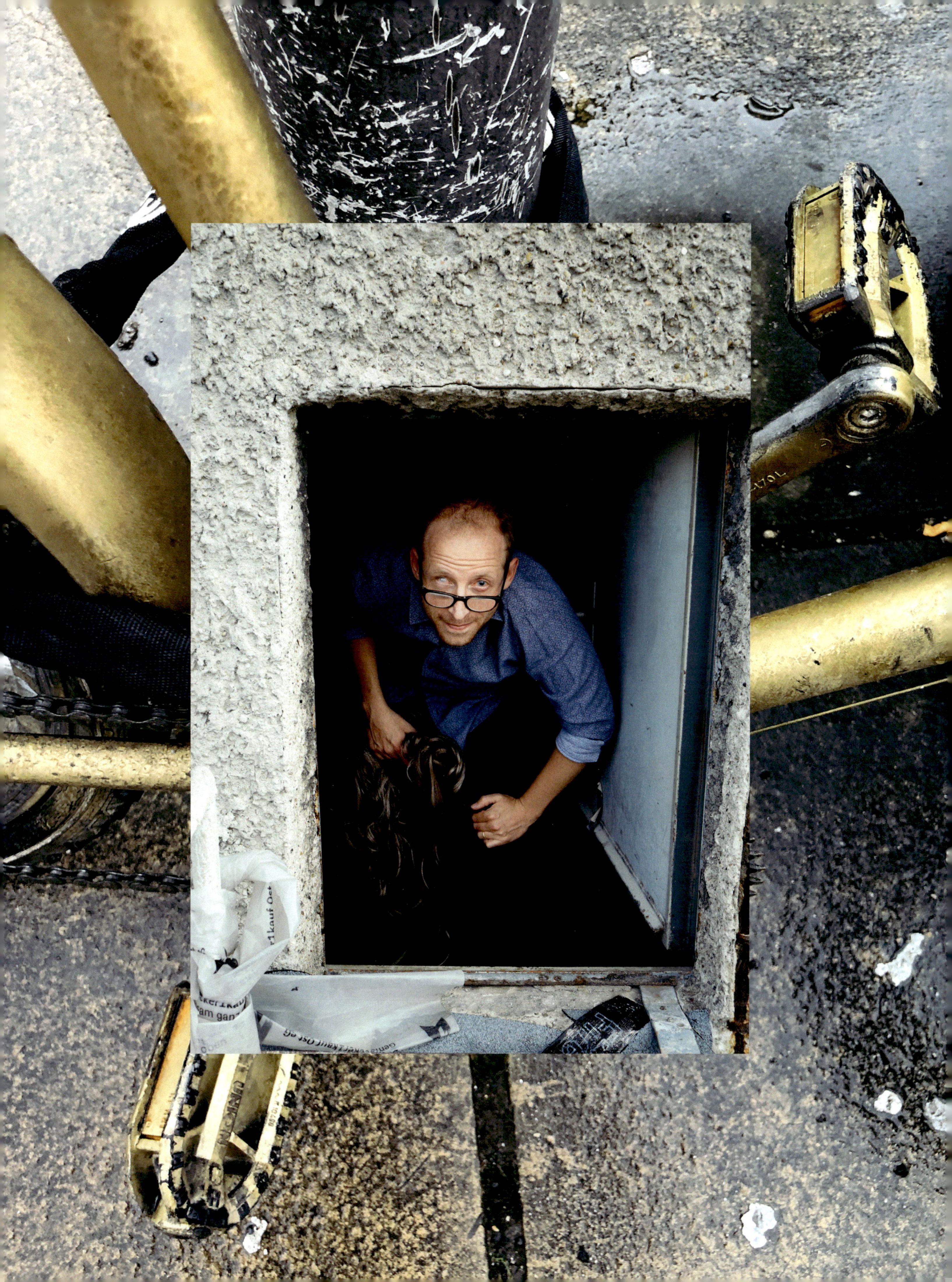

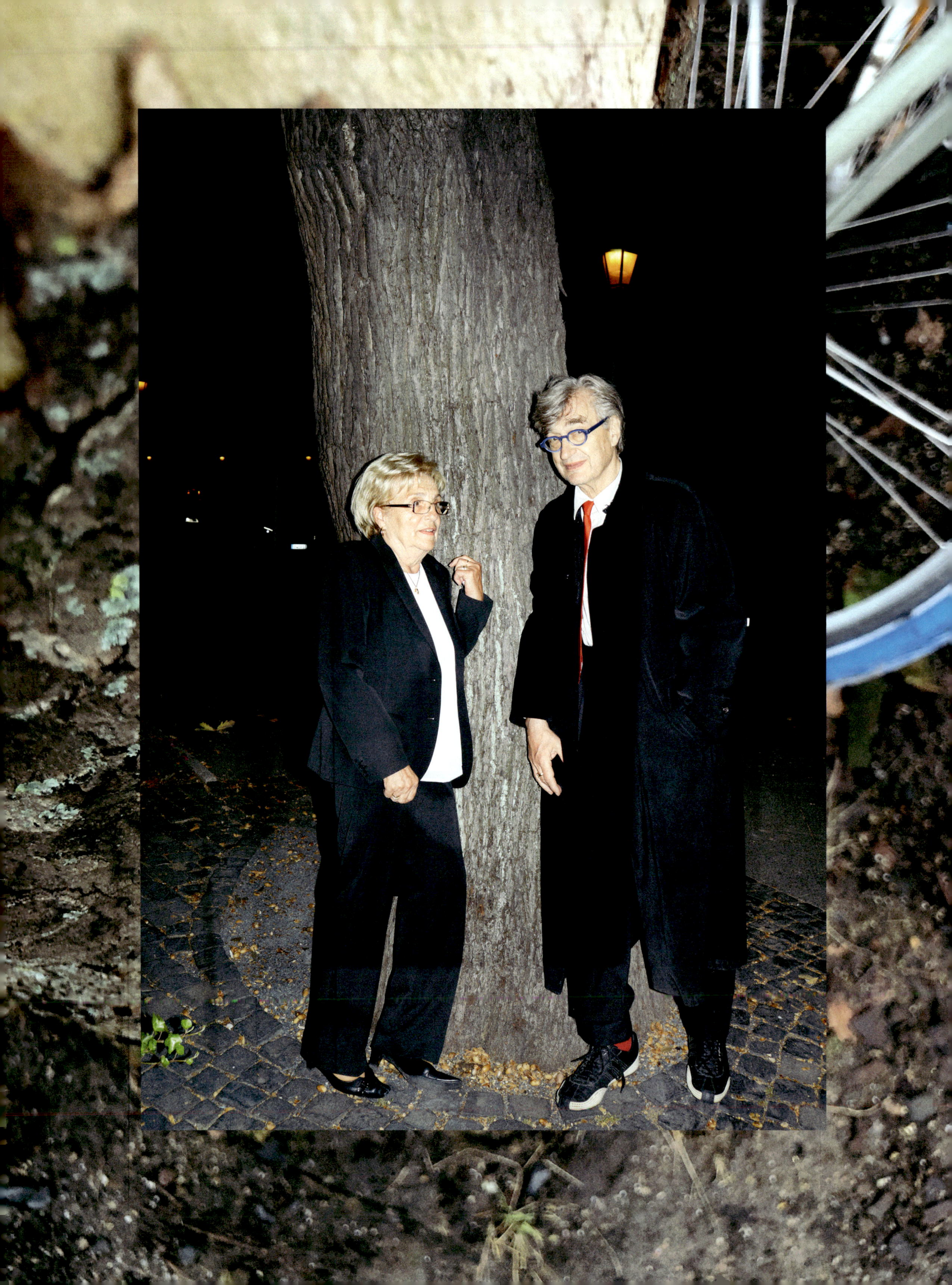

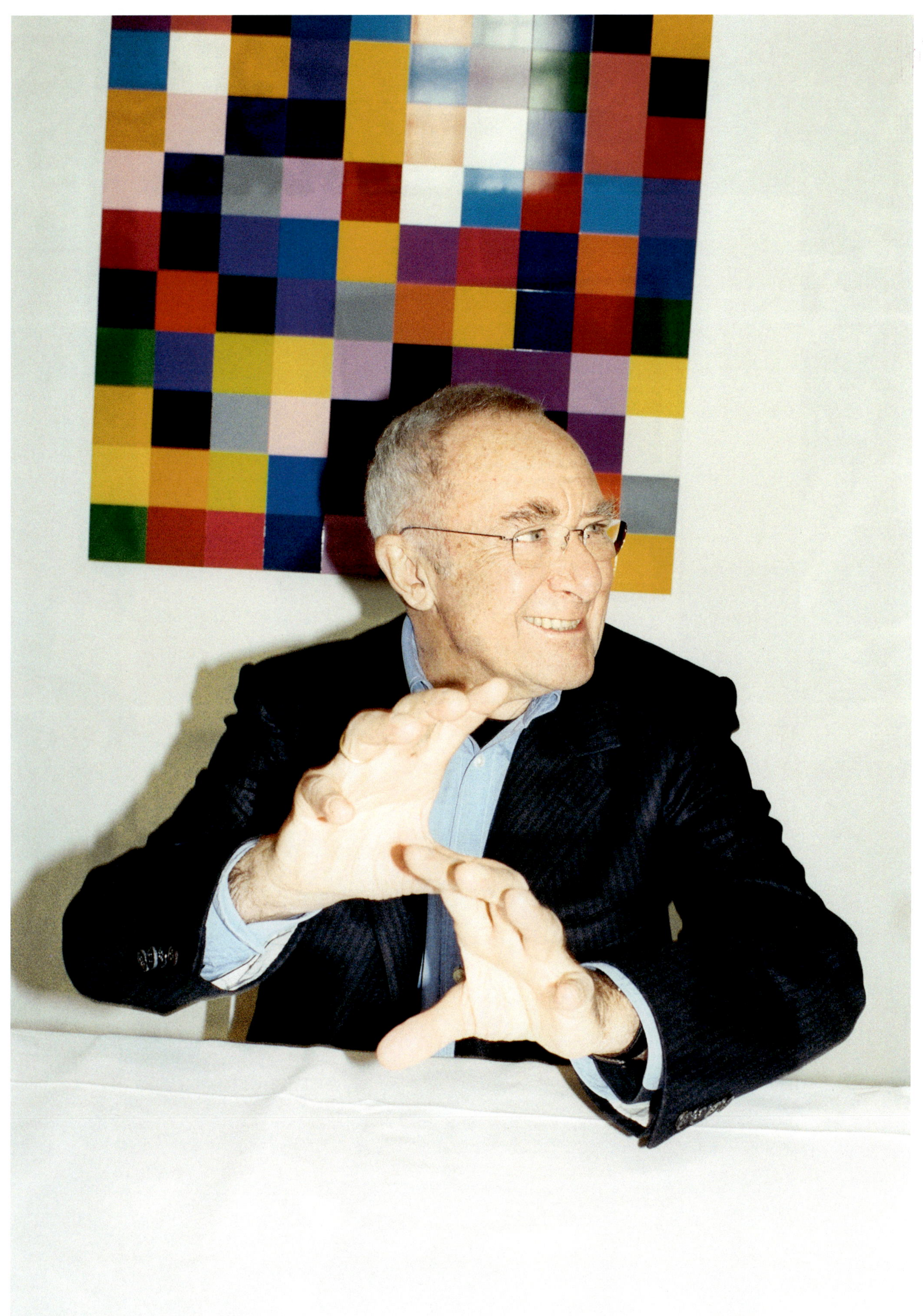

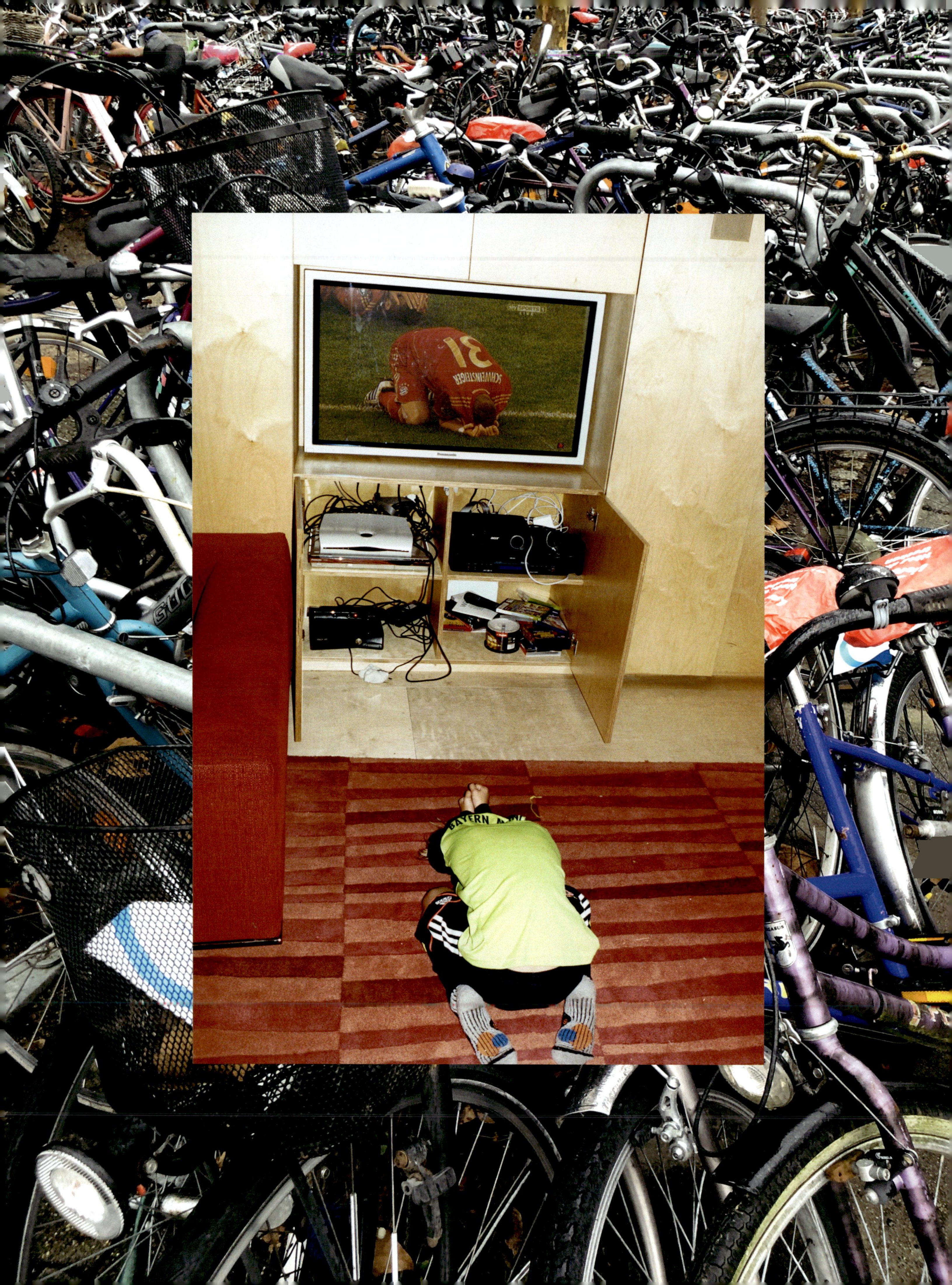

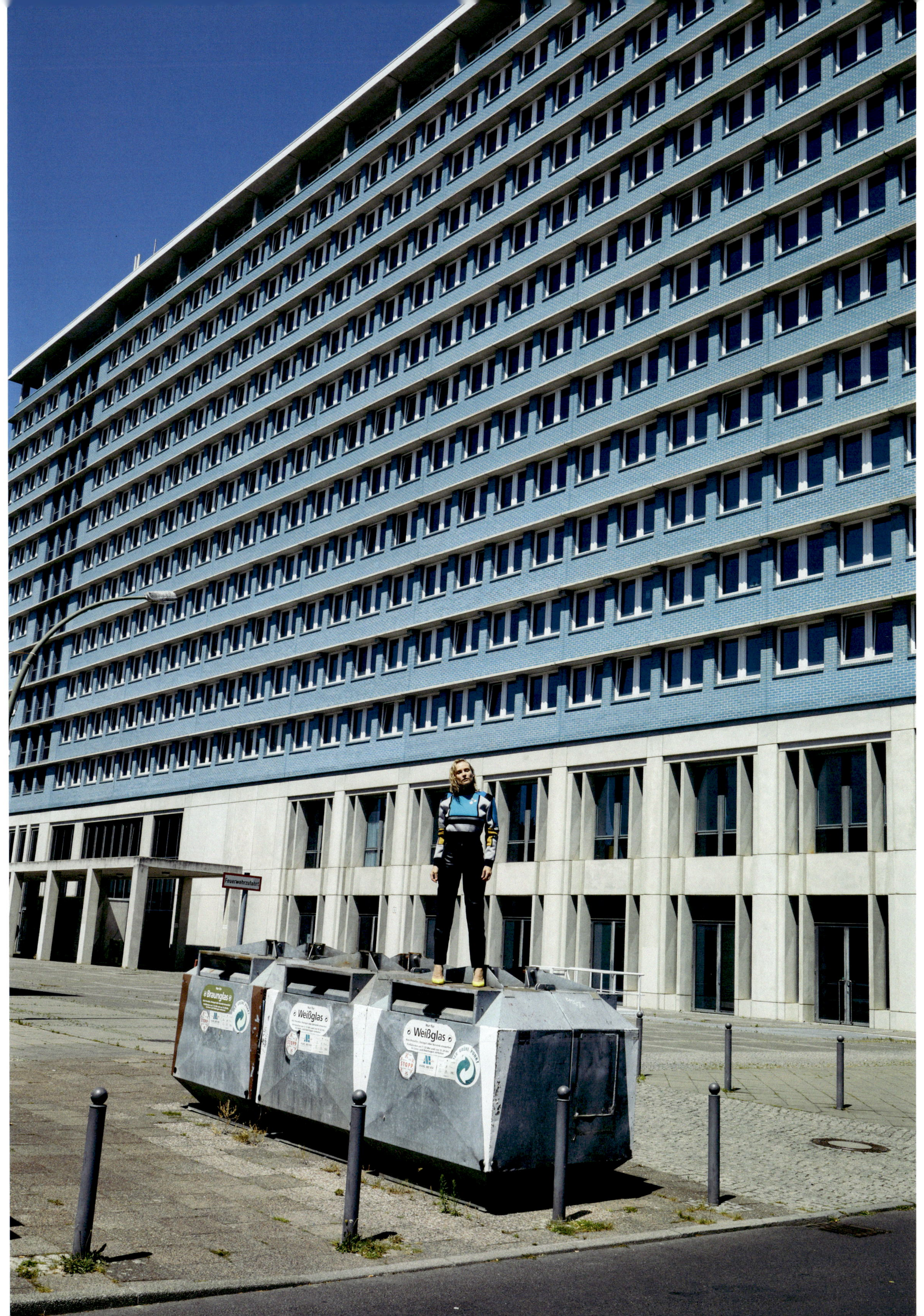
Feuerwehrzufahrt
Braunglas
Weißglas
Weißglas

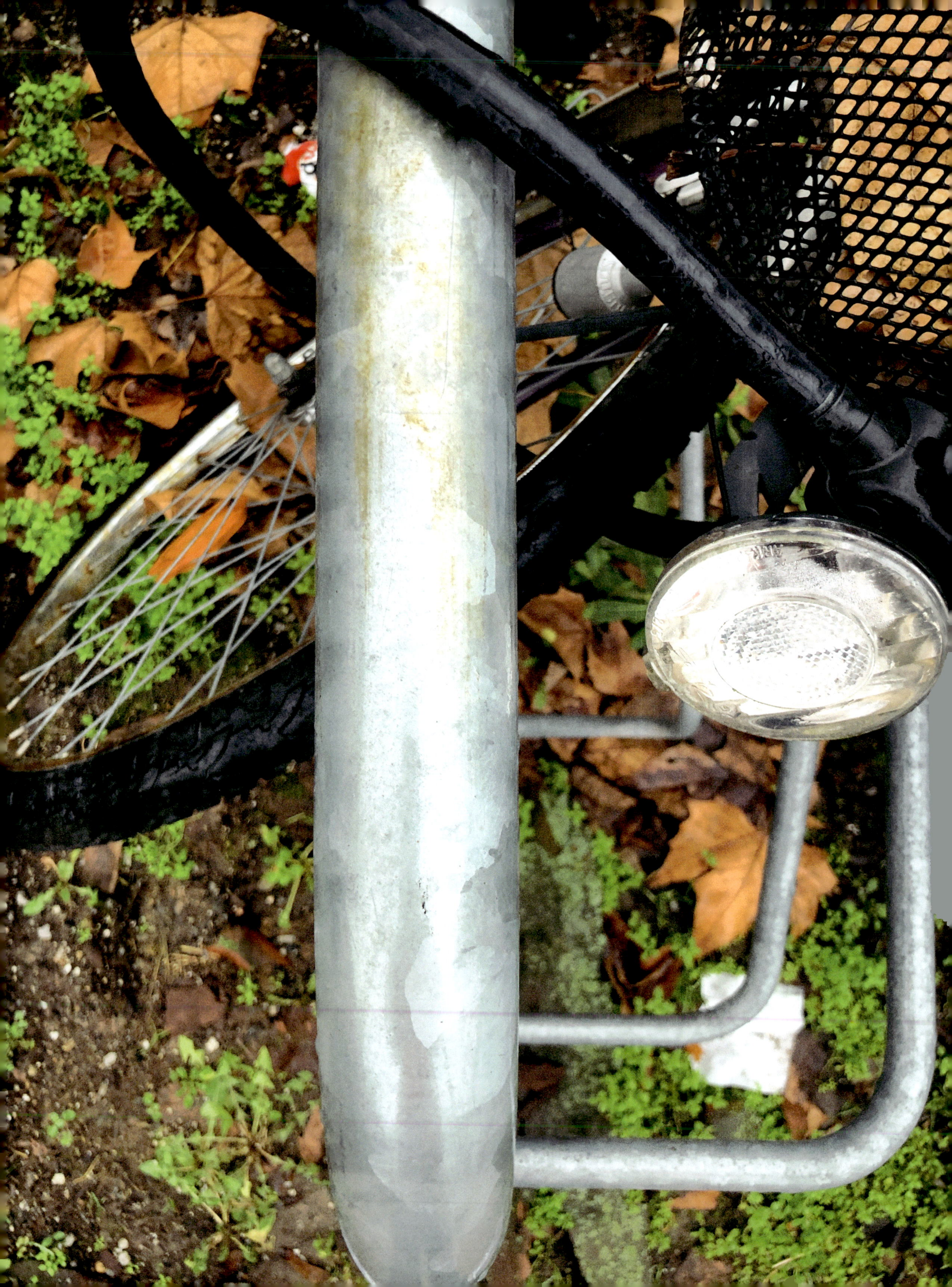

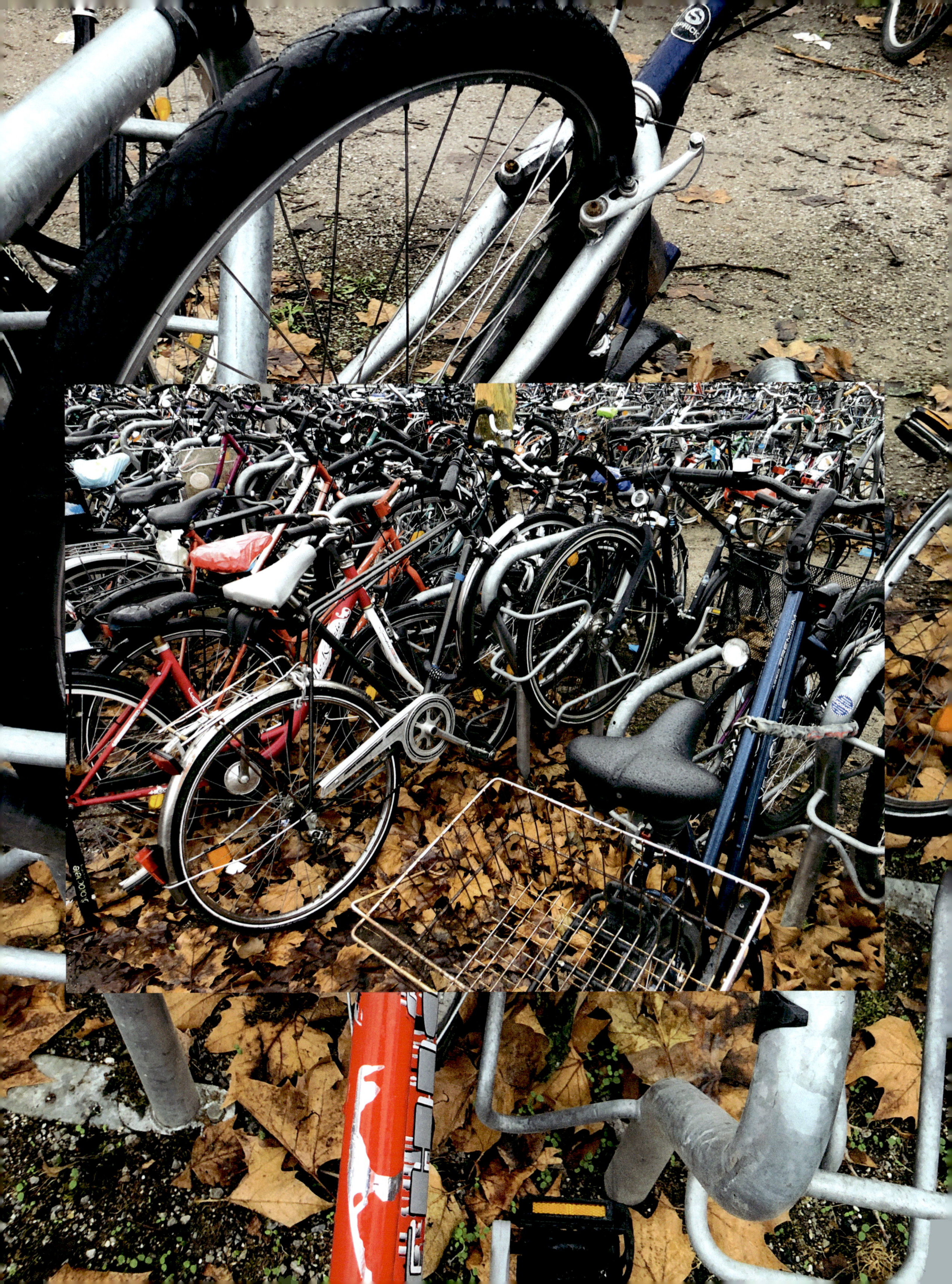

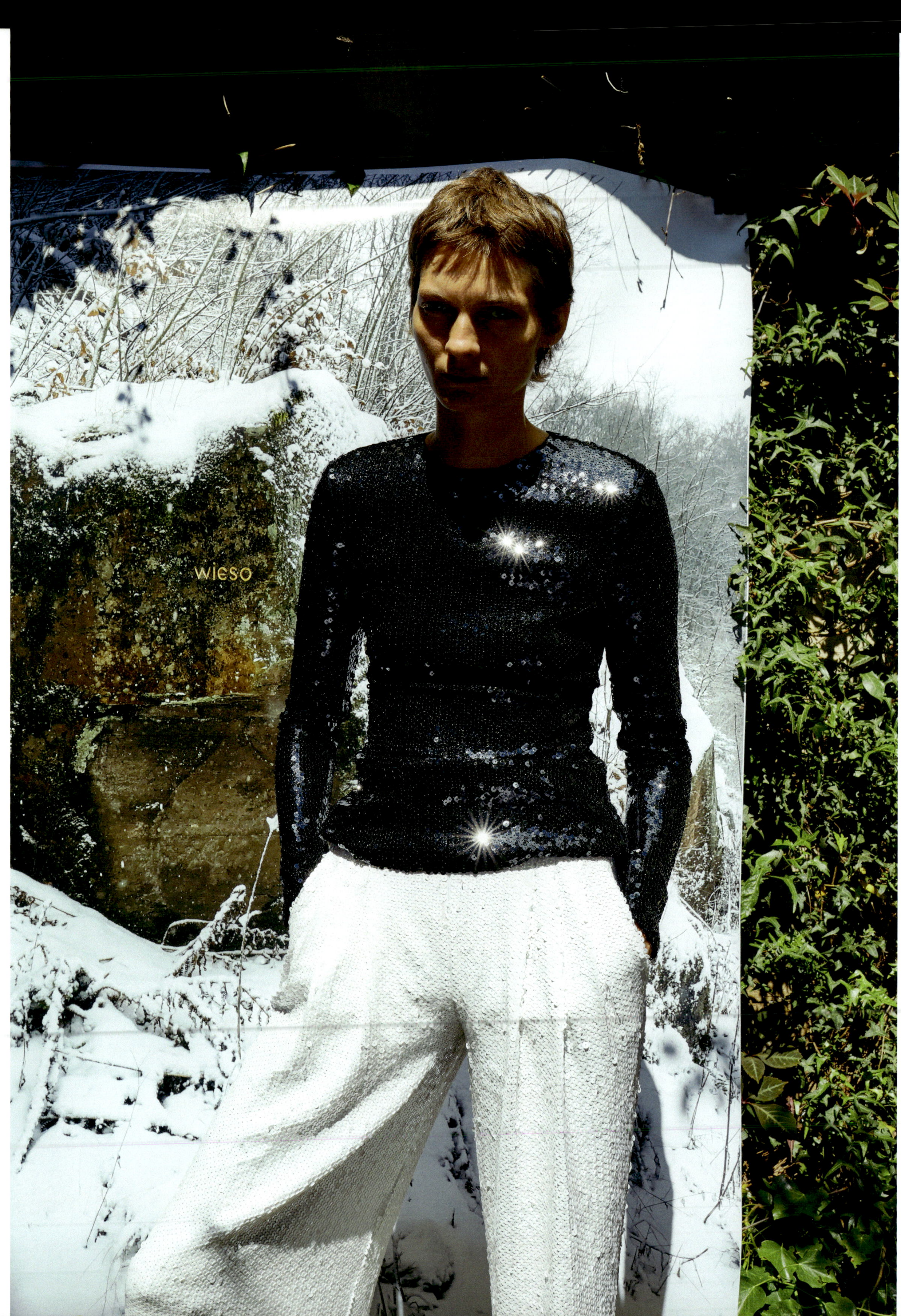
wieso

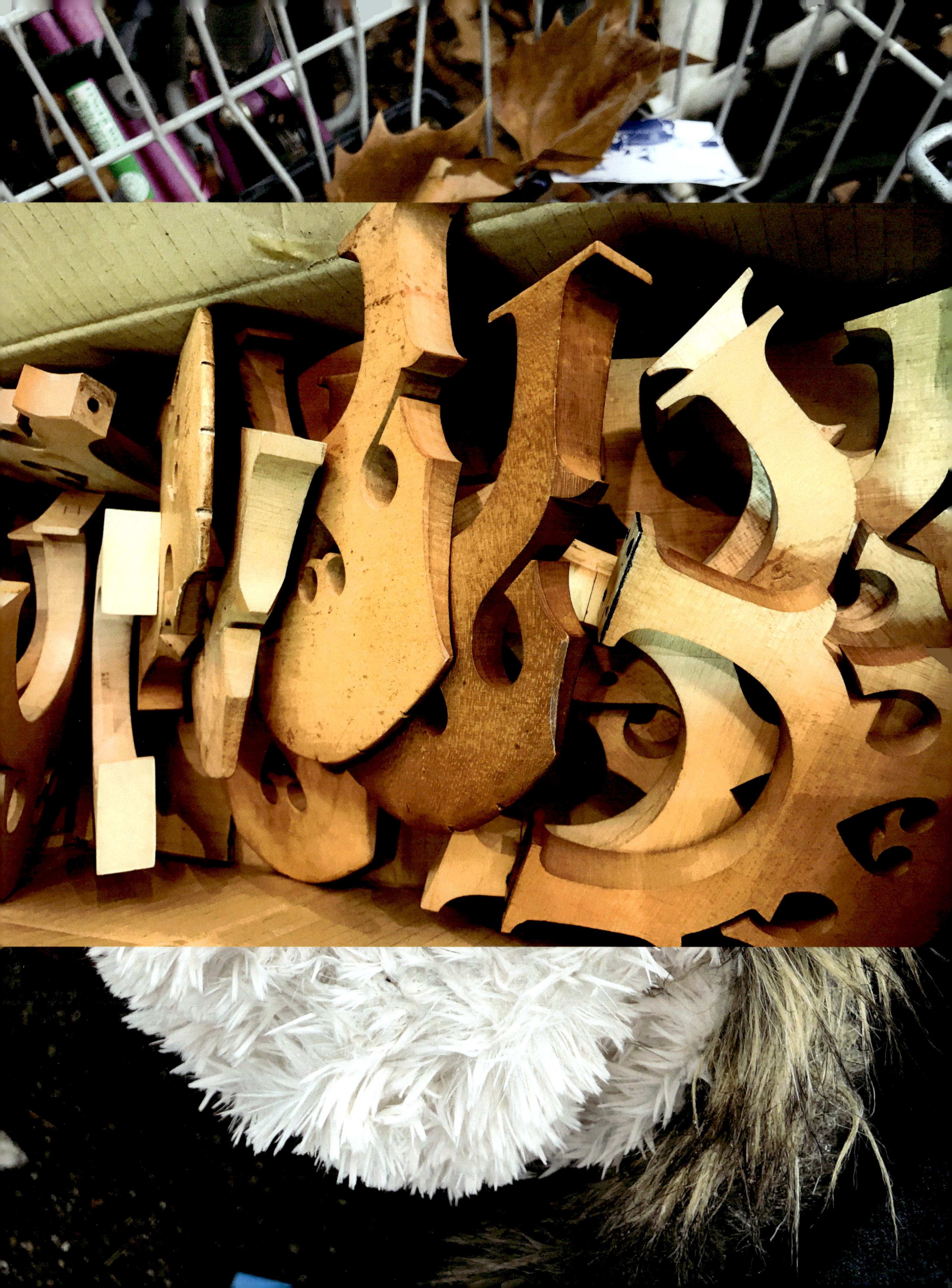

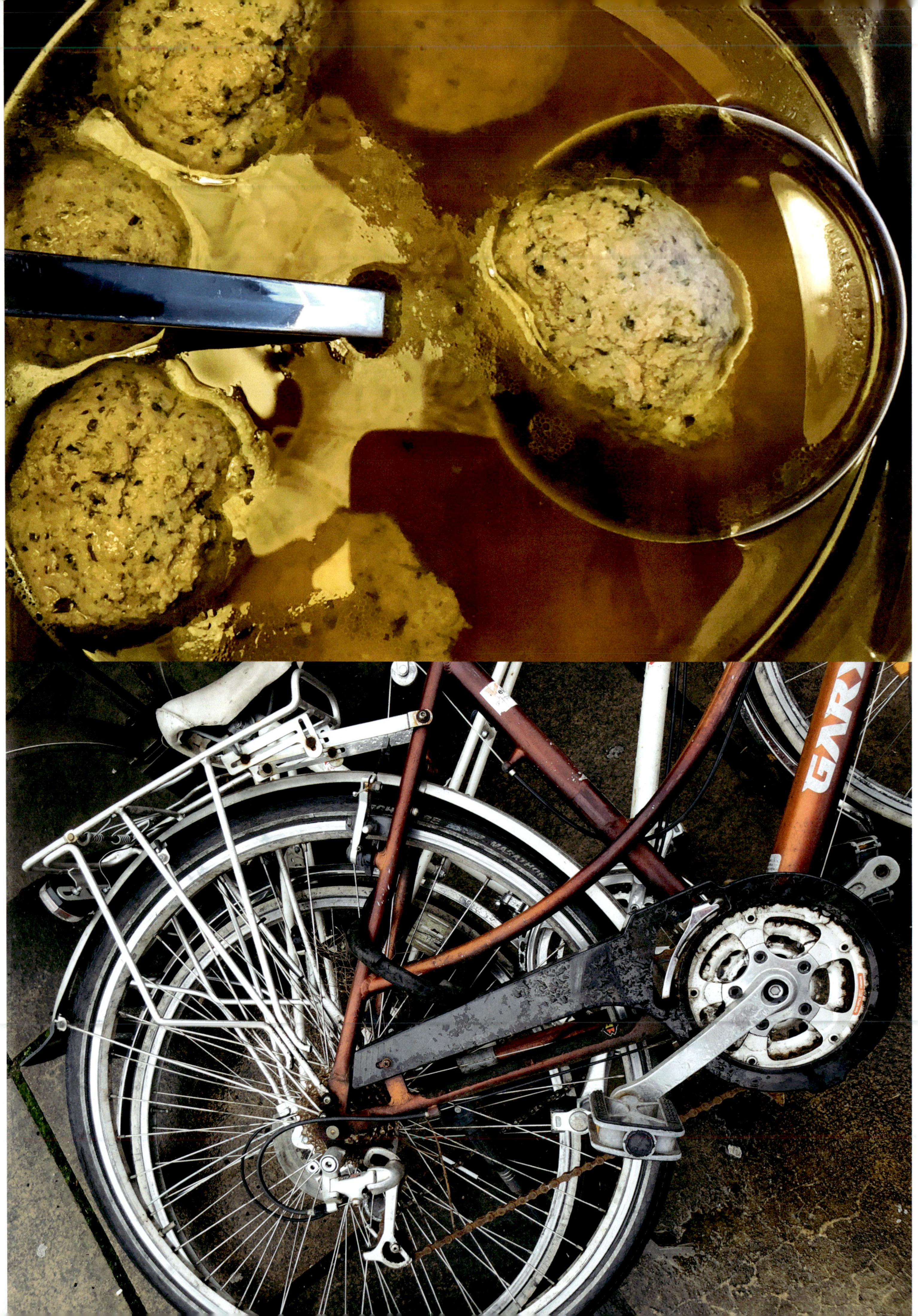

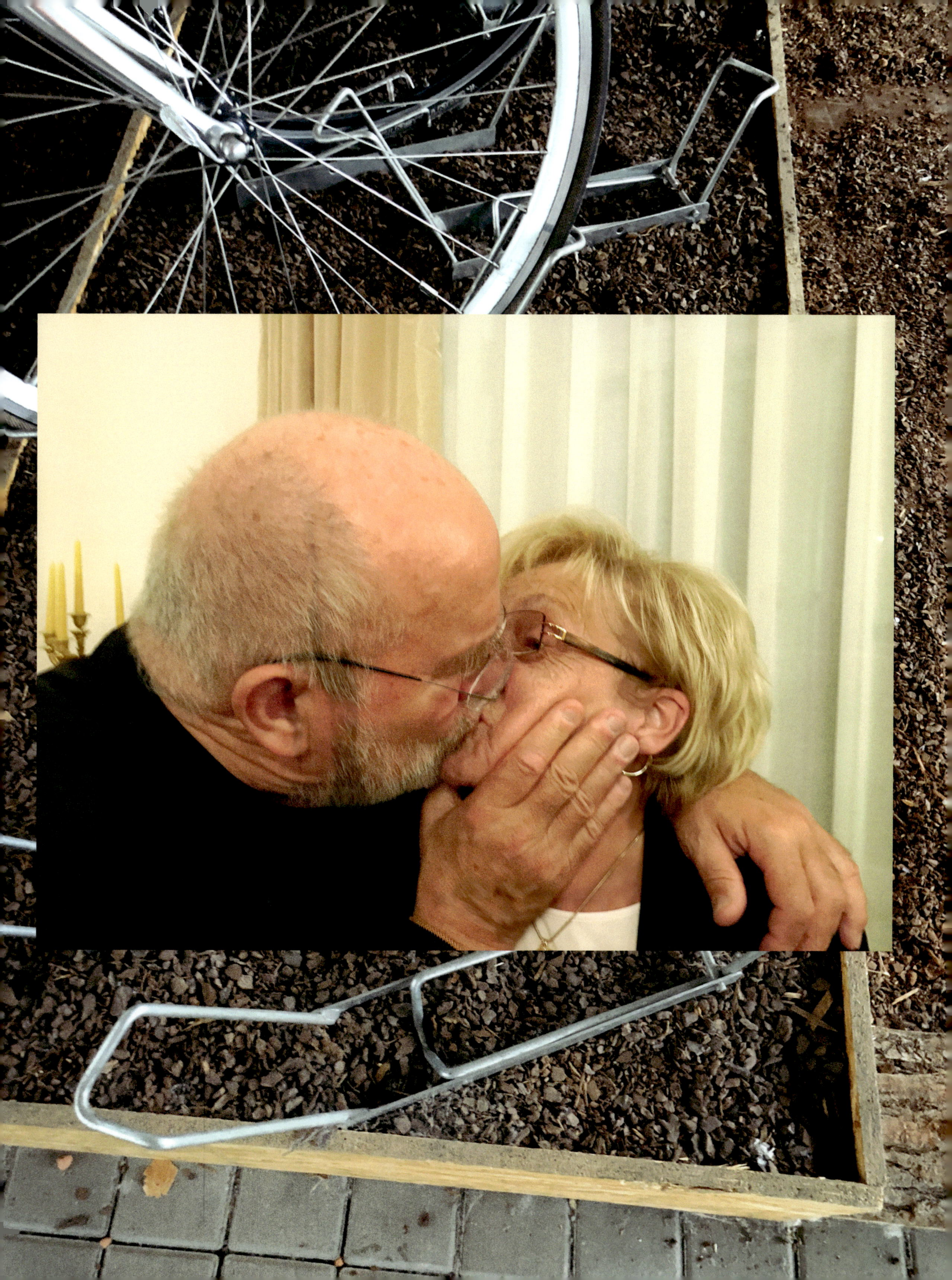

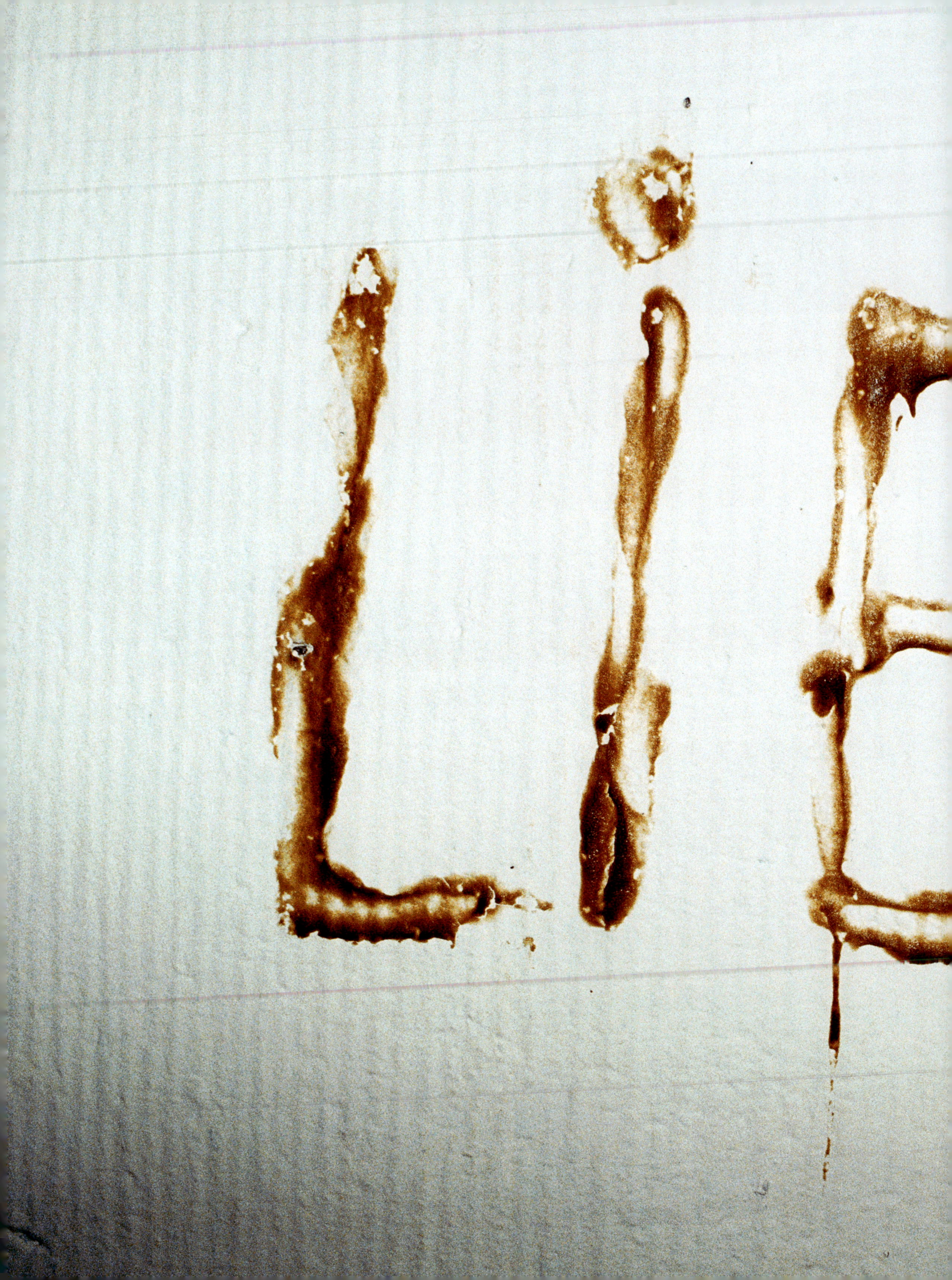
Li

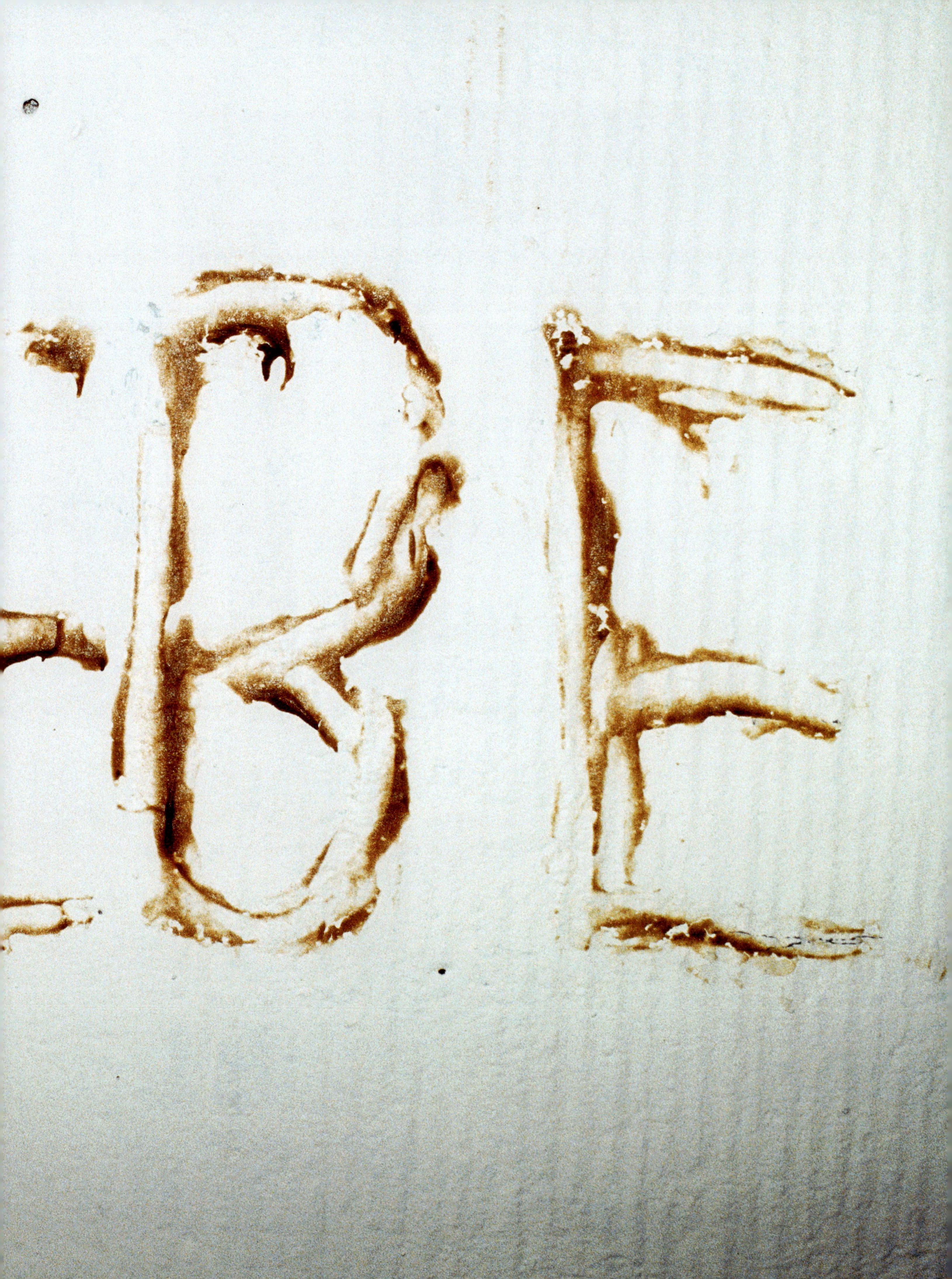
BE

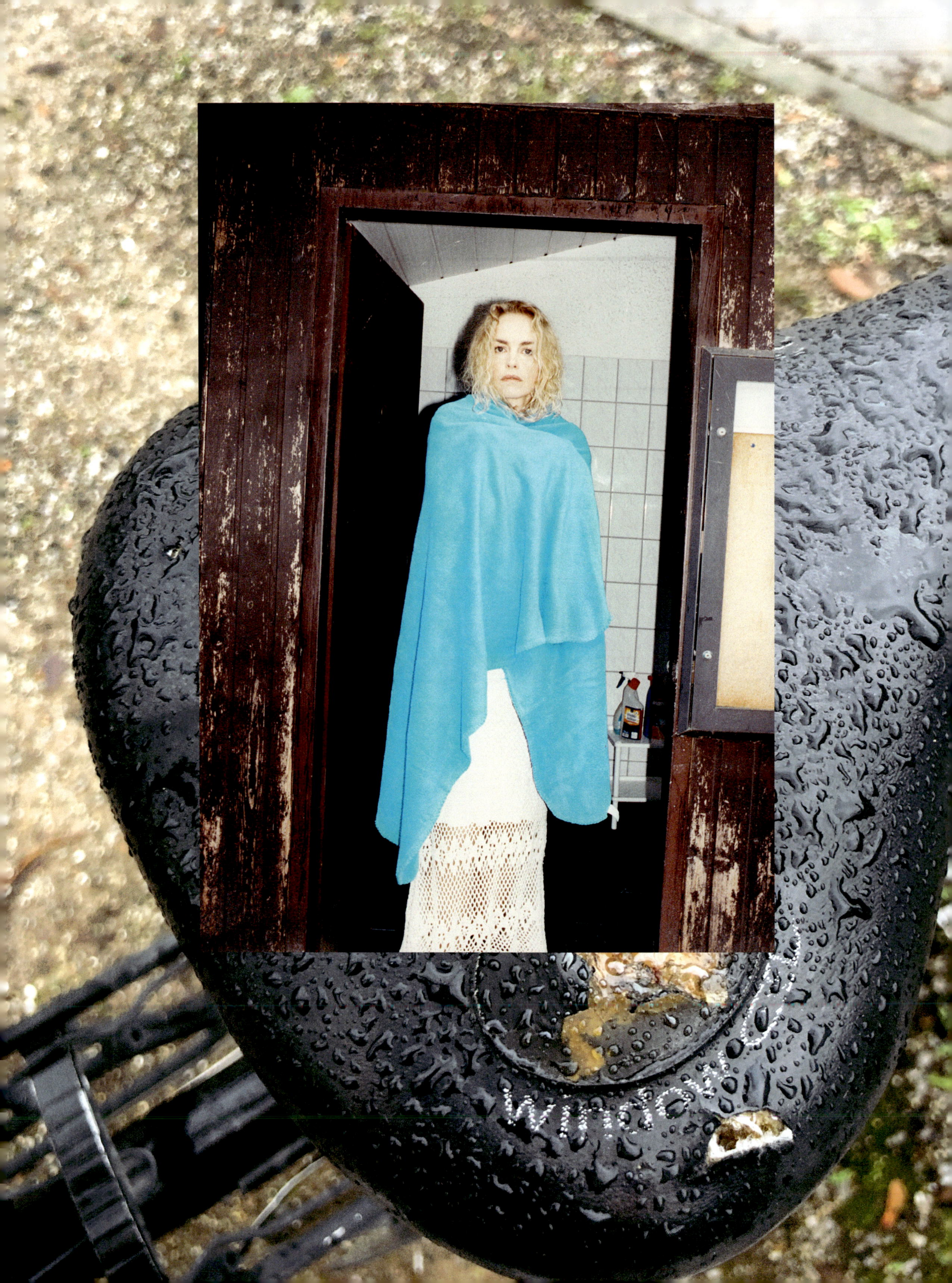

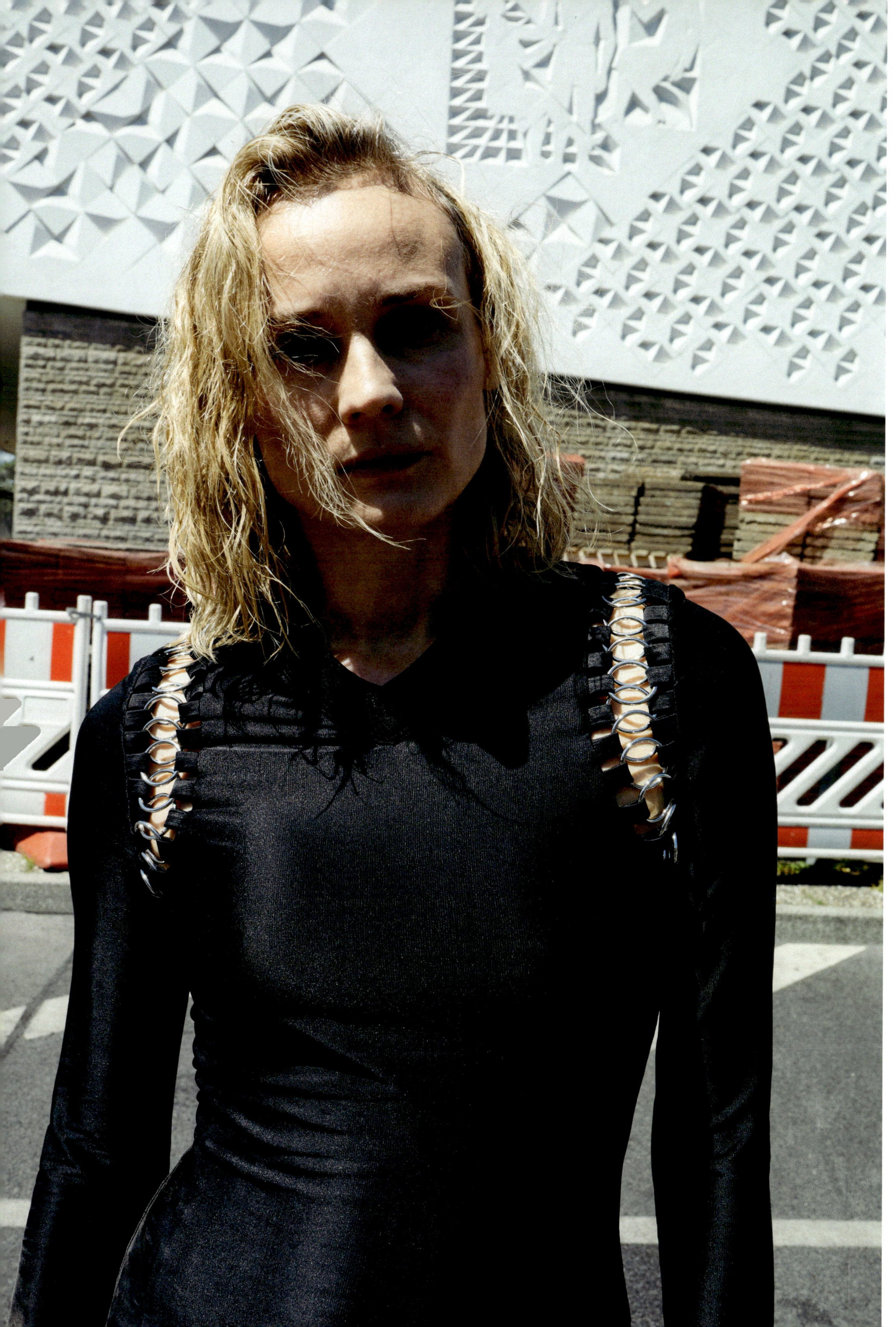

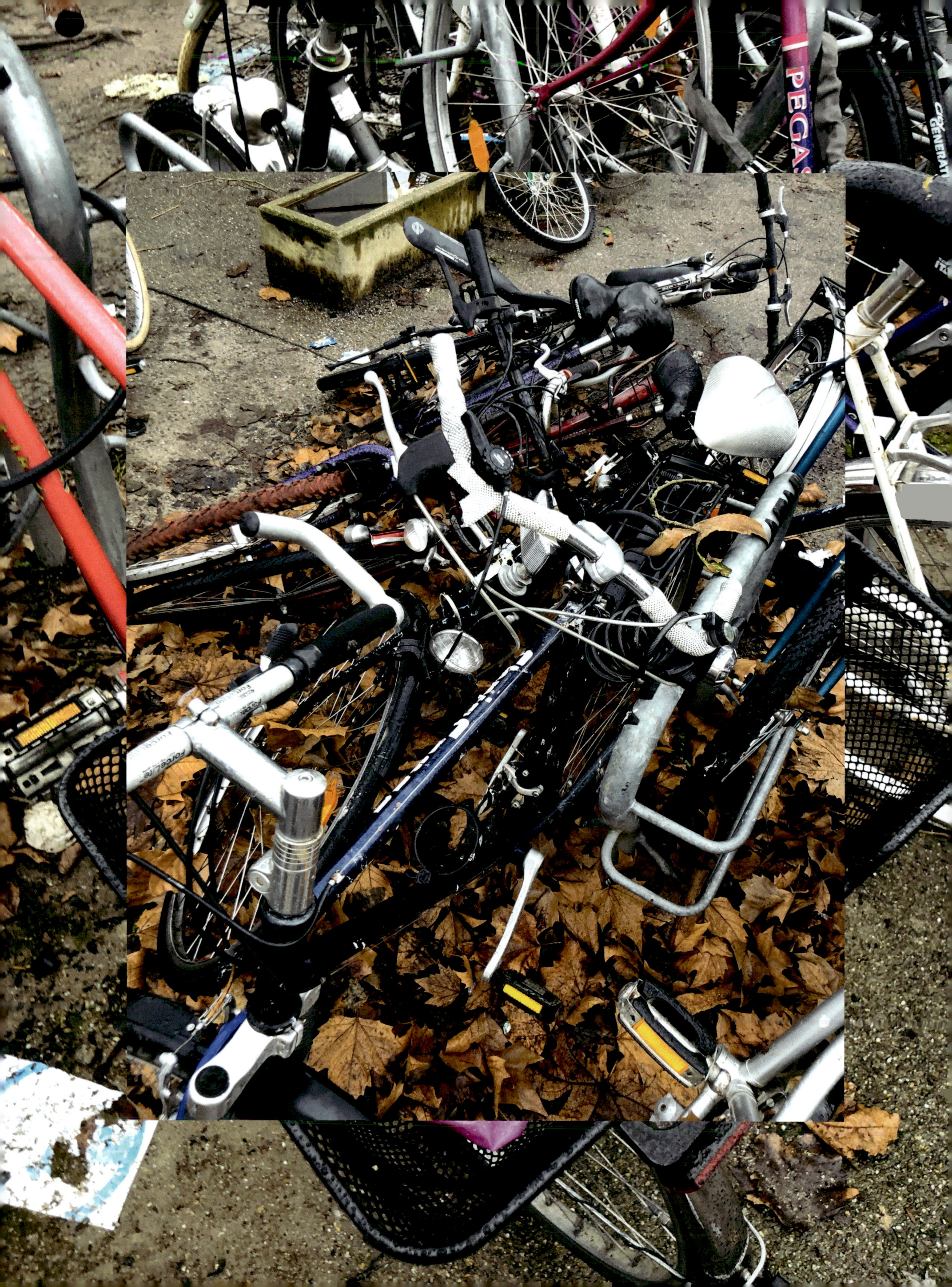
PEGAS

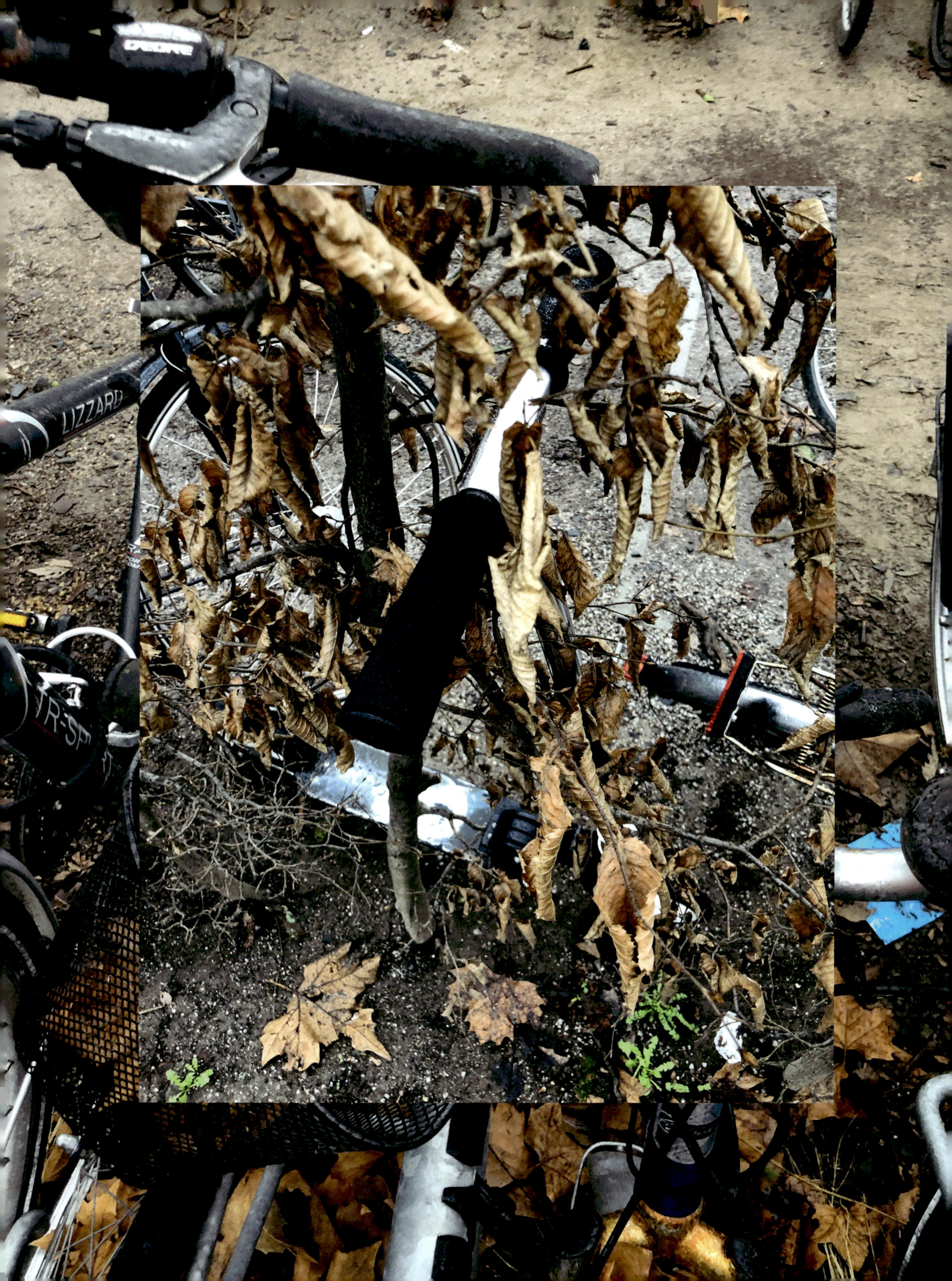
DEORE
LIZZARD

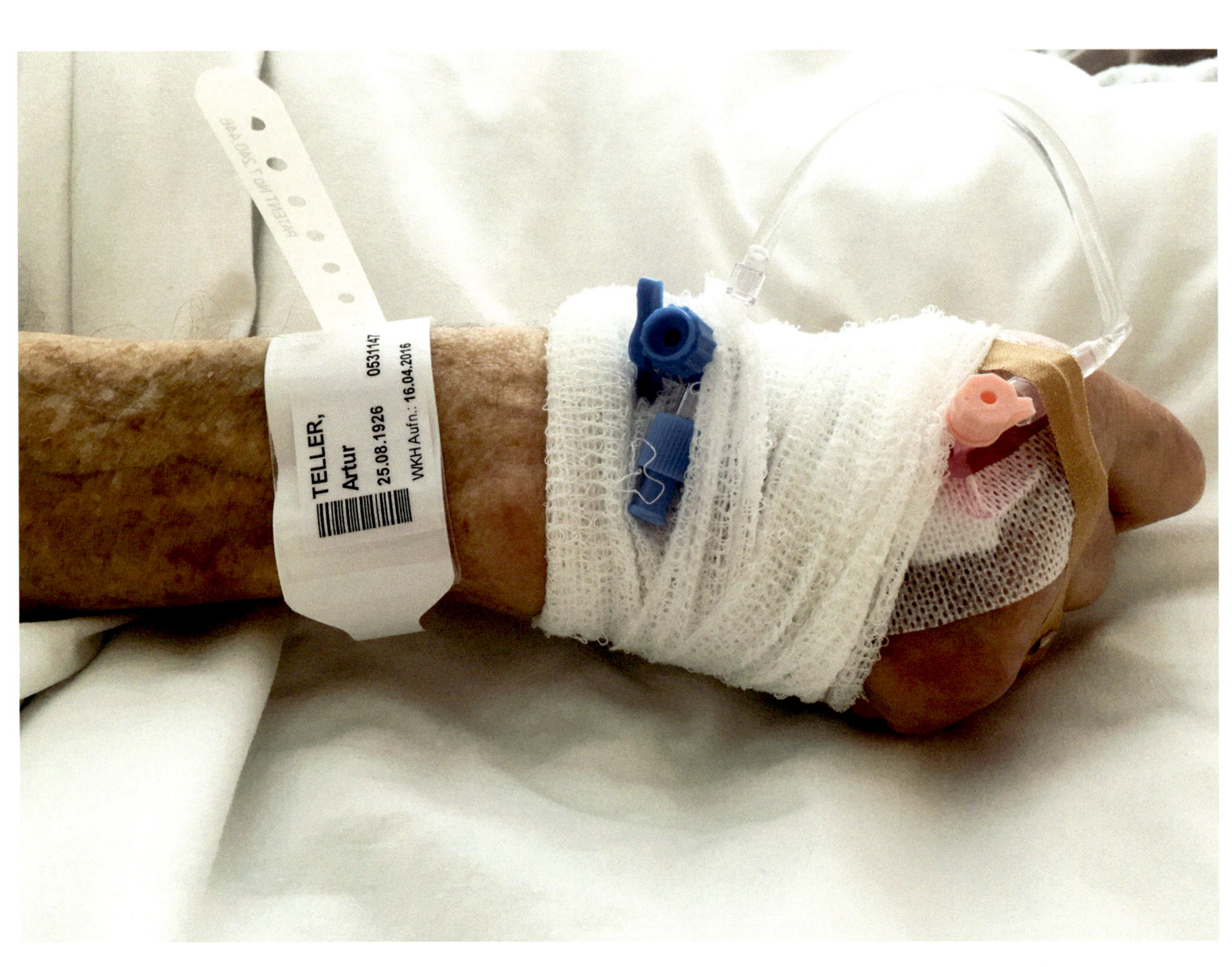
TELLER,
Artur
25.08.1926
0531147
WKH Aufn.: 16.04.2016

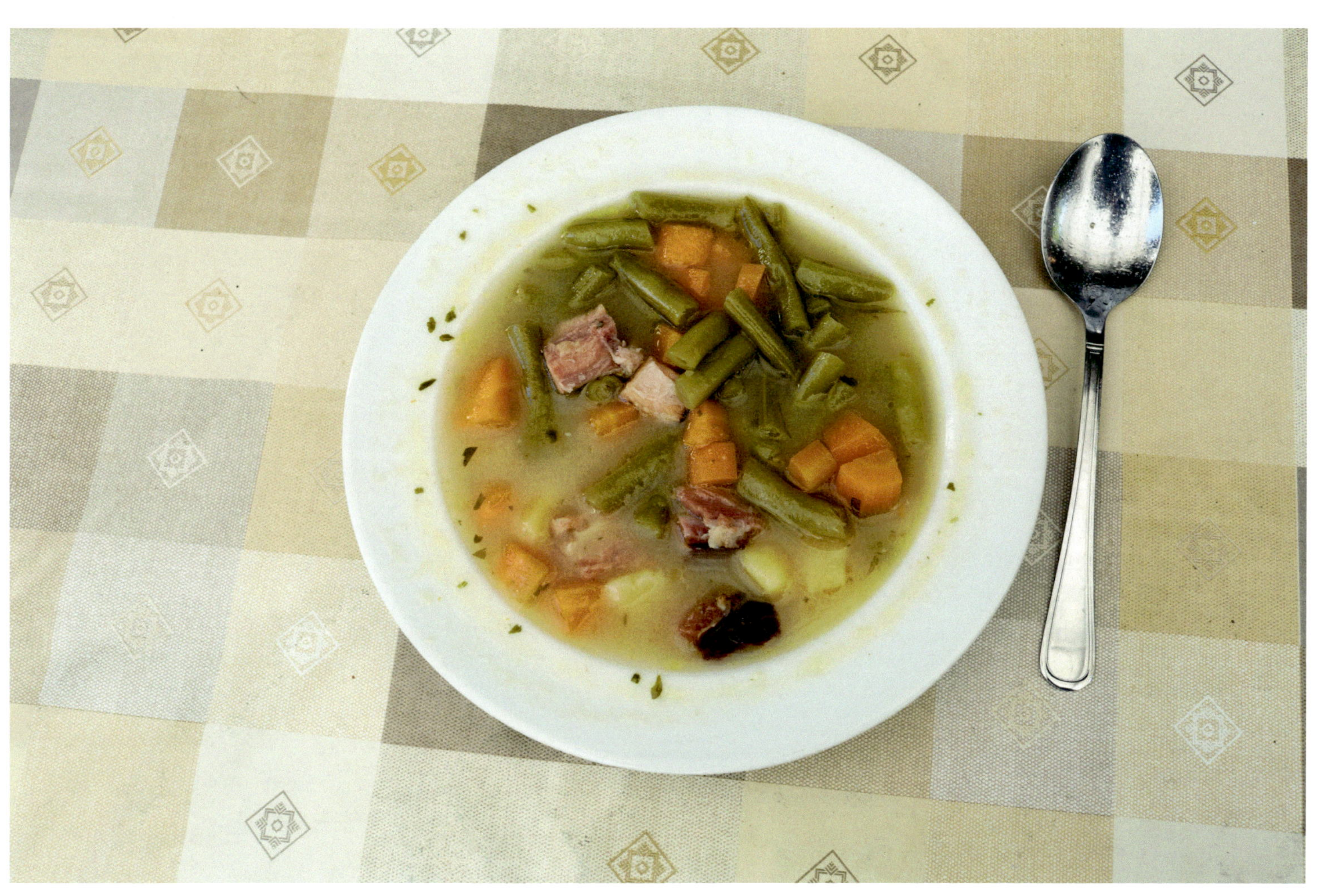

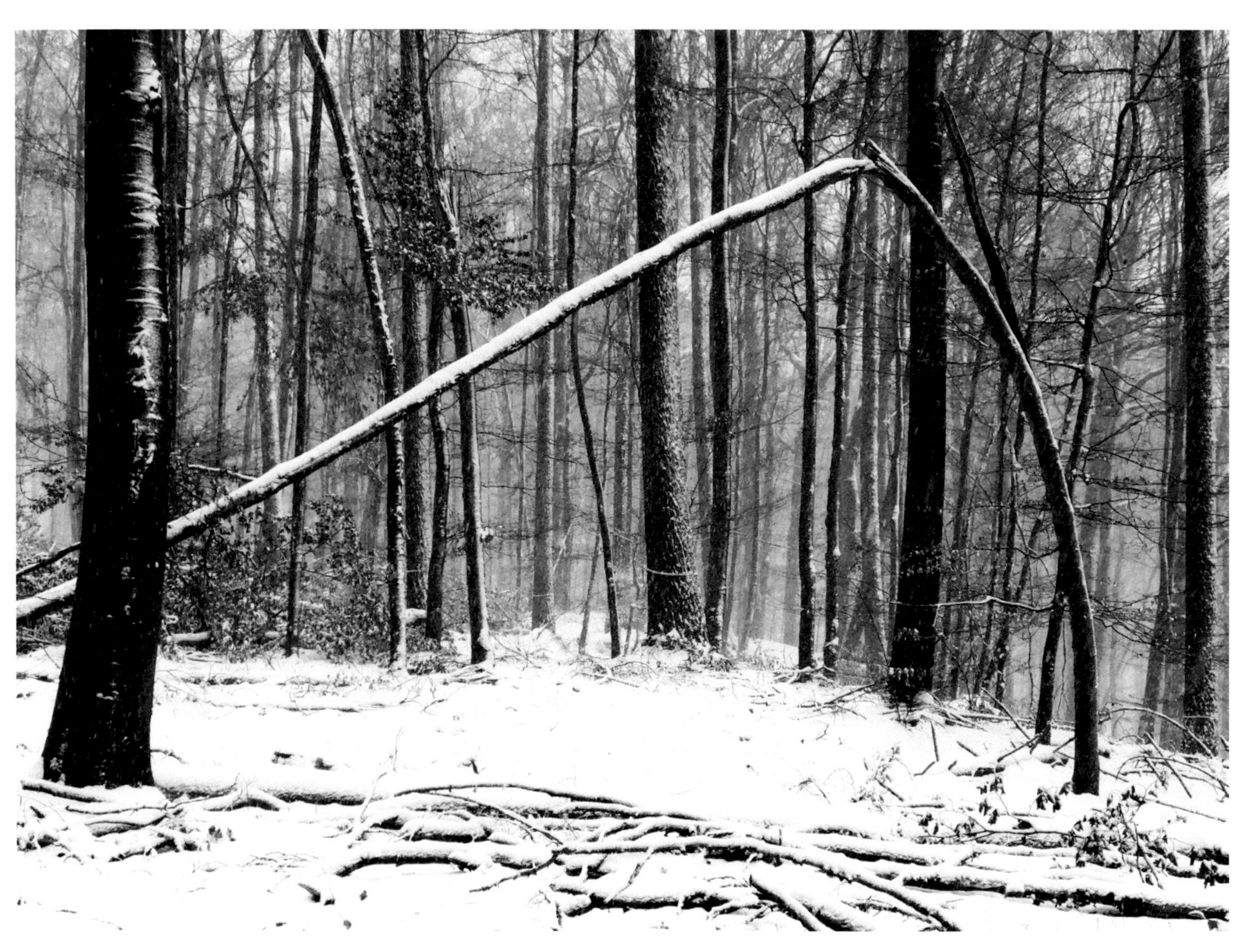

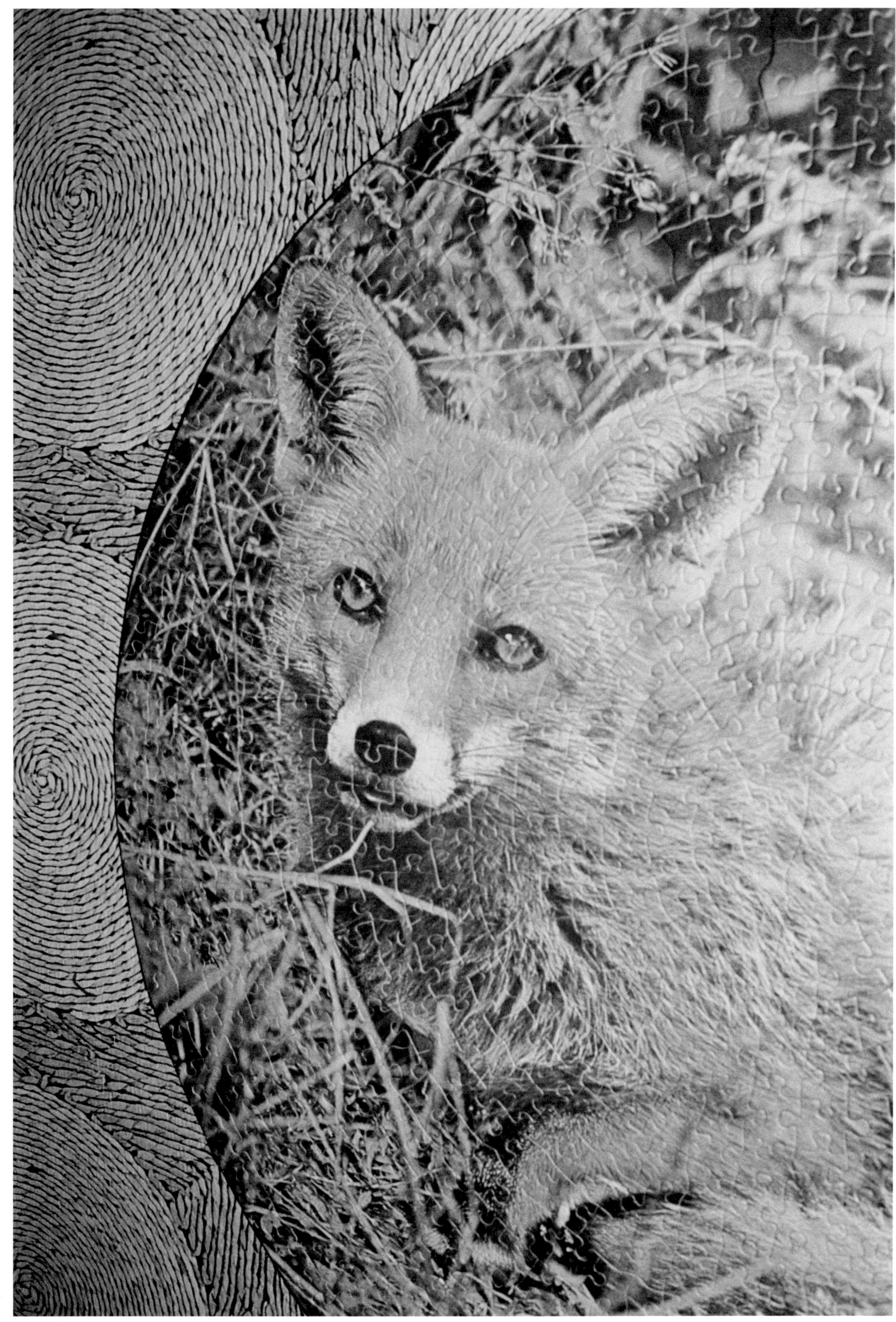

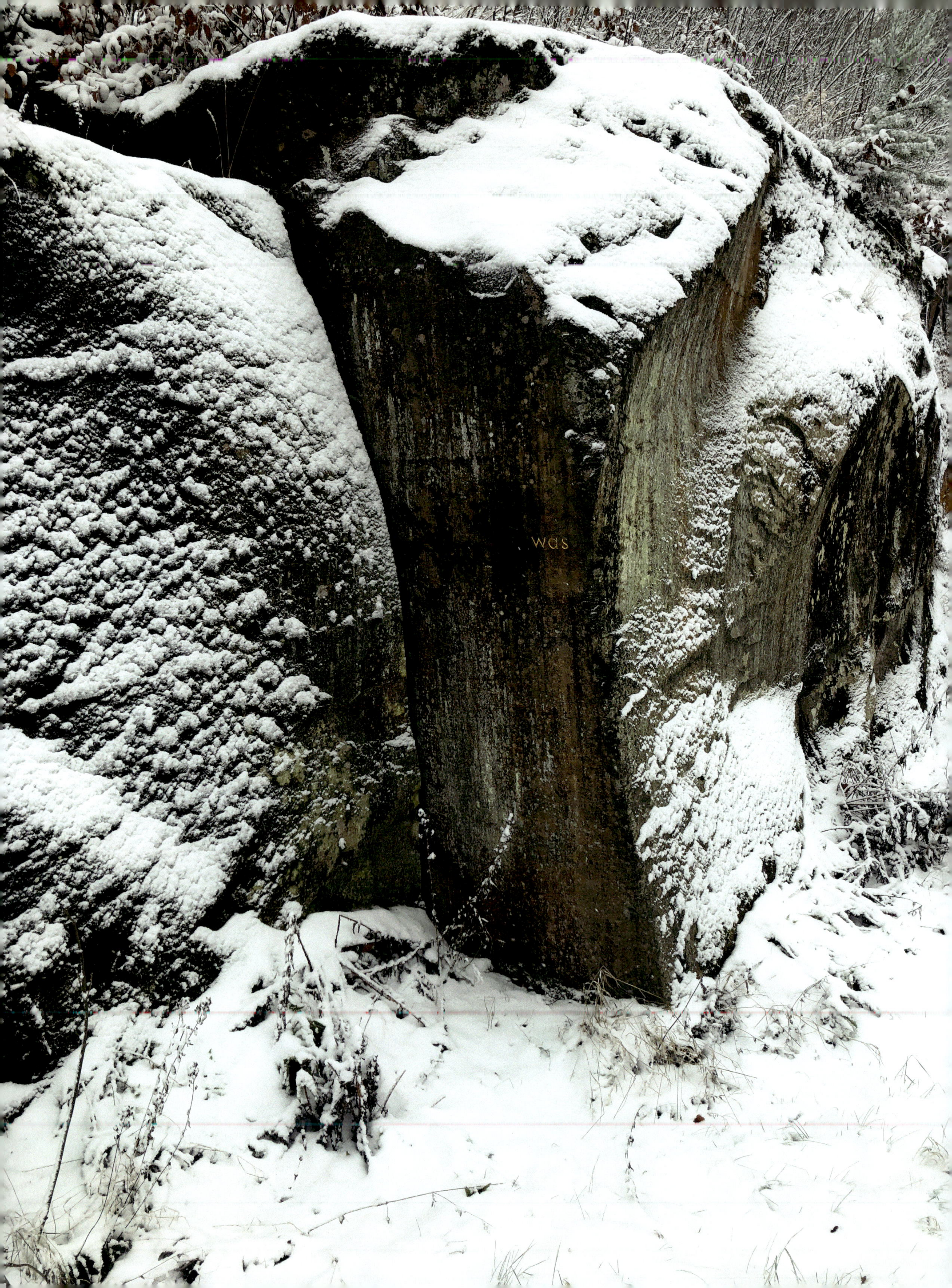
was

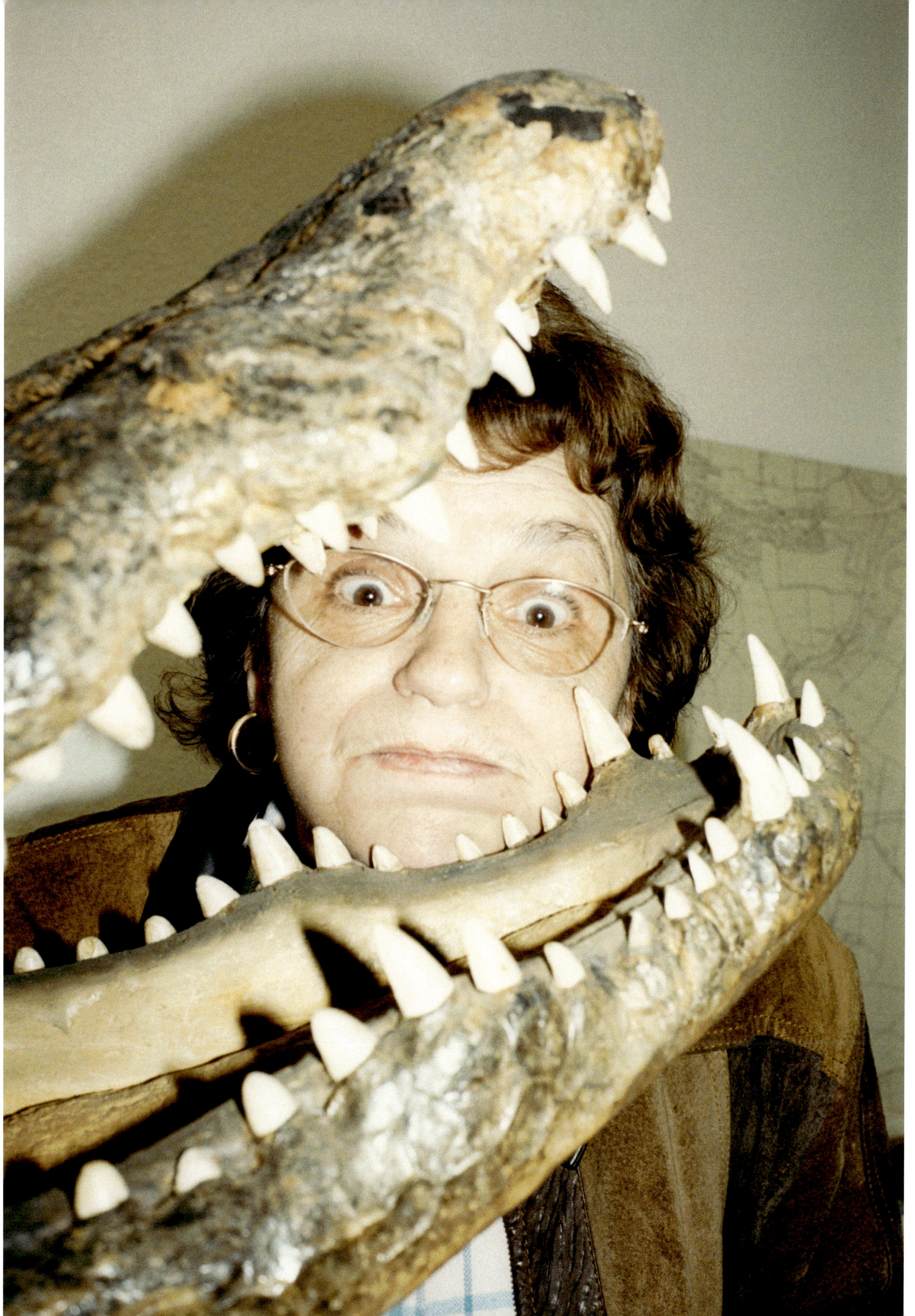

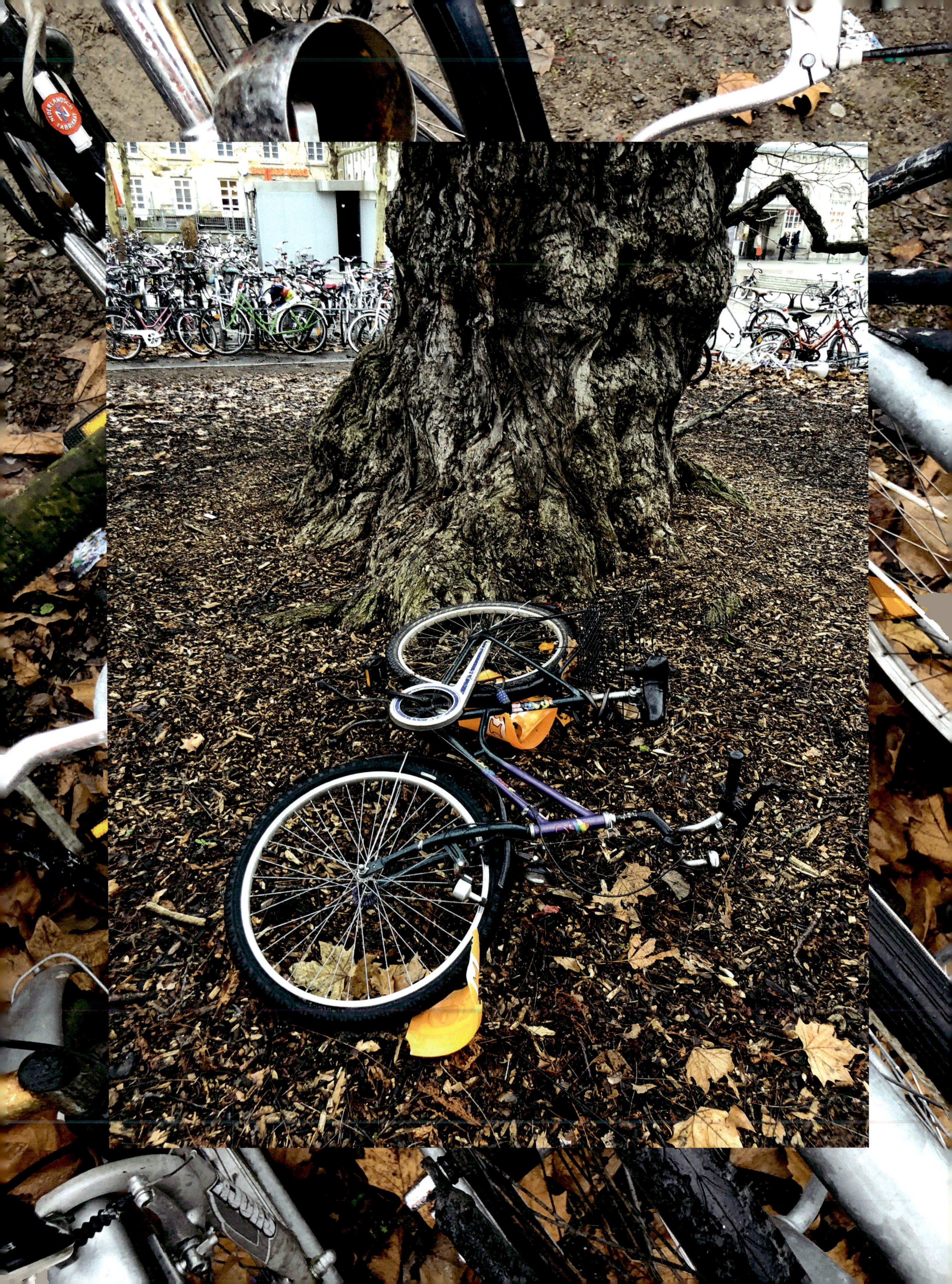

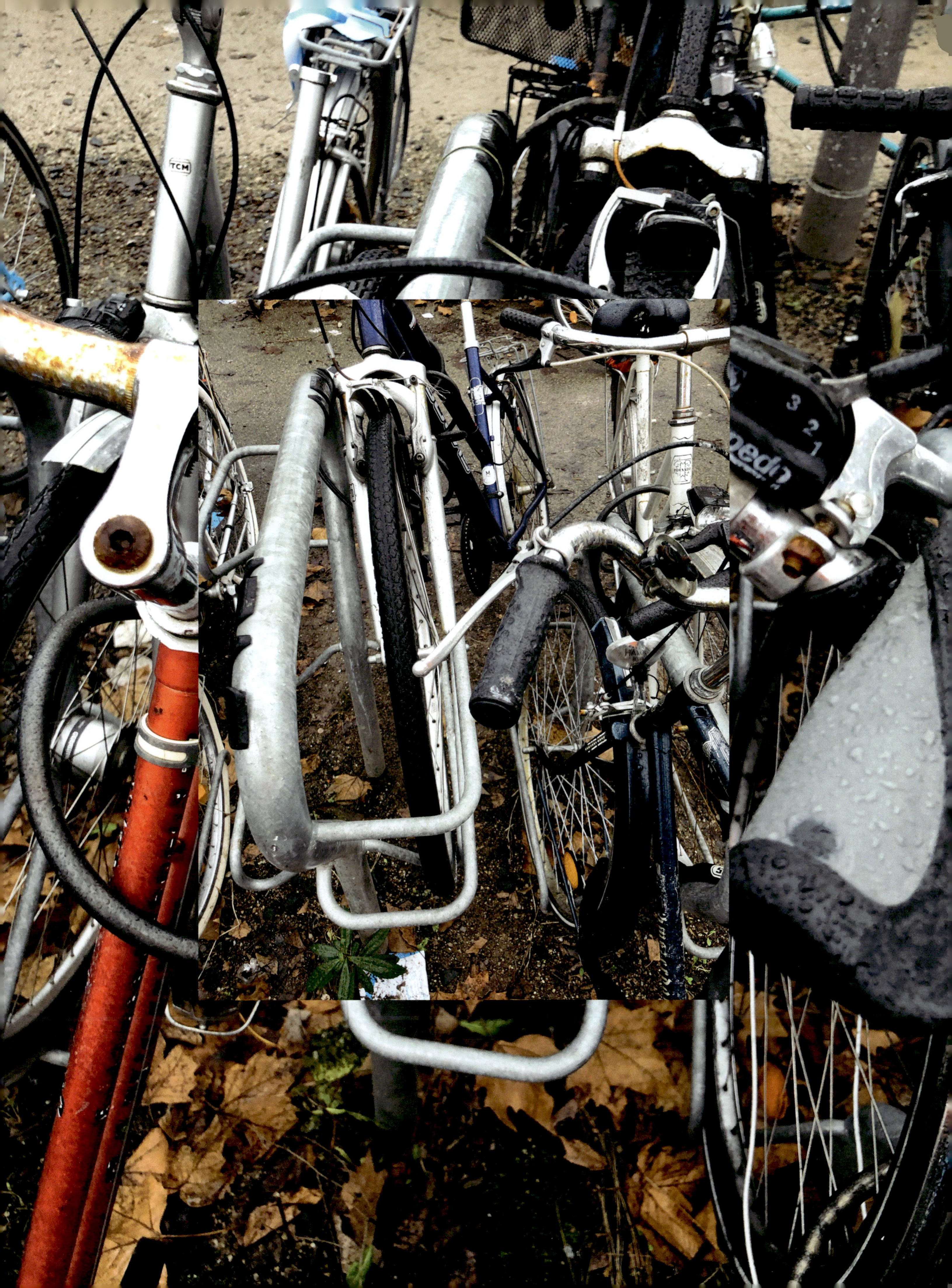
TCM
3 2 1

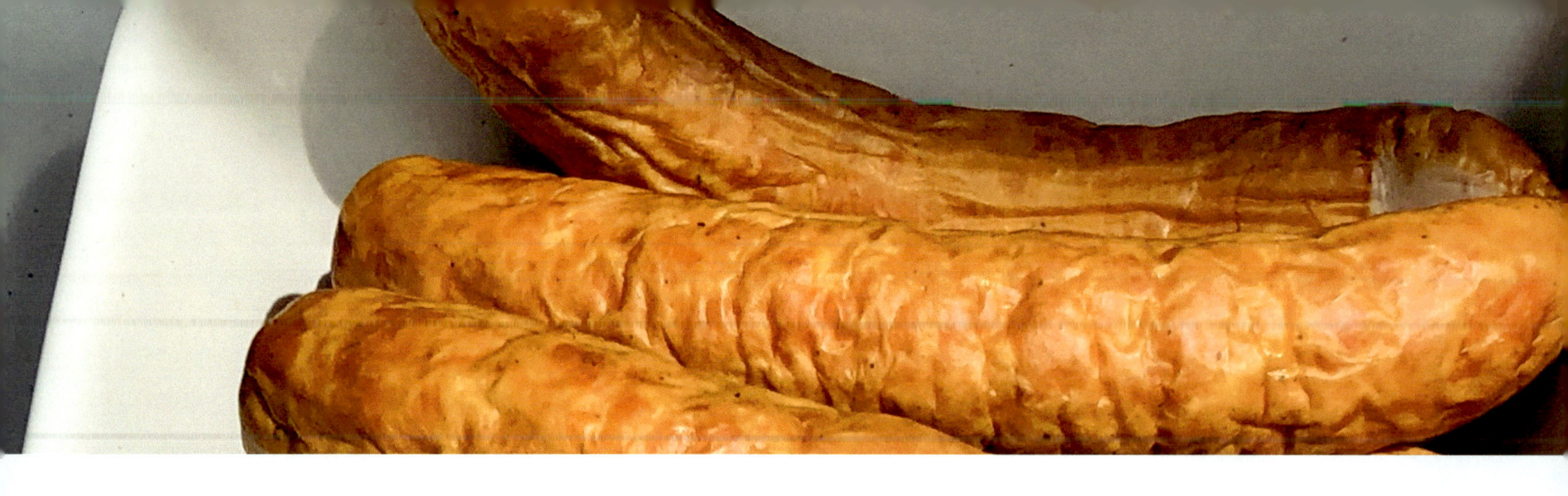

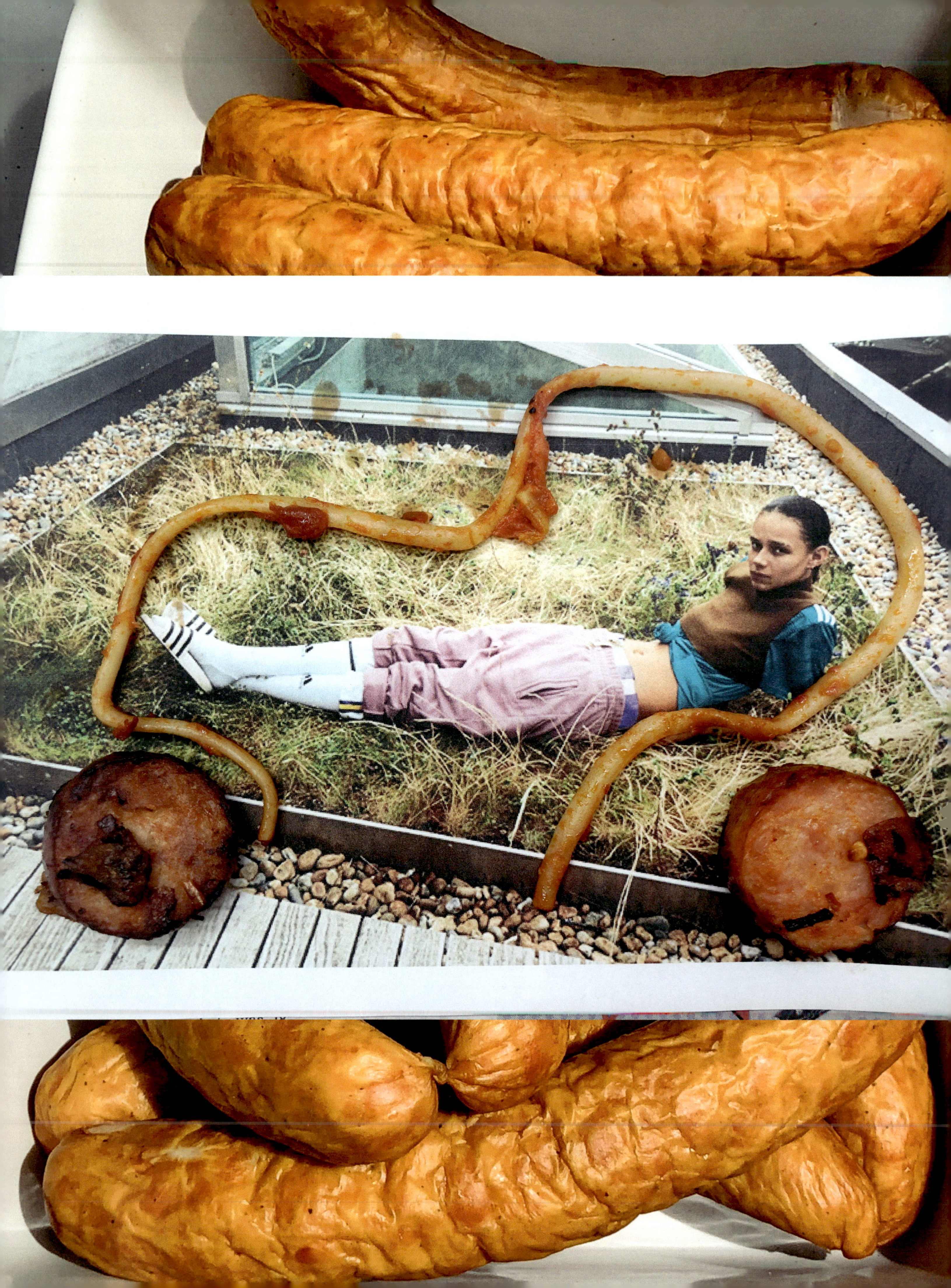

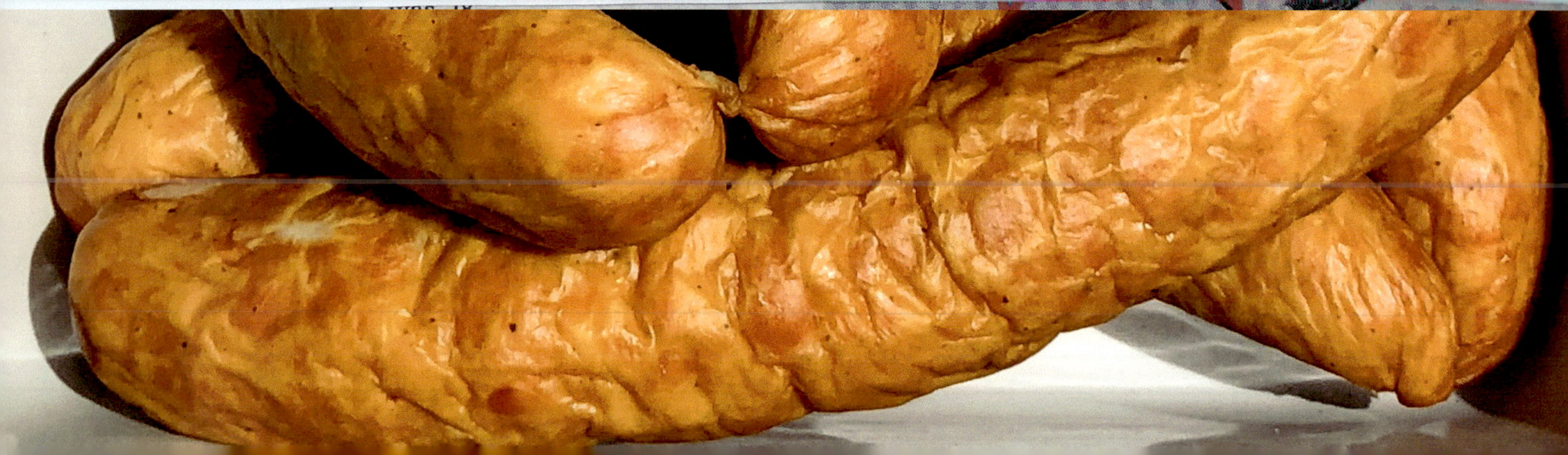

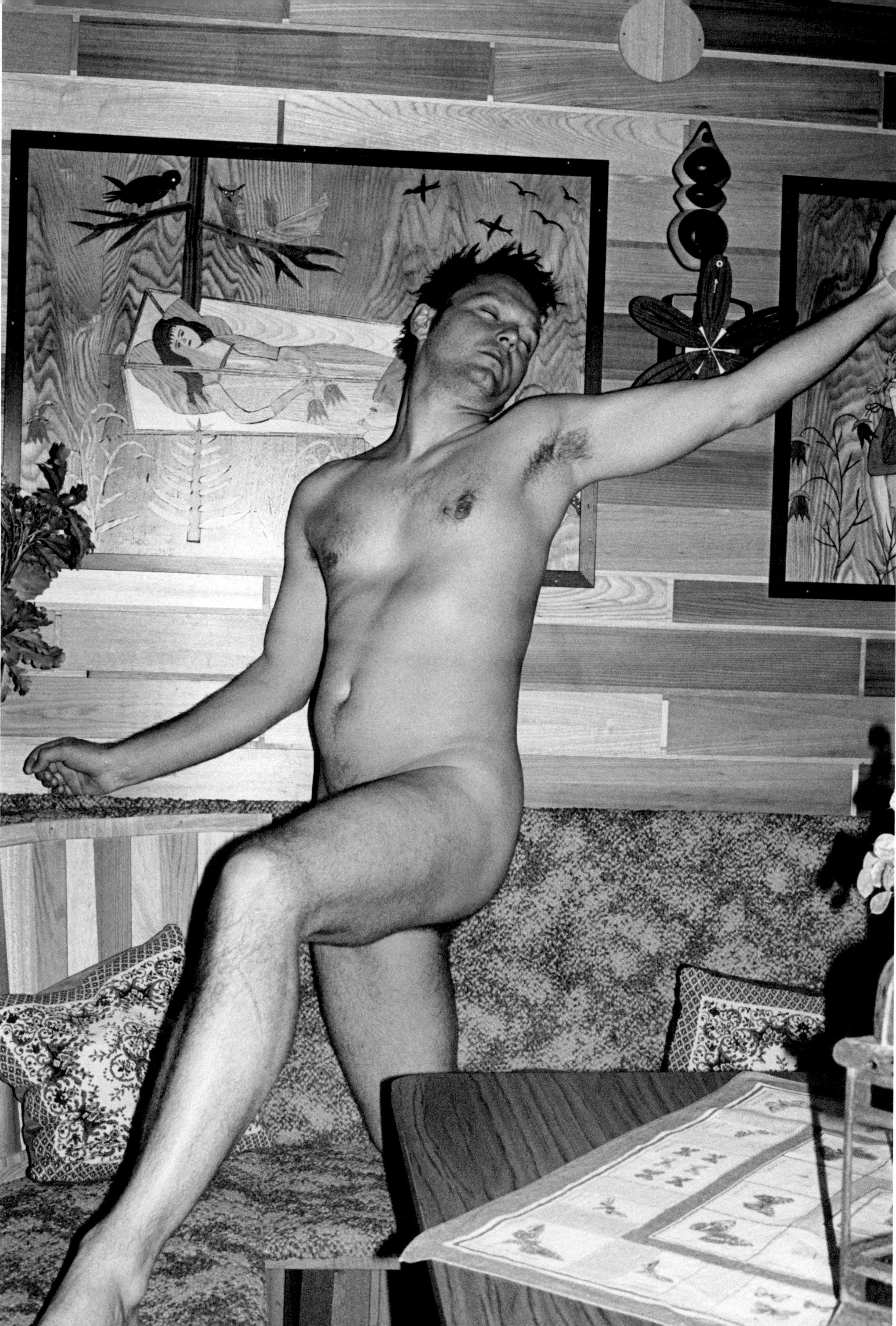

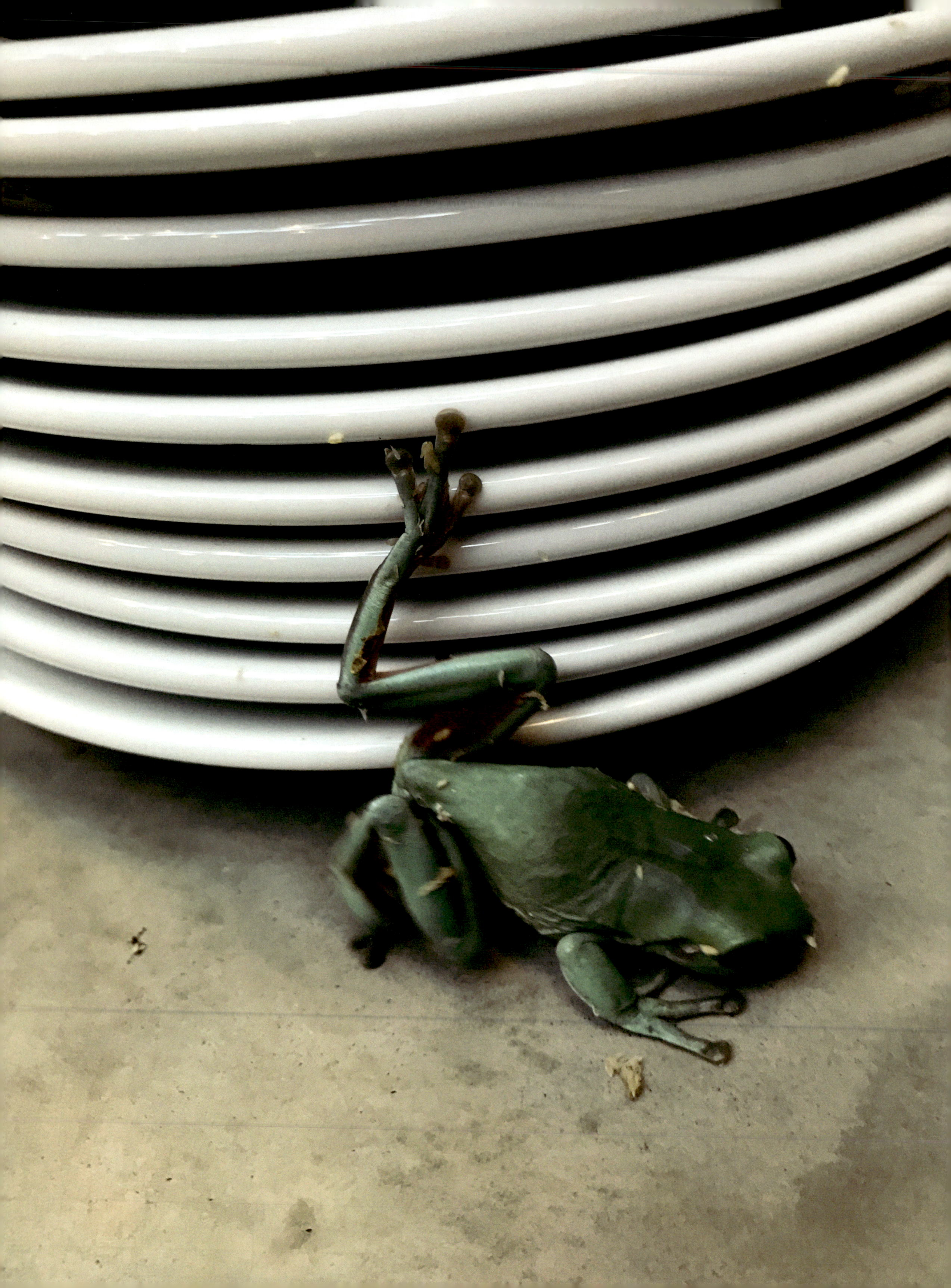

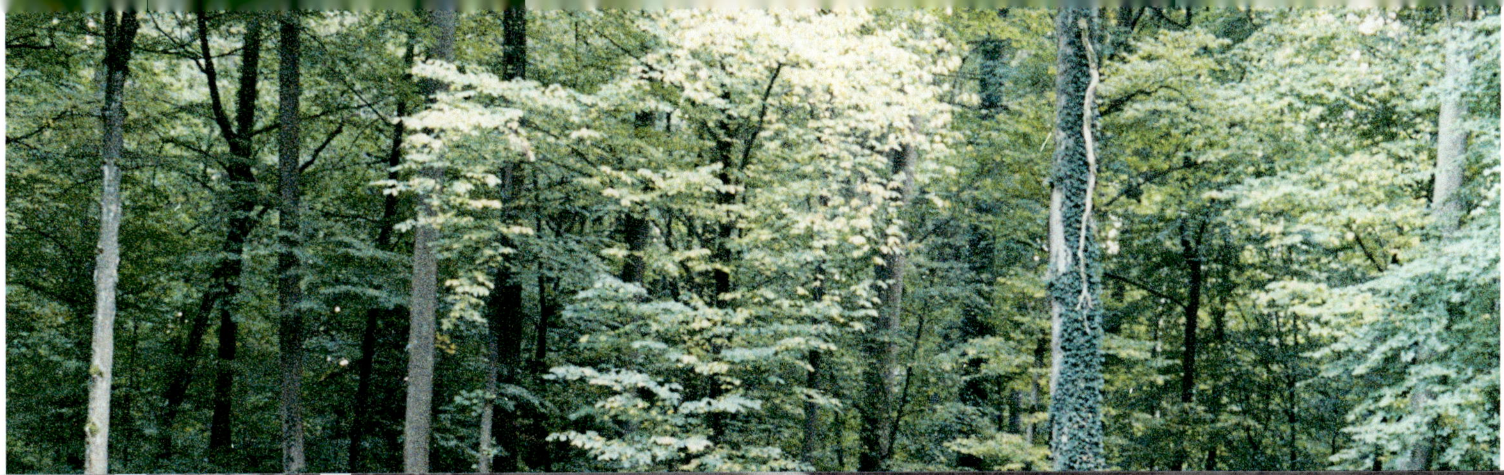

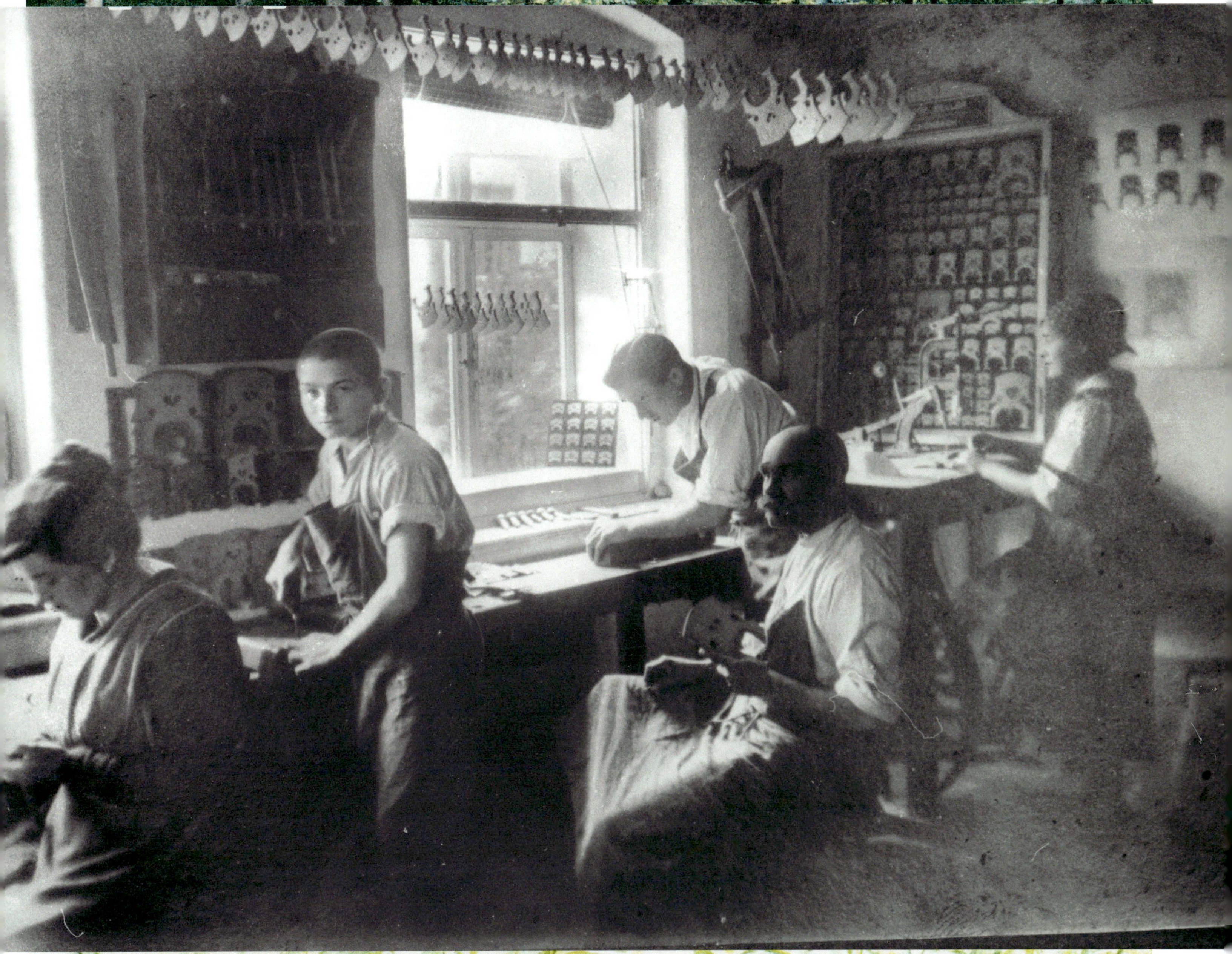

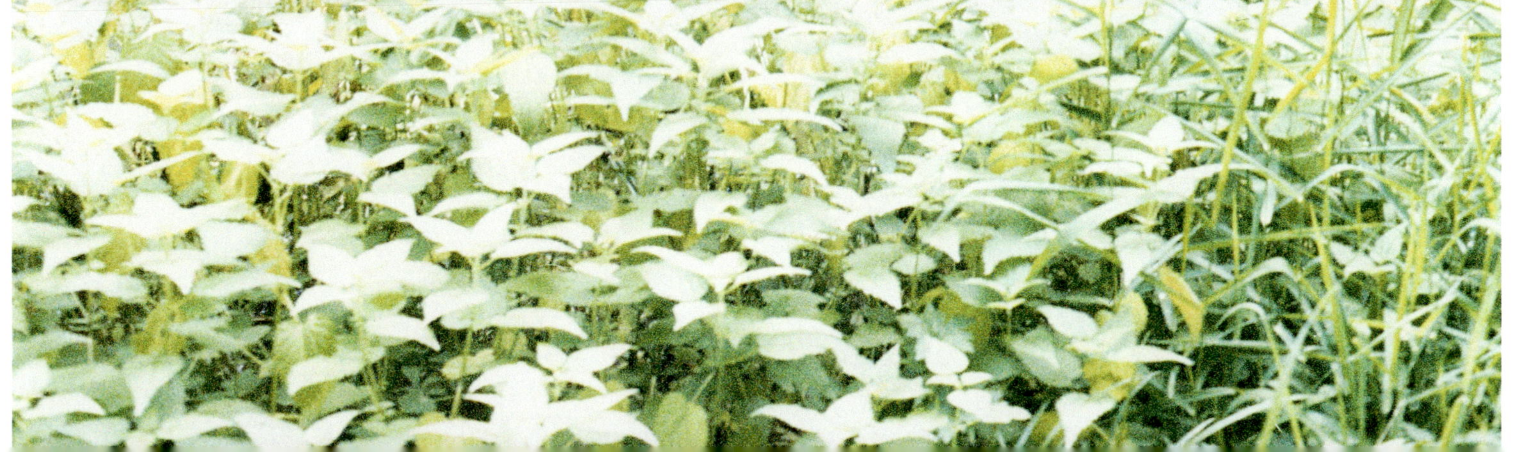

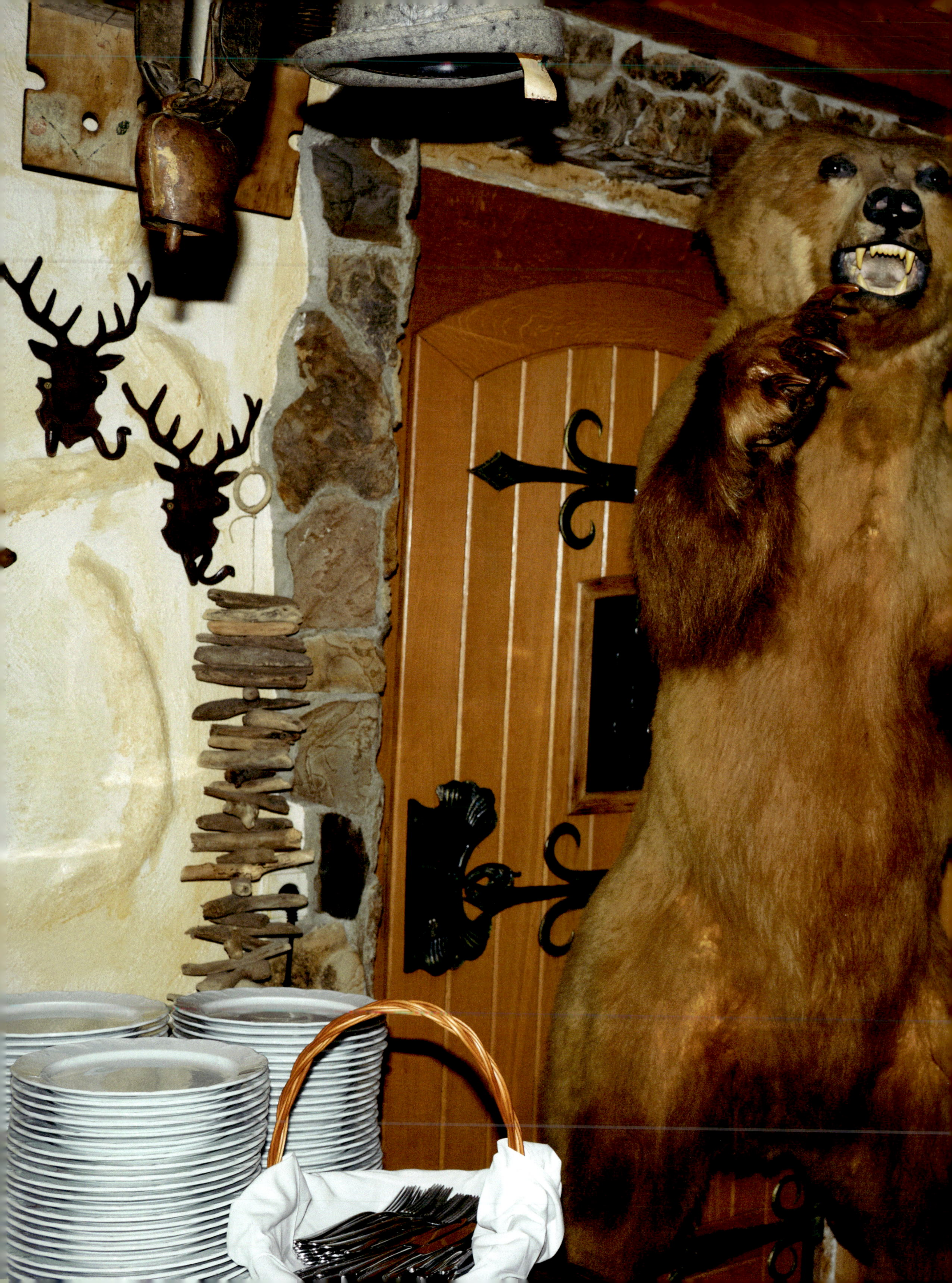

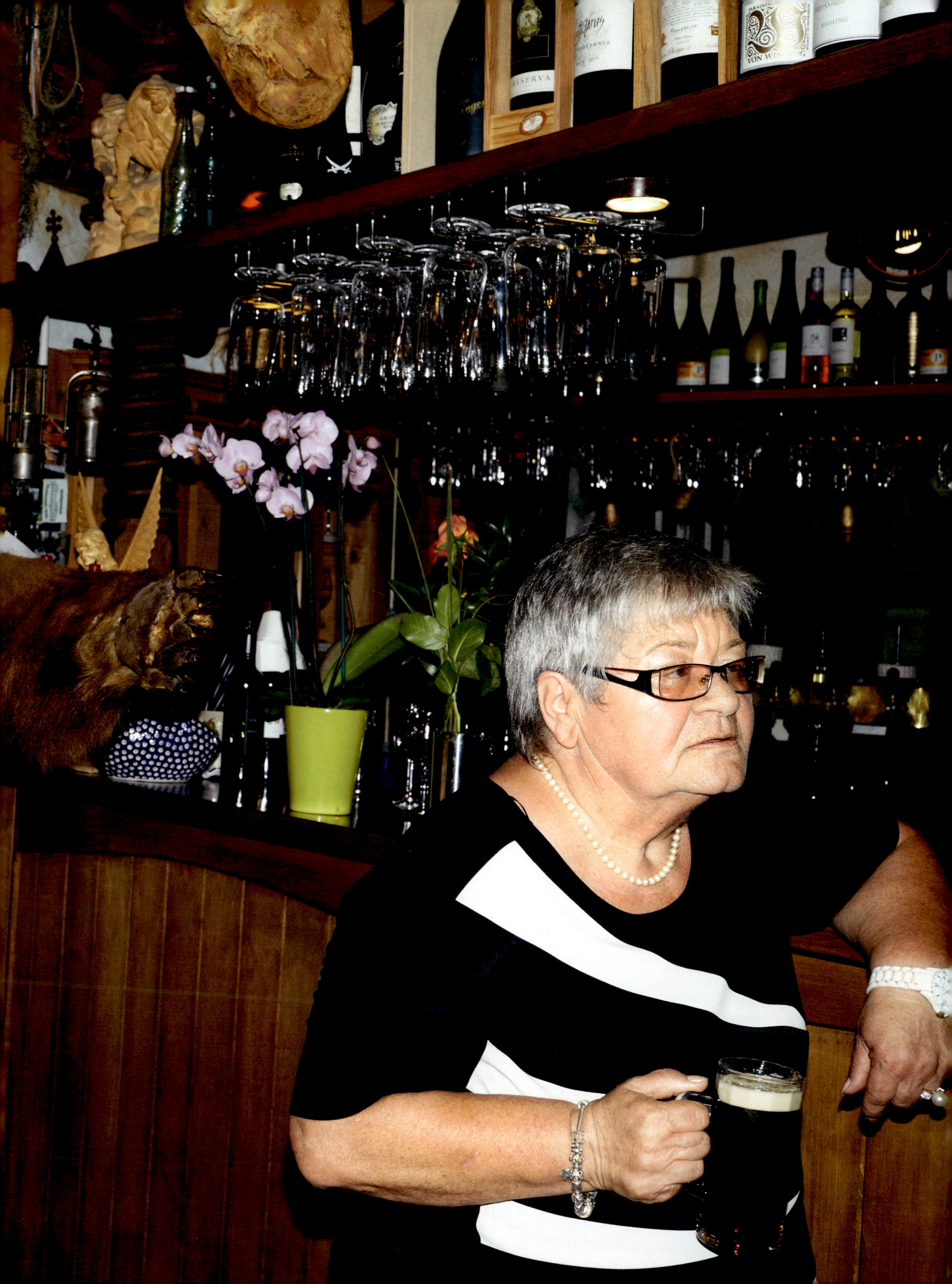
RESERVA
RIESLING

Artworks in order of appearance:

Self-portrait for Business of Fashion, London, 2015

Football Fan, London, 2018
Sandra Hüller No.1, Bochum, 2019

Wurstplatte, Weimar, 2014
Diane Kruger No.1, Berlin, 2019

Demokratie leben!, Göttingen, 2019
Wolfgang Joop, Berlin, 2019

Leni Riefenstahl, Starnberger See, 2002
Wurstfrühstück, Baden-Baden, 2019

Diane Kruger No.2, Berlin, 2019
Coco/Nicolette Krebitz, New Order album cover, London, 2001

Anne Imhof and Eliza Douglas, Paris, 2016
Poster for Anne Imhof, 'Sex', Tate Modern, London, 2019
Lars Eidinger, London, 2016

Bicycles, Göttingen, 2019

Gloria von Thurn und Taxis, Regensburg, 2005
Irene Teller, Bubenreuth, 2016

Herman de Vries Sculpture No.2, Steigerwald, 2019
Herman de Vries Sculpture No.1, Steigerwald, 2019

Birkenstock Factory, Görlitz, 2018
Diane Kruger No.4, Berlin, 2019

Sosein, Heroldsberg, 2019
Joachim Löw, Düsseldorf, 2018

Bicycles, Göttingen, 2019

Bamberger Symphoniker, Bamberg, 2016

Drainpipe, München, 2014
Scab, Bonn, 2016

Siegerflieger, Berlin, 2014
Boris Becker, Wimbledon, 2014

Herman de Vries Sculpture No.3, Steigerwald, 2019
Thomas Ostermeier, Berlin, 2013

Sandra Hüller No.2, Bochum, 2019
Birkenstock Factory, Görlitz, 2018

Mum and Dad, London, 2015

Sandra Hüller No.3, Bochum, 2019
Angela Merkel, Bonn, 2016

Raucherraum, Schauspielhaus Bochum, Bochum, 2019

Bicycles, Göttingen, 2019

Diane Kruger No.7, Berlin, 2019
Self-portrait, Fußball ist unser Leben, Bubenreuth, 2019

Hermann Teller, Bubenreuth, 2002
Karolin Wolter No.2, London, 2019

Claudia Schiffer, Cannes, 1999
Karl Lagerfeld, Paris, 1997

Currywurst, Göttingen, 2019

Höhle, Fränkische Schweiz, Germany, 2002
Stella Tennant, London, 2014

Diane Kruger, Berlin, 2019
Spieß, Erlangen, 2005

Self-portrait, 6th consecutive title, Bayern München, London, 2018

Bicycles, Göttingen, 2019

Anna Ewers, Berlin, 2017

Bicycles, Göttingen, 2019
Karpfen, Bubenreuth, 2001

Karl Lagerfeld, Paris, 2009
Eva Herzigova, Kanzlerbungalow, Bonn, 2016

Pope Benedict XVI with Angel, Regensburg, 2005
Johann König, Berlin, 2015

My Mum with Wim Wenders, Berlin, 2016
Gerhard Richter, London, 2008

Ed Teller and Bastian Schweinsteiger, London, 2012
Diane Kruger No.12, Berlin, 2019

Bicycles, Göttingen, 2019

Karolin Wolter No.4, London, 2019
Stege, Tokyo, 2016

Irene Teller's Leberknödelsuppe, Bubenreuth, 2019
Peter Lindbergh kissing my Mum, Schloss Bellevue, Berlin, 2016

Liebe, Nürnberg, 2004

Nina Hoss, Berlin, 2013
Diane Kruger, No.14, Berlin, 2019

Bicycles, Göttingen, 2019

Artur Teller, Erlangen, 2016
Suppenteller, Bubenreuth, 2016

Wald, Steigerwald, 2019
Puzzle, Bubenreuth, 2018

Herman de Vries Sculpture No.4, Steigerwald, 2019
Mother with Crocodile, Bubenreuth, 2002

Bicycles, Göttingen, 2019

Binx, London, 2018
Self-portrait with Snow White, Bubenreuth, 2002

Frogs and Plates No.12, London, 2016
Josef and Isidor Teller, Sudetenland, 2008

Gisela Teller, Hannover, 2015

Asparagus, Gebhards Hotel, Göttingen, 2019

Imprint

This special issue is published on the occasion of the exhibition *Heimweh* by Juergen Teller at KÖNIG TOKIO, MCM Ginza Haus 1, Tokyo, Japan (November 2019 – January 2020)

Publishing Editors: Juergen Teller & Dovile Drizyte and Johann & Lena König
Exhibition Coordinators: Julie Hottner, Josselin Merazguia, Tatsuya Yamasaki
Translation: April von Stauffenberg
Layout of Artworks: Juergen Teller Studio
Art Direction: Louisa Hölker

First published by Koenig Books, London
Koenig Books Ltd
At the Serpentine Gallery
Kensington Gardens
London W2 3XA
www.koenigbooks.co.uk

Printed in Germany

Distribution:

Germany, Austria, Switzerland / Europe
Buchhandlung Walther König
Ehrenstr. 4,
D - 50672 Köln
Tel: +49 (0) 221 20 59 6 53
verlag@buchhandlung-walther-koenig.de

UK & Ireland
Cornerhouse Publications Ltd. - HOME
2 Tony Wilson Place
UK – Manchester M15 4FN
Tel: +44 (0) 161 212 3466
publications@cornerhouse.org

Outside Europe
D.A.P. / Distributed Art Publishers, Inc.
75 Broad Street, Suite 630
USA - New York, NY 10004
Tel: +1 (0) 212 627 1999
orders@dapinc.com

ISBN 978-3-96098-736-9
ISSN 2626-9856

Special Thanks:

MCM Worldwide
Sung-Joo Kim
Dirk Schönberger
Hiroaki Nakamura
Harrie Kim
Catalin Plesa
Sally Waterman
Karin Xiao
Peter Sayn-Wittgenstein